Sunshine in the Dark

UNIVERSITY PRESS OF FLORIDA

Florida A&M University, Tallahassee
Florida Atlantic University, Boca Raton
Florida Gulf Coast University, Ft. Myers
Florida International University, Miami
Florida State University, Tallahassee
University of Central Florida, Orlando
University of Florida, Gainesville
University of North Florida, Jacksonville
University of South Florida, Tampa
University of West Florida, Pensacola

University Press of Florida

Gainesville · Tallahassee · Tampa · Boca Raton · Pensacola · Orlando · Miami · Jacksonville · Ft. Myers

Sunshine in the

DARK

Florida in the Movies

Susan J. Fernández and Robert P. Ingalls

Copyright 2006 by Susan J. Fernández and Robert P. Ingalls
Printed in the United States of America on recycled, acid-free paper
All rights reserved

11 10 09 08 07 06   6 5 4 3 2 1

Library of Congress Cataloging-in-Publication Data

A record of cataloging-in-publication data is available from
the Library of Congress.

ISBN 0-8130-2990-2

The University Press of Florida is the scholarly publishing agency
for the State University System of Florida, comprising Florida A&M
University, Florida Atlantic University, Florida Gulf Coast University,
Florida International University, Florida State University, University
of Central Florida, University of Florida, University of North Florida,
University of South Florida, and University of West Florida.

University Press of Florida
15 Northwest 15th Street
Gainesville, FL 32611-2079
http://www.upf.com

To Allison for her inspiration
And Sally for her support
and assistance
Susan J. Fernández

To Joèle with love
Robert P. Ingalls

Contents

Illustrations

Color Plates *follow page 142*

The lynch mob that terrorizes African-Americans in *Rosewood* (1997)

C. J. Sanders as the young Ray Charles and Sharon Warren as his
mother in front of their north Florida home in *Ray* (2004)

Elvis Presley in a publicity shot for *Girl Happy* (1965)

Nathan Lane in *The Birdcage* (1996)

Ashley Judd (*right*) and Allison Dean play clerks in a tourist shop in
Ruby in Paradise (1993)

Eddie Murphy in *The Distinguished Gentleman* (1992)

Diane Keaton and her nephew (Leonardo DiCaprio) driving on the
beach in *Marvin's Room* (1996)

Richard Dreyfuss, Seymour Cassel, Dan Hedaya, and Burt Reynolds play
retired mobsters in *The Crew* (2000)

Jim Morris (Dennis Quaid) pitching in Orlando in *The Rookie* (2002)

Dan Marino (*center*) with his kidnapper (Sean Young) and Ace Ventura
(Jim Carrey) in *Ace Ventura: Pet Detective* (1994)

Danny Glover (*top*) and Joe Pesci in *Gone Fishin'* (1997)

Acknowledgments

A number of people deserve recognition for their generous assistance in helping us complete this project. We thank Lisa K. Bradberry for her help in identifying and locating some of the films included in the book and for the many discussions that contributed to our interpretation of the films. By sharing her knowledge not only with us but also with many others, she has expanded the interest in Florida films. The students in the Florida History in Film class, offered during 2004 at the University of South Florida, St. Petersburg, also contributed insights and observations about some of the films covered here. We thank them for their diligence and excellence. Gary Mormino kindly provided a number of valuable references.

We would also like to thank reference librarian Madeline Matz at the Motion Picture, Broadcasting, and Recorded Sound Division of the Library of Congress for her assistance, as well as that of other staff members at the archive. A travel grant awarded by the Humanities Institute at the University of South Florida provided the opportunity to view films at the Library of Congress, and we greatly appreciate the support of the Institute.

Two other archives provided invaluable assistance in locating photographs that illustrate this book. We are indebted to the very cooperative staffs at Photofest in New York City and at the Wisconsin Center for Film and Theater Research at the University of Wisconsin—Madison. At the University of South Florida, Richard Bernardy generously assisted in making digital copies of still photographs.

The University of South Florida Publications Council provided significant financial support for illustrations, and we are especially grateful to the members of the council for their role in improving the quality of the final publication.

The editors and staff of the University Press of Florida continued their tradition of extraordinary guidance and assistance, and we are proud to publish this book with a press committed to Florida history and culture. We particularly want to thank Meredith Morris-Babb for her early endorsement of this project and for her continued efforts on our behalf.

Finally, thanks to our friends and relations, especially Sally and Joële, who not only watched some of the films with us, but also endured our endless discussions about good and bad Florida films.

Introduction

Ah, Florida! Sunshine. Beaches. Palm trees and orange blossoms. Winter warmth and winter green. Orange sunsets. Blue water. Pink flamingos. Spanish moss. Hibiscus. Key West. South Beach. The Everglades. Flipper. Swimming, fishing, and sailing. Weeki Wachee. Silver Springs. Disney World. Cape Canaveral. Relaxation. Recreation and re-creation. The Fountain of Youth.

Oh, Florida! Heat. Humidity. Skin cancer. Crowded beaches. Sharks. Red tide. Citrus canker. Developers. Mosquitoes. Cockroaches. No-see-ums. Sinkholes. Lightning. Hurricanes. Alligators. Traffic. Nursing homes. Migrant labor camps. Disney World. Tourists. Chads.

Florida. This place of multiple images and multiple realities has been portrayed in a variety of contradictory ways since the first Spanish conquerors traveled across the peninsula in the sixteenth century. Visitors have arrived with expectations based on their hopes, dreams, and desires. Some migrants have stayed to build a new life, others to quietly live out their remaining years in the sunshine, cooled by balmy breezes.

Early travelers searched for gold, and finding none, moved on. By building garrisons, the Spanish attempted to protect the territory from competitors. The natives were subdued, exploited, then moved west, and finally isolated or assimilated. Slaves escaping from neighboring British colonies worked at Spain's Fort Mose, built their own communities, and found sanctuary with Seminoles. Other slaves worked on plantations and ranches or in logging and turpentine camps. The European settlers migrating for new opportunities were housed, employed, and governed by Spain, Britain, and ultimately, the United States.

By the mid-nineteenth century, Florida had become a destination for the ailing who believed in the recuperative powers of the sun, sea air, and the warm waters of the Gulf of Mexico and Atlantic Ocean. Travelers wrote about the delightful climate, the birds, the forests, the mangroves, and the fishing, as well as the mosquitoes, alligators, swamps, water moccasins, and "crackers." The earliest images of Florida portrayed the area as either an unspoiled paradise or a wilderness begging to be transformed into ever-changing views of paradise.

By the time the motion picture developed at the end of the nineteenth century, settlements dotted the shores of the state. The Edison Manufacturing Company teamed up with publisher William Randolph Hearst and competed with Billy Bitzer's American Mutoscope and Biograph Company to produce and distribute footage of the Spanish-American War in 1898. Their efforts gave audiences around the country their first moving pictures of Florida, as cameras captured brief shots of soldiers against a backdrop of bustling ports, tall pines, palm trees, and cigar factories. Troops from around the country were filmed training at military camps, handling supplies, disembarking from railroad cars, and boarding ships. Films of the action in Cuba were also produced, showing U.S. troops landing at Daiquiri and Santiago, wounded soldiers being transported from rowboats to a hospital ship, and Cuban civilians freed from detention centers and awaiting relief at U.S. military camps.

These films were part historical documentary and part staged drama, and so should be considered the first fictional war movies. Directors mixed actual footage and reenactment without differentiation. Scenes of Cubans ambushing Spaniards, Spaniards shooting insurgents, and Rough Riders skirmishing with the enemy were actually performed in New Jersey by the National Guard. In Thomas Edison's New York studios, a model of the USS *Maine* was exploded in a water tank, and a miniature U.S. flag was raised over a picture backdrop of Havana's fort, El Morro. What mattered, after all, was the impact of the image, its ability to arouse emotions, strengthen values, and even prompt action. Like still photography, the motion picture camera first framed a reality perceived by the operator, and then film became a medium for creating and portraying fictional events and characters. Movies provided a new means of telling stories, and like the written word and still photographs, moving pictures produced images of Florida that continually evolved in the twentieth and the twenty-first centuries.

For early filmmakers Florida offered a natural setting requiring few alterations. The climate, particularly in north Florida, was hospitable almost year-round, and movie producers saw opportunities to film outside, in Spanish-moss-draped forests, on white sand beaches, on tropical islands just offshore, and in St. Augustine—the oldest city in North America. By World War I Jacksonville hosted thirty production companies, providing work for a thousand local actors and extras. Famous silent movie stars, including Theda Bara, Rudolph Valentino, Francis X. Bushman, Gloria Swanson, and John Barrymore, made films in Florida through the 1920s.[1]

The film genres produced during the silent era encompassed comedy, drama, adventure, romance, detective, fantasy, and even horror films. However, in most cases, the stories had nothing to do with Florida. St. Augustine, with its preserved fort (Castillo de San Marcos) and Spanish-style houses from the 1700s, provided a perfect set for films about the exotic far-off lands of Egypt, South America, and India. Movies about royalty and pirates (*Don Cesar de Bazan*, 1915; *The Undying Flame*, 1917; *The Gulf Between*, 1918) took advantage of beach settings, as well as locations in St. Augustine and Jacksonville. Morality dramas and comedies, most now lost or disintegrated, were by far the favorite genre of early filmmakers, although Florida was not integral to their story lines.

Nevertheless, early films about Florida occasionally provoked local outcries about their alleged distortions of reality. A 1913 movie, *The Wine of Madness*, tells the story of a Pennsylvania man who goes to Florida after investing in real estate, only to discover that he's bought an acre of barren swampland with an old dilapidated shack on it. Clearly worried that distribution of this film and others like it would scare away potential out-of-state investors, the *Tampa Morning Tribune* published an editorial, entitled "Films That Lie," urging Florida theater owners to boycott such pictures because they spread "misrepresentation and falsehood throughout the country."[2]

Ironically, Florida figured more prominently in movie plots after most of the production companies relocated to Hollywood in the 1920s. Although often shot elsewhere, movies started to tell more stories set in the Sunshine State. South Florida's remarkable growth after World War I gradually caught the attention of filmmakers, who incorporated the state into their plots. As wealthy northern tourists and permanent residents streamed in, accessing Palm Beach and Miami through Henry Flagler's train service on the east coast, some silent films focused on Florida's upper-class playgrounds, critiquing the behavior of wealthy tourists and residents by depicting them as shallow or nefarious. Occasionally movie plots also included working-class Floridians trying to exploit upper-class tourists.

During the 1930s and 1940s, most Florida films were escapist musicals or dramas about heroes, criminals, or war veterans. Light comedy and musicals tended to romanticize the state as an ideal destination for either opportunity or escape from troubles. In Florida men migrating from other states could train for war or find jobs after military service, and women could find wealthy husbands. In Florida tourists could board planes and boats to South America and the Caribbean. The new ability to produce movies in color also drew filmmakers to the state to capture its natural beauty and take advantage of settings in (then) sparsely developed coastal areas. With few exceptions, the films that were set in Florida had little to do with the state or with any popular perceptions about the state, other than its beauty and tendency to suffer hurricanes.

That limited film identity began to change in the postwar era. To some extent, national trends in films helped determine the direction of plots that would work in Florida settings. The popularity of movies about war heroes in the late 1940s, westerns in the 1950s, and postwar crime dramas ensured that Florida would find a place in these trends. Light musicals and comedies in the late 1950s and early 1960s found Florida settings appropriate for highlighting the growing tourist industry. The tourists now, however, included not only families and manipulative gold diggers, but also the first wave of boomer college students. Spring-Break films appealed to a growing new segment of moviegoing audiences—teenagers, who wanted to see stories about their peers on the big screen. From the beginning, filmmakers have shown a special interest in Florida tourists, sometimes representing the ambivalence that Floridians themselves feel about these strangers in their midst.

On another level, the realities of Florida's postwar boom also inspired some film plots of the 1950s. More migrants meant urban growth that also led to more crime. As officials focused on eradicating organized crime's expansion into illegal gambling and other outlawed enterprises in Florida, filmmakers dramatized these efforts in fictional stories. In addition, tales of migrants who went in search of legitimate work also attracted the attention of moviemakers after the war, and plots about newcomers to the state have persisted in Florida films.

While migrants from other states continued to change the Florida landscape, immigrants from other countries helped forge new visions of the state. After the 1959 revolution, Cubans arrived in Florida in larger numbers, and very gradually, filmmakers included them in the migrant mix. Later groups of migrants from other areas of the world occasionally appear in Florida movies, but with less frequency than Cubans.

From noir to neo-noir, filmmakers employed the classical dark style of the 1940s to portray antiheroes, femmes fatales, and criminals as some of Florida's most intriguing characters. Gradually Florida films also showed illegal activities by men and women in rural areas or small towns, adding them to the list of cinematic criminals. In addition, local cops and federal agents inevitably found their way into crime films. Stories about convicted felons provided the opportunity for filmmakers to show valid and invalid images of conditions in Florida prisons.

During the last forty years of moviemaking, changes in the industry have affected the images and themes in Florida films. Following the protest movements of the 1960s, the baby-boomer generation wanted more relevance and greater realism in movies. The old Hollywood formula of very expensive productions could no longer guarantee profits for major studios. New directors, actors, and ideas emerged, influenced by European and Japanese directors who used innovative plots and camera work that broke with dominant conventions. After filmmakers like Roger Corman and John Cassavetes began an independent film movement on shoestring budgets, other directors and performers followed, expanding in directions that major Hollywood studios had avoided. Many of these small-budget films emphasized the search for individual self-expression, allowing audiences to identify more closely with the characters. Independent films also blurred the lines of traditional genres.[3]

For many ethnic groups and for women, roles changed as well. In retelling American frontier conquest stories, film portrayals of Native Americans lost some, but not all, of their violent stereotypes. African-Americans shed the traditional roles of maids, servants, and entertainers, and portrayed crime fighters and other professionals. Previously, most films cast women primarily in conventional roles of whore, wife, or victim. While some Florida movies in the 1920s featured women whose experiences reflected the emerging "new woman," their ultimate goals remained marriage and family. This theme continued in films through the 1950s. But changes in the 1960s and 1970s brought expanded roles for women as independent and powerful characters, often concerned with issues beyond the realm of personal relationships.

Following the Vietnam War and the Watergate scandal, more films critical of politics emerged, along with adventure movies and other escapist fare. Story lines dispersed in many different directions. With *Jaws* (1975), the "mega-blockbuster" film era began in the 1970s. Movie studios became hugely profitable enterprises and, as a result, targets of takeovers by big corporations. Profits from merchandising products associated with films, product placement, and soundtracks drew new investors into the industry. Focus groups were used to help select marketable movie endings. To further expand profit potential, some studios also contracted with formerly independent filmmakers.

In the 1980s and 1990s, the development of VHS cassettes and DVDs, along with the expansion of film festivals, produced new opportunities for filmmakers, especially independents. Some could avoid the uncertainty of box office returns and the high costs associated with theater distribution by making films that could appeal to a large enough audience to recoup limited production expenses, at the very least. These changes resulted in more films in all genres and subgenres, contributing to an increased number of films set in Florida.

Filmmakers have been attracted to the state for more than its climate, or the recent efforts of state and local governments to lure them. Over time Florida has meant many different things to people, and filmmakers have played a part in either reinforcing or undermining popular images of the state. Wherever actually filmed, movies provide more than images of Florida; they also project ideas about Florida. For some the state has been perceived as a fantasy land, where natural and embellished habitats and constructed sites draw vacationers seeking respite from work, commuting, gray skies, or snow. As a tourist site the Sunshine State attracts all classes of visitors, and their widely varying experiences are both dramatized and lampooned in films.

Florida has also historically drawn transplants who envision the state as the land of opportunity, a place that always offers possibilities for starting over. In this view Florida can accommodate and improve the lives of new arrivals. So many film characters either dream about or actually travel to Florida in search of re-creation that it has become associated with an epic quest. Prior to the 1960s these trips often produced positive outcomes in films, but since the 1970s results have been less certain.

For others, including many who have never visited the state, Florida is viewed as the example of "what's wrong with America." To them the state represents environmental degradation, overdevelopment, overindulgence, crass commercialism, crime, corruption, and sheer wackiness. Because these criticisms have some basis in reality, writers and filmmakers also find these themes ideal for dramas and comedies. As Carl Hiaasen, one of the Florida novelists whose books have been adapted for film, said in a recent interview, "The Florida in my novels is not as seedy as the real Florida. It's hard to stay ahead of the curve. Every time I write a scene that I think is the sickest thing I have ever dreamed up, it is surpassed by something that happens in real life."[4]

Film images of Floridians, the people who actually live in this novel state, range from characterizations that are realistic and accurate to many that are fanciful, even insulting. Portrayals of Floridians have, of course, changed over the past century of filmmaking, enriched by knowledge, familiarity, and the extraordinary growth in the number of people making films.

This book traces the images of Florida and Florida characters from the earliest movies to the present. In three separate sections we analyze the changes that have taken place in Florida movies by examining film settings, plots, and characters. Settings include both the natural and constructed environments that movies portray. Plots or story lines are the narrative themes that predominate in Florida movies and that cross many genres or film types. And characters include the dominant types of roles that appear in Florida films, attempting to portray natives, migrants, and visitors.

Filmmakers who select a Florida setting for their plots and characters allow us to see changes over time both in the physical landscape and in perceptions of the environment. Since the early films shot in Florida, movie images of cities, coastlines, and roadways have obviously changed radically, as have the meanings attached to growth. Increasingly Florida has become paradise lost, both in the popular imagination and in film. The Everglades and its inhabitants are still associated with danger and mystery, but just as encroaching development has reduced the size of Florida's "river of grass," so too the significance of the region in films has diminished in comparison to urban settings.

A consistent element pervades the landscape in Florida films. With its extensive coastline and many swamps, rivers, natural springs, lakes, and swimming pools, Florida is usually depicted in films as a place with water always present or nearby. Even more than other aspects of the environment, water carries many possible meanings, making it especially attractive as a setting for filmmakers. Water can be viewed as a place for reflection, cleansing, survival, entertainment, or death. The more remote and natural the environment portrayed in film, the more likely it is that

1. Frank Sinatra on a Miami waterway in *Lady in Cement* (1968). By permission of Photofest.

the water there harbors danger. More accessible waters, especially those lapping white, sandy beaches, commonly invite romance, relaxation, or introspection. Water can also be imagined as rejuvenating, whether it springs from the Fountain of Youth or contains life pods from another planet. In contrast to such visions, water can be a site where crimes are committed and fears are confronted. Fears of drowning, of what lurks beneath the surface, of being swept away or lost are faced or repressed in movies.

In addition, dreams are formulated, and goals achieved by way of water. Countless actors in countless scenes pause to contemplate by gazing out across the vast, endless space of ocean or gulf. Others trudge through knee-deep or waist-high muck to get to their destination, every sloggy step representing the difficulty of the journey. By battling with nature on the water, men find themselves, earn the respect of family, and fall in love. Wading or diving into the surf, troubled souls are cleansed. Using the water as a means of escape, men and women are freed. Others just drift.

On land, cinematic images of Florida as either an environmental paradise or an ecological nightmare are sometimes subtle, sometimes blatant.
At one extreme the beaches are lightly populated, the sun shines brightly,
and the wildlife is picturesque. At the other extreme the state is overrun by wall-to-wall condos, motels, and tourist attractions. Increasingly,
public debates about how Florida chooses to use its land—and the impact
of growth—have entered film plots. Movie-made Miami can be a chic,
neon-lit, art deco dream, bordered by beautiful beaches filled with beautiful people. However, it can also be a congested, dangerous city populated
with menacing characters. As Robert Sherrill put it in a review of a book
by Carl Hiaasen, "Heavy drug traffic, corrupt judges, corrupt police, corrupt politicians, corrupt bureaucrats, violent crime on a massive scale
and greedy destruction of the natural environment—why, land's sake,
Miami and its neighboring communities have everything you could ask
for."[5]

Plots in Florida films generally center on tourism, starting over, and
crime. The first includes stories about singles and families enjoying the
rejuvenating, reinvigorating, or relaxing aspects of their visits. Increasingly dramas and comedies about Florida vacations depict tourists whose
experiences do not meet their expectations, to say the least. The second

2. Kim Dickens takes a purifying swim in the Atlantic Ocean in *Things Behind the
Sun* (2001).

common plot device in Florida movies emphasizes the experiences of people who go there to establish new careers, escape their pasts, re-create themselves, or retire. By far, the most common plots focus on crime, highlighting murder, theft, drug trafficking, political corruption, real estate scams, and foreign intrigue.

Within these plots, a wide array of peculiarly Florida characters appear—Seminoles, crackers, retirees, Cuban immigrants, astronauts, Spring Breakers—along with various heroes, criminals, warriors, and athletes. African-Americans, Greeks, and other ethnic groups representing all classes and many jobs have their special places in Florida films. In major and minor roles, women desperately look for husbands, revenge, jobs, easy marks, or a good time, while others enjoy highly paid occupations, opportunities for personal growth, and peace. Characters project attitudes, make sacrifices, experience success and failure, and engage in activities that allow us to trace the history of gender relations and roles over the past century. By analyzing stories and characters over time, we get a sense of not only the social, political, and economic changes that took place, but also the pace of those changes and how they are perceived.

During and after the election of 2000, Florida arguably became the subject of more jokes than any other state in the nation. Only with the 2003 recall of the governor of California did the focus begin to shift appreciably. After the rash of hurricanes that tore through the state in 2004 and 2005, residents often echoed a common sentiment: it's the price of living in paradise. Perhaps most Floridians accept the contradictions of Florida living; if so, they should appreciate the contradictory images about the state that appear in movies.

Over the course of the last century, some significant changes have occurred in the settings, plots, and characterizations of major studio and independent films. In fact, the idea for this book developed from *Things Behind the Sun* (2001), an independent film by award-winning director and screenwriter Allison Anders.[6] Based on her personal experiences as a migrant from Kentucky to Florida, Anders's film tells the story of a young woman who is gang-raped after her family moved to Cocoa Beach to "start over" in the 1960s. Although set in the same era as Elvis Presley's film *Follow That Dream* (1962), *Things Behind the Sun* is not the lighthearted story of opportunity and re-creation experienced by Presley's Georgia family.

We assume that films not only reflect popular images but also affect how viewers interpret people, events, and even places. Moreover, viewers' perceptions of the same film undoubtedly change as times change. While this book focuses on our perceptions of how filmmakers have viewed Florida and its people, we realize that films have multiple messages that speak differently to different people in different eras. Nevertheless we are convinced that a number of dominant themes have become so much a part of films about Florida that in many cases they are accepted conventions. Whether these images are accurate or not depends in part on the audience's point of view, and we frequently comment on what we see as particularly notable insights or inaccuracies in films. However, we make no attempt to gauge the possible impact of movies on other viewers. So-called reception theory, which looks at how audiences may receive and act on cinematic images, is a complex and hotly debated subject that we leave to others. Our modest goal is to analyze what we see as dominant messages of films about Florida and to examine how these messages have changed over time. The book is not specifically directed at academics or specialists in film studies, but rather at general readers with an interest in images of Florida and Floridians.

At the end of the book, we have included a list of over three hundred films set entirely or partly in Florida. The length of this list is itself evidence of the significance of the topic in movies. In the text we also mention films that have some dialogue referring to Florida, even though all the action occurs elsewhere. The list and the book itself were made possible by the Web sites of the Internet Movie Data Base (*IMDB.com*) and the American Film Institute (*AFI.com*), as well as the film archive of the Library of Congress. The *IMDB* Web site lists filming locations and other relevant information about films, providing an invaluable source for researching and writing this book. The site of the American Film Institute contains lengthy synopses of many Florida films, including some no longer available. Still, we are aware that some films may have been overlooked. If so, add them to the list and think about how they fit into our interpretations. In addition, new films about Florida continue to appear, and we hope this book will need to be updated in a few years.

We are excluding any consideration of movies that were filmed in Florida but had plots that set the story somewhere else. With many silent films, the exact setting of the plots is difficult to determine. Even though many films were made in Florida during the first two decades of the industry, most are no longer available, and surviving descriptions do not always indicate where the story took place. With one exception, we have also omitted foreign films about Florida people and places, although these films might provide an interesting subject for future research.

Documentaries and docudramas have also been excluded, as well as movies made for television and so-called X-rated films. Certainly, made-for-TV films have enjoyed large audiences and have no doubt affected perceptions about the state and its people, but their limited availability for viewing would make it difficult to include them in a thorough analysis. We are also aware that X-rated films have been widely produced in Florida, but even if the state itself were somehow integral to their plots, settings, or characters, we doubt that those movies would suggest different interpretations than we offer here. We do include many other low-budget films, produced by independents, as well as by major and minor studios. Some of these went straight to video without any theater distribution, and others premiered at film festivals before being released on video.

In some places we have noted films that are no longer available for viewing. We have included information gleaned from *IMDB.com*, newspaper reviews, and other sources when discussing these films. Where appropriate we have also included comments from professional film critics.

Watching these many films has enhanced our appreciation for filmmakers and for the state. We hope this book will encourage readers to watch more Florida movies and think about images of the state and its people on the screen. We invite you to share our experience by buying or renting one of the films on our list. Close your curtains or drapes to block out the sunshine, turn down the air conditioner to cool off, make some guacamole dip with Florida avocados, grab some chips, pour a glass of Florida orange juice or wine, sit back, and enjoy the film.

Part 1

Settings

Early film companies flocked to Florida to take advantage of its good weather for year-round shooting outdoors. As a result the state's natural and constructed environment provided settings for numerous silent movies, including many that related tales about faraway places. Florida's beaches, forests, and rural countryside appear as backdrops for early films supposedly set in exotic parts of the world such as Africa and the South Pacific. The state also inspired some moviemakers to use the natural and built environments in order to dramatize historical or contemporary tales about Florida itself. Vacation cities like Palm Beach and Miami and natural settings like beaches and the Everglades provided ready-made backdrops for stories about the Sunshine State and its people. These images undoubtedly resonated with national audiences that were increasingly familiar with Florida's reputation as a place for vacations, romance, land speculation, and economic opportunity. California became the center of the film industry by the late 1920s, but wherever actually produced, movies about Florida continued to reflect certain perceptions about the state's physical environment and its significance.

Over the years, changes in Florida's landscape, as well as its meaning, have been captured by moviemakers. Like any other state, Florida has its own particular characteristics, and filmmakers have focused on those readily identified with the state. Specific architectural designs, land features, and places associated with particular experiences have been used in movies to establish notions of behavior, class, and even mood. Indeed, elements of the state's environment, such as swamps and freeways, have become part of the story line in some films.

Seeing Florida's landscape through the lens of filmmakers reveals not only how they view the state, but also what perceptions the movie-going public might harbor. After all, screenwriters and directors share with their audiences common frames of reference that make film story lines believable whether told as drama, comedy, action/adventure, or horror. Even fantasies set in Florida usually build on some recognizable physical reality about the state. Needless to say, cinematic portrayals of the environment may also grossly, even if unintentionally, distort reality, as evidenced by shots of mountain ranges in movies supposedly set in Miami. Nevertheless, the settings of movies provide clues to their messages about Florida's natural and manufactured environment.

Chapter 1

*"Hey, would you get a load of the sunshine?
I feel like a teenager."*
Cocoon: The Return (1988)

"I hate Florida—too much sun."
Great Expectations (1998)

Paradise Framed

The Natural Environment

"The climate of Florida is undoubtedly its chief charm," noted a travel writer in 1875.[1] As far back as Ponce de León's search for the Fountain of Youth, Florida's primary attraction has been its environment. Even the name *La Florida* that Ponce de León gave the area in 1513 refers to "the land of flowers." For centuries the peninsula has been commonly associated with bright sun, sandy beaches, and warm water. However, Florida's natural environment also harbors threats, given the dangers posed by dark swamps, menacing alligators, man-eating sharks, and killer hurricanes. In reality the same phenomenon may be viewed as either a blessing or a curse. The sun, for example, can be a source of vitamin D or a cause of cancer.

Cinematic images of Florida's environment tend to alternate between the extremes of dream and nightmare, leaving little room for subtlety. With notable exceptions, beaches and sunshine (or sunsets) appear in most movies set in Florida. It seldom rains, and few people sweat, even in the absence of air conditioning. By portraying the Atlantic Ocean and the Gulf of Mexico from the perspective of sunbathers on beautiful beaches, films often overlook the wall-to-wall condos and hotels that line Florida's coasts. Significantly, few films question the impact of growth in the state. Instead wildlife appears to present the greatest danger to residents and tourists. The cinematic paradise that coastal Florida evokes has its counterpart in the Everglades, which films represent as dark and mysterious with a variety of natural threats like alligators that can bring hell on earth.

An early expression of the conflicting images of Florida appears in the Marx Brothers' film *The Cocoanuts* (1929). One of the first talking pictures about Florida, *The Cocoanuts* captures the decidedly contradictory sentiments about the state's environment in two lines of dialogue written by George S. Kaufman. "Florida—sunshine, sunshine, perpetual sunshine all the year round," says Groucho Marx as he tries to sell some worthless land in south Florida. "Let's get the auction started before we get a tornado."

The extremes of the state's semitropical climate propel the action in *The Yearling* (1946). Based on the novel by Marjorie Kinnan Rawlings, the classic film won Academy Awards for best art direction and best cinematography in color. Taking full advantage of Technicolor, *The Yearling* opens with a panorama that shows bright sunlight filtered through a moss-laden oak tree on a spit of land beside a lake of shimmering blue water. In a voice-over, Penny Baxter (Gregory Peck) declares, "Lake George, Florida. April 1878." As the camera swings from this lake in central Florida and moves up a river, Baxter explains that after fighting the Yankees in the war, he "came down this broad river, goin' back into the wilderness, away from civilization, looking for a place to settle . . . back into the scrub country. It got wilder as I got deeper into the woods. . . . Even wilder . . . as I got back closer to the sources, to the beginnin' of things, further away from towns and wars." At the end of his journey, Baxter says that he found a village and a wife, and the two of them "cleared and cultivated a little piece of half-fertile ground." Despite the qualifier "half-fertile," the opening shots of *The Yearling* portray an unspoiled paradise.

The first scene with Baxter's son Jody (Claude Jarman Jr.) reinforces this image. The eleven-year-old lies dreamily in a glen, watching deer and raccoons as they come to drink from a stream beside him. Upon returning home, he tells his father of his longing to have an animal as a pet. The wish is fulfilled when Jody finds an abandoned fawn and brings it home

3. Claude Jarman Jr. in *The Yearling* (1946). By permission of Photofest.

in his arms. The two bond together as they frolic in the wild and even sleep together in Jody's bed. Nature, it seems, can be tamed.

After framing Florida as a dreamland, *The Yearling* reveals that nature can also bring death and destruction. A marauding bear kills several of the Baxters' farm animals. Soon thereafter, Penny almost dies from a snake bite. At another point Jody hears a wolf howl in the night. The biggest threat to the family comes from the weather. Six days of heavy rain ruin their food crops. When the rain finally stops and the trio emerges from their cabin, Jody's mother (Jane Wyman) weeps at the sight of their flooded land. Trying to restore their spirits, Penny Baxter says, "There ain't much of a world left for us, but it's all we got. Let's be thankful that we got any world at all." On cue the sun then breaks through the clouds, and the next scene shows a blue sky and flowers in bloom.

However, nature soon offers a new challenge. After Jody's pet deer, Flag, grows into a yearling, he destroys first the family's tobacco plants and then the corn crop. "That settles it," Jody's mother says, "that deer has got to go." After Jody and his pet get one more reprieve, the boy replants the corn and builds a high fence around it. The yearling, of course, simply jumps the fence and once again tramples the family's corn. Deer, like the weather, cannot be controlled. "You know we depend on our crops to live," Penny tells his son. "And you know there ain't a way in the world to keep that wild yearling from destroying them." He then orders Jody to take the yearling out and shoot him.

As Jody leads the yearling away on a rope, he says, "You gotta' go away and never come back. . . . We can't live together like I planned." He then releases the deer. When the yearling returns to the farm, Jody's mother shoots him. The wounded animal is finally shot dead by Jody who immediately runs away from home. After several days without food, he is rescued on the river by the crew of a steamboat. Returning home, he has clearly learned the hard lesson that life in Florida is not easy, and it requires recognizing that nature can be destructive and beyond human control. "He ain't a yearling no longer," Penny Baxter says of his son at the end of the film.

Despite the havoc that nature can cause in Florida, most films show the sun shining brightly. Photographed at dawn or sunset, the sun offers a benign and beautiful backdrop, especially in the Keys as depicted in *92 in the Shade* (1975), *Up Close and Personal* (1996), and *Blood and Wine* (1997). The promise of sun (and good food) brings a visitor to Miami in the comedy *Big Trouble* (2002), which features a hippylike character, named Puggy (Jason Lee), who leaves Boston after he reads "an article in Martha Stewart's *Living* that said sunny Miami had some of the finest Cuban restaurants in the entire world." Within minutes of his arrival in Miami, Puggy was thinking, according to the film's narrator, "that this had to be the warmest and friendliest place on earth." The desire to escape from bad weather in the north to Florida's semitropical climate figures as a plot device in numerous films, including *The Big Street* (1942), *Midnight Cowboy* (1969), *Stranger than Paradise* (1984), and *Running Scared* (1986).

Favorable images of Florida's environment are often countered in films by decidedly negative aspects of the state's climate. In the days before air conditioning, the heat is considered unbearable in summer. Even though characters rarely sweat, they complain about the hot weather. In *Key Largo* (1948), Frank McLoud (Humphrey Bogart) arrives in the summer and comments to locals, Nora Temple (Lauren Bacall) and her father-in-law (Lionel Barrymore), that "the Keys are different than anything I've ever seen. And hotter." Barrymore's character warns that it will not get any cooler until November, when "the thermometer will go down to about a hundred, and the sand flies and mosquitoes will disappear, and it'll be right livable for about three months." In another scene with rain falling outside, the gangster played by Edward G. Robinson says, "You'd think

4. Michelle Pfeiffer and Robert Redford in the Florida Keys. *Up Close and Personal* (1996).

this would cool things off, but it don't." Ceiling fans provide the only relief.

A Flash of Green (1984), an independent film by Victor Nuñez, is set in the 1950s and deals realistically with a number of Florida themes, including the weather. The title refers to the phenomenon that is supposedly visible on rare occasions just as the sun dips below the horizon, and the film shows spectacular sunsets along Florida's west coast. In the absence of air conditioning, the heat is ever present, but no one complains. They just sweat, and the lead character (Ed Harris) always wears his tie loose at the neck.

Films actually made in the 1950s rarely show the effects of Florida's humidity. In *Miami Exposé* (1956), male characters often sweat, but women appear untouched by the heat. The swimmer Esther Williams frequently gets wet in her Florida films, but never from perspiration. *Where the Boys Are* (1960) also dates from pre-air-conditioning days, but no one sweats, even on the beach. Nevertheless the hot weather apparently affects people. Observing tourists doing the limbo on the beach and a cop arresting a drunk, someone comments, "It's the climate."

Despite the annual threat of hurricanes in Florida, only a few films use them as a plot device. *Reap the Wild Wind* (1942), a Cecil B. DeMille movie set in the Florida Keys during the 1840s, opens with hurricane-force winds under a clouded sky. A voice-over narrator announces that along the lines of seagoing commerce "lie the sharklike teeth of the Florida Keys, where savage hurricanes come screaming out of the Caribbean and drive tall ships onto the destroying shores." When a hurricane strikes in *Key Largo*, the aging hotel owner (Lionel Barrymore) recalls that "the worst storm we ever had was back in '35. The wind whipped up a big wave. . . . Eight hundred people were washed out to sea." Upon hearing this, the frightened gangster played by Edward G. Robinson responds, "You're a liar. Nobody would live here after a thing like that happened." The year after *Key Largo* first appeared on the big screen, another movie used the menace of tropical storms in its title. *Slattery's Hurricane* (1949), based on a novel by Herman Wouk, stars Richard Widmark as a pilot who regains his self-confidence by flying into the eye of a hurricane approaching Florida. In *Hurricane Island* (1951) a ferocious storm wipes out the villains.

Perhaps surprisingly, the longest and most realistic treatment of a hurricane striking Florida appears in *Flipper* (1963). Before the beloved dolphin ever makes an appearance, the entire first third of the movie covers the course and impact of "Hurricane Hazel" as it strikes the Keys. The story begins with Porter Ricks (Chuck Conners), a professional fisherman, out on his boat with his son Sandy (Luke Halpin). When the hurricane unexpectedly changes course, they make for shore, plowing through high waves. As they approach their home port on a Florida key, a water spout hovers behind them. Meanwhile, with the winds increasing, people on the key are shown boarding up buildings, piling up sandbags, and tying down trailers. Porter and Sandy outrun the worst of the storm, and along with several dozen other residents, they take shelter in the small town's post office, which has wooden shutters over the windows. As wind speeds surpass one hundred miles per hour, the roaring sound gets louder, and flying debris crashes against the outside of the post office. Finally the storm passes, the sun comes out, and people emerge to survey the damage. One building is destroyed, and tree limbs litter the area. A local fisherman's boat washes up with no trace of any survivors.

The remake of *Flipper* (1996) reduces the hurricane scene to about one minute, but a few other films depict hurricanes in Florida. In *Treasure of Matecumbe* (1976), a Disney production, nineteenth-century treasure hunters travel to the Florida Keys, where they suffer through a horrendous hurricane. The climactic scene of *The Mean Season* (1985) takes place during a hurricane that causes intermittent blackouts in south Florida.

Inclement weather rarely plays a significant role in movies about Florida. It occasionally rains in recent films such as *Folks!* (1992) and *The Specialist* (1994), but tropical downpours almost never occur. However, exceptions make interesting use of bad weather. *The Yearling* and *Yellowneck* (1955) are two early films that show torrential rain storms contributing to the harshness of life in Florida. In *Any Given Sunday* (1999), a professional football game in Miami's Orange Bowl is played in such heavy rain that a sportscaster (Oliver Stone) refers to it as "the Monsoon Bowl." *Fair Game* (1995) and *Held for Ransom* (2000) dramatize chase scenes with rain and lightning. In *Summer Rental* (1985) and *Gone Fishin'* (1997) rain is one of the many unexpected developments that disappoint Florida vacationers. Another comedy, *Caddyshack* (1980), shows a golfer struck dead by a bolt of lightning. A thunderstorm provokes the climactic crisis in the family movie *Because of Winn-Dixie* (2005), which tells the story of a young girl living in a small Florida town.

The most significant and distinctive use of Florida weather by film-makers appears in films noirs, and John Huston's *Key Largo* established the pattern. As one study of the style points out, most films noirs of the 1940s use dark city streets and urban settings to produce the somber mood, but *Key Largo* features "exotic scenery, the storm at sea, and the closed-in feeling of the hotel lounge . . . [to] create a heavy, humid atmosphere that is laden with claustrophobic tension."[2] In *Key Largo*, Florida's heat and humidity become oppressive, and the hurricane frightens even hardened criminals.

In the 1970s and 1980s, the state's weather caught the attention of filmmakers who revived the noir style in what became known as neo-noir or Florida noir. The revival began with the long overlooked film *Night Moves* (1975), directed by Arthur Penn. As the title suggests, much of the action occurs after sunset, thus avoiding the sunlight of the Keys, where most of the film is set. The female lead (Jennifer Warren) is described as "edgy," which she attributes to "the heat and low wages." She works at an isolated fish camp that has rustic cabins with no sign of air conditioning. The movie's private eye (Gene Hackman) travels from Los Angeles to the Keys in search of a sixteen-year-old runaway, played by Melanie Griffith in her first film role, and when he finds her, she explains life in Florida in terms of the weather. "There's been some great storms here," she says. "It feels like everything's gonna blow away." More ominous, according to another character, is the so-called Devil's Triangle, a stretch of water near the Keys that is "a bad area for accidents. . . . They got more missing planes and boats there than you can count." The film's plot revolves around a downed plane discovered in those waters.

Six years after *Night Moves* was released, *Body Heat* (1981) became the classic neo-noir film set in Florida. From the title through virtually every

5. Gene Hackman, Jennifer Warner, and Melanie Griffith in *Night Moves* (1975). By permission of Photofest.

scene, Florida's oppressive summer weather plays a leading role in the film, provoking dialogue and even action. Set in a small fictional town in south Florida, the film opens at night with a sweating, bare-chested man looking out an open bedroom window. "My God, it's hot," a woman standing behind him says in the movie's first line. "I just stepped out of the shower," she continues, "and started sweating again." The action then shifts to a courtroom with defense attorney Ned Racine (William Hurt) and a local prosecutor (Ted Danson) in conference with the judge. A fan blows ineffectively in the background, and the faces of the three men are shiny with perspiration. After this scene the attorneys adjourn to a crowded diner where they sit with their coats off, ties loosened, and shirt collars open. A wall air conditioner provides so little relief that Danson's character says to the waitress, "When are you going to get a real air conditioner in here?" For the most part, air conditioning is conspicuously absent in the film.

The inescapable heat and humidity, even after sunset, dominate much of the dialogue in the early scenes of *Body Heat*. Ned Racine first encounters Matty Walker, the femme fatale played by Kathleen Turner in her first movie role, at an outdoor concert in the evening, and the spectators are fanning themselves as they listen to the music. Spotting Matty for the first time as she leaves the concert, Ned approaches her and uses the weather to break the ice. "You can stand here with me if you want," he says, "but you'll have to agree not to talk about the heat." During the playful banter that ensues, the two stop for sno-cones, and Matty spills some of the shaved ice on her blouse. "At least it's cool," she says, "I was burning up." Matty and Ned part, and when he encounters her some days later, she says, "You're the one who doesn't like to talk about the heat. Too bad—I'd tell you about my chimes." Encouraged by him, she continues, "The wind chimes on my porch—they keep ringing, and I go out there expecting a cool breeze—that's what they've always meant, but not this year. This year it's just hot air." After the couple later makes love at her waterfront mansion, which has no air conditioning, they take a bath in ice water, a cube of which Matty rubs sensuously on her face. In another scene Ned goes to his refrigerator to get a beer, and he stands there in a familiar Florida pose, trying to cool off with the door wide open.

Body Heat makes it clear that Florida's unrelenting heat raises not only the body temperature but also the crime rate. In his first appearance, a local detective (J. A. Preston) joins Ned and the prosecutor at their table in the diner. As the three men sit with ties loosened and shirt sleeves rolled up, the detective talks about the increase in his workload due to the weather. "When it gets hot, people try to kill each other," he explains. "It's that crisis atmosphere, ya' know. People dress different, feel different,

6. Kathleen Turner and William Hurt cool off with sno-cones in *Body Heat* (1981).

sweat more, wake up cranky, and never recover." In words and images, especially the perpetual coat of perspiration worn by its characters, *Body Heat* gives viewers the feel of Florida's sticky, semitropical climate.

Despite the success of *Body Heat*, the potential of Florida's weather for creating a noir setting did not capture a following among screenwriters and directors until the 1990s. The wave arrived with *China Moon* (1994), which one observer dismissed as faux noir because he found it neither a work of art nor even interesting.[3] Nevertheless, it was followed by a number of films, including *Blood and Wine*, *Palmetto* (1998), *Wild Things* (1998), *Big City Blues* (1999), and *Out of Time* (2003), that use the dark side of Florida's climate to provide much of the atmosphere. "Weather frequently acts as an unspoken character in film noir," one reviewer pointed out, noting that "the rain pours constantly in *China Moon*."[4] Some Florida films, like *Wild Things*, emphasize the sharp contrasts in the state's environment with shots of bright sunshine and blistering heat along the beach that alternate with dark scenes in the Everglades.

Palmetto, directed by Volker Schlöndorff, mirrors *Body Heat* by using heat and sweat to evoke a steamy, sensual atmosphere. The local bar and a cabin on the beach have no air conditioning, and the film's antihero, Harry Barber (Woody Harrelson), wears a permanent layer of sweat. A reviewer for the *New York Times* wrote that this "juicy film noir" vividly depicts "semitropical rot in southern Florida. . . . Filled with steamy tropical downpours, shots of dripping palm leaves, and glistening cockroaches, the movie makes the most of the location, and after a while you feel the heat and humidity begin to settle over you." In the opening scene, Harry Barber watches a palmetto bug crawl across his prison cell, and more roaches are shown in later scenes, leading a San Francisco reviewer (apparently unaware of palmetto bushes) to assert that the film "takes its title from a Florida town named after the palmetto bug."[5] Although the film has one shot of a beautiful sunset on Florida's west coast, rain falls throughout much of the second half of *Palmetto*. With rain still coming down as Harry runs from police at the end of the film, he reflects wistfully that he "was hoping the rain was going to wash away the whole dirty business." Rain also helps create the dark mood of *Out of Time*, which is set in the Keys. The film features many shots of Florida's lush environment of beaches, palm trees, mangroves, and sunsets, but heat, humidity, and rain provide the gloomy atmosphere for this noir thriller. In the film's denouement, the villains are dispatched during a horrific rainstorm.

A few movies emphasize the impact of air conditioning on life in Florida. The film *Up Close and Personal* uses sunsets for romantic backdrops

7. Hume Cronyn in *Cocoon: The Return* (1988). By permission of Photofest.

for stars Michelle Pfeiffer and Robert Redford, but Pfeiffer's character, a fledgling weather reporter at a Miami TV station, makes it clear in her first on-camera appearance that indoors is the place to be in south Florida. "It's heat, heat and more heat. . . . The five-day forecast is more, more, more, hot, hot, hot. Stay inside. Cuddle up. Cuddle up and enjoy the air conditioning." Air conditioning not only brings more people to Florida, but it also keeps them alive, according to an amusing victim of Alzheimer's disease in *Folks!* The character, played by Don Ameche, says Florida is "wall-to-wall old people," who stay alive because "air conditioning keeps them in cold storage."

While air conditioning makes indoor Florida more livable, it appears to make the outdoors less tolerable, especially with growing concern about skin cancer. In the fantasy film *Cocoon: The Return*, when a retiree (Hume Cronyn) goes to the beach, he declares, "Hey, would you get a load of the sunshine? I feel like a teenager." However, when another retiree (Jack Gilford) prepares for the beach, he puts on a hat, long pants, and a jacket. "We'll have to stop at a pharmacy," he says. "If I don't have zinc oxide, I'll burn to a crisp. . . . Did you bring juice? I'll get dehydrated." In *Police Academy 5: Assignment Miami Beach* (1988), the Florida sun is so brutal that one of the visiting cops gets a wicked sunburn, as does the character played by John Candy in *Summer Rental*. A New Yorker in *Great Expecta-*

tions declares, "I hate Florida—too much sun." In *Forever Mine* (1999), a hotel employee warns a sunbather in Miami, "Be careful. This can be deceiving. . . . Florida sun—rays today, raisins tomorrow." Negative views of Florida's environment are projected into the past in *Cabeza de Vaca* (1991), a film about the sixteenth-century Spanish conquistador who encounters a harsh, uninviting climate during his brief stay in Florida.

The Sunshine State's most distinguishing physical feature is undoubtedly water. Florida not only has over one thousand miles of coastline, but it is also dotted with lakes, rivers, and huge swamps. Although these waters appear in virtually every movie set in Florida, they can be used to invoke very different images and themes. The state's waters can depict paradise or nightmare and provide characters with a variety of experiences, ranging from cleansing and entertainment to death.

The state's coastline is commonly used by filmmakers to establish a Florida setting. Silent films made in Florida, notably *A Florida Enchantment* (1914), take advantage of the location to show pristine beaches and oceanfronts. *It's the Old Army Game* (1926), a silent film starring W. C. Fields, includes a brief scene of a deserted Florida beach. By the 1950s films often used aerial views of Florida's coastline as the establishing shot to set the scene. Both *Miami Story* (1954) and *Miami Exposé* open this way. Even when filmed elsewhere, early movies about Florida, such as *The Big Street*, *The Chase* (1946), and *Some Like It Hot* (1959), have requisite scenes of beaches that are presented as romantic places. Except for *Reap the Wild Wind* and *Key Largo*, which depict Florida waters as menacing, even deadly, most movies from the 1940s and 1950s simply use the coastal waters as a backdrop.

By the 1960s, with Florida tourism flourishing, beaches became the defining image for escape and fun. While movies about Spring Break like *Where the Boys Are* helped popularize Ft. Lauderdale among college students, *The Bellboy* (1960) and *Tony Rome* (1967) portray Miami Beach as a waterfront playground for adults. Independent films later rendered a more realistic view of beaches, especially in north Florida. *Stranger Than Paradise*, directed by Jim Jarmusch, plays the perception of Florida against its reality. Two friends (John Lurie and Richard Edson) stuck in Ohio with snow on the ground dream about going "to some warm place." One suggests Florida because "it's beautiful down there—white beaches and girls in bikinis." However, when they arrive in north Florida in the middle of winter, they discover that it is so cold that they need jackets and sweaters to walk on the beach. Similarly, *Ruby in Paradise* (1993) shows how dreary and cold the beaches of Panama City can be in winter.

Films frequently portray Florida beaches as either deserted or peopled largely by attractive young women in skimpy bathing suits. In *A Murder of Crows* (1999), when the character played by Cuba Gooding Jr. visits Key West, he sits alone on the beach. More commonly, babes in bikinis are Florida icons who appear even in dramas that are not beach movies, such as *Scarface* (1983), *Donnie Brasco* (1997), and *Any Given Sunday*. Comedies in particular exploit this association. *Cocoon: The Return, Summer Rental,* and *Revenge of the Nerds II: Nerds in Paradise* (1987) all show scantily clad women on the beach. In *Running Scared* Billy Crystal and Gregory Hines play Chicago cops who vacation in Key West, where they easily pick up one woman after another (white for Crystal and black for Hines!). Back in Chicago, Crystal's character reminds his partner that they "have an obligation to the lovely ladies of Key West. Remember them—the long legs, flat bellies, the tight buns, and those tanned tits."

Much of the natural beauty of Florida lies under water. Two early films about sponge divers in Tarpon Springs take viewers *Down Under the Sea* (1936) and *Sixteen Fathoms Deep* (1948). In addition to showing how sponges are gathered by hand, *Sixteen Fathoms Deep* captures beautiful underwater panoramas with turtles, sharks, and other fish. The film's shots of dolphins jumping out of the water hint at why this creature comes to represent the dream of man and nature living in harmony in Florida.

Flipper turns that dream into cinematic reality. The film's star is a dolphin called Flipper, who was actually a trained dolphin named Mitzie (1958–1972). The story line has twelve-year-old Sandy Ricks find the dolphin washed ashore after he and his family survive Hurricane Hazel. Wounded by a spear from a spear gun, Flipper is nursed back to health by Sandy, who forms a close bond with this supposedly wild mammal. The pair spend days frolicking together, eventually performing tricks for local kids. Disappointment sets in when Sandy's father insists on releasing the healthy dolphin back into the wild. From the fisherman father's point of view, dolphins are "a deadly enemy," because "they tear our nets, they eat our fish, they chase the rest away. . . . If they come, we'll kill them. . . . Even Flipper." However, after returning to ocean waters, Flipper proves a savior when Sandy is attacked by a shark, and Flipper kills the shark by repeatedly head-butting it. This leads Sandy's father to decide "to share with the dolphins, not to kill them." The success of this story about the bond formed between a boy and a dolphin turned Flipper into a TV star with his own series. It also helped create a mania for dolphin studies and dolphin-watching.

8. Luke Halpin in *Flipper* (1963). By permission of Photofest.

Several films portray the mammals as friendly creatures. *Cocoon* (1985) uses dolphins on the surface of the Gulf of Mexico to suggest something magical about the waters in the film's opening scene. Later in the movie, they swim alongside a boat and frolic with divers. In *Cocoon: The Return*, dolphins on the water's surface make a chirping sound, as though they are trying to communicate. A subplot in *Night Moves* appears to mock the fixation with dolphins. When the character played by Gene Hackman arrives in the Keys, he finds a woman (Jennifer Warren) feeding dolphins enclosed in a pen alongside a dock. "There's a big demand for dolphins," she explains. "Lots of people want them. You'd be surprised. People buy them for their swimming pools. They think it's chic to have a dolphin for a pet."

Manatees, the newest darling of animal lovers, have thus far at-tracted little attention in Hollywood, probably because, unlike dolphins, they cannot be trained as performers. An obscure movie, *Point of Impact* (1993), has a reference to endangered manatees, which do not actually appear in the film. Instead a Miami retiree spends his time trying to pro-tect manatees and explains, "They're sensitive creatures. They're a dying breed. They don't take too kindly to the prop of an outboard." Thus, unlike dolphins, which reinforce the view of Florida as paradise, the endangered manatee serves as a marker of paradise lost.

Despite the cinematic allure of Florida's beaches and surrounding waters, they have always harbored danger. In *The Cocoanuts* Groucho Marx engages in some wordplay about a Florida fruit he calls "alligator pears," and he asks, "how many alligator pears [pairs?] are sent out of this state every year and told not to come back?" His answer: "All they can get hold of." *The Barefoot Mailman* (1951) tells the story of a mail carrier (Jerome Courtland) who braves more than rain, sleet, and snow to deliver the mail in south Florida during the 1890s. The physical obstacles he faces daily include a swamp with alligators that kill a "beachcomber" and attack the mail carrier who wrestles one of the creatures to save his own life. Films in the 1980s bring increasing signs of menace in Florida waters. *Spring Break* (1983) includes plenty of women in bikinis, but when a young man goes to relieve himself in a wooded area along Ft. Lauderdale's famed beach, he is attacked by an alligator that steals his pants. In *Eyes of a Stranger* (1981), the opening scene has a wildlife photographer on an isolated beach stumble upon the nude body of a dead woman floating in the water with a belt around her neck. Cinematic dangers on and near Florida's beaches suggest a perception of paradise lost by the 1980s.

The greatest living threats in Florida clearly lurk under water. One of the first images of man-eating monsters below the surface comes in *Reap the Wild Wind*, an epic from the early 1940s that has a giant squid squeeze the life out of the film's star, John Wayne. In *Beneath the 12-Mile Reef* (1953), a huge octopus attacks sponge divers from Tarpon Springs. A very real underwater threat—at least for fish—provides a subplot in *Flipper* when fishermen encounter the effects of "red tide," a microorganism that causes enormous fish kills. Like a giant squid or octopus, red tide may make a convenient plot device for movies about the deep sea, but it hardly presents a threat to the average swimmer on a Florida vacation.

Instead sharks loom as the biggest menace in the ocean, a role played by alligators in the state's fresh waters. Like beach movies that began in California locations, the shark movie, of course, started elsewhere with *Jaws* (1975), but this man-eater becomes associated with Florida, especially with increased media coverage of shark attacks in the Sunshine State. Significantly, few sharks appeared in Florida movies until *Jaws* made people think twice about swimming in the ocean. *Flipper* depicts one of the first shark attacks on the big screen, and the opening scene of *Lady in Cement* (1968) shows sharks, but they simply circle the dead body

9. The star of *Jaws 3-D* (1983), prowling at Sea World. By permission of Photofest.

of a woman, encountered by Tony Rome (Frank Sinatra) while deep-sea diving near Miami. The potential impact of sharks on Florida tourism elicits some humorous dialogue in *Absence of Malice* (1981), which was made a few years after *Jaws*. In the Florida film Sally Fields plays a Miami reporter who overhears a colleague on the phone asking a cop about the possible presence of sharks in a news story. "You might want to go a little easy on the sharks," Fields's character advises. "Don't scare the tourists. The rule is it's a shark if it walks out of the water, stops traffic, and bites a cop. If they're just swimming around, we call them fish."

Jaws 3-D (1983) brings the menace of sharks to Florida in a far-fetched plot. The movie opens with the familiar *Jaws* theme music and a serene underwater shot of fish that is suddenly disrupted by a burst of blood. A killer shark has found its way into an amusement park on Florida's coast. Among the fantasies perpetrated by the film is the illusion that sharks can growl and swim backward. The white hats in the film are worn by dolphins, the good underwater creatures, who try to warn divers about the presence of sharks. In spite of its silly story line, *Jaws 3-D* undoubtedly serves to reinforce the image of Florida waters filled with danger.

Newspaper headlines about periodic attacks also contribute to the fear of sharks, but the actual threat is remote. Since 1990 Florida has annually averaged twenty-one shark attacks that have caused a total of four deaths. By comparison, lightning has injured an average of forty-five people annually in the state since 1959, resulting in an average of nine deaths each year.[6]

Despite the infrequency of shark attacks, films highlight the threat. The nightmare vacation in *Summer Rental* includes sharks swimming in Gulf waters. In *Licence to Kill* (1989) James Bond's longtime friend, CIA agent Felix Leiter (David Hedison), is seized by an evil drug lord who has him lowered into a shark tank in the Keys. Instead of killing Leiter, the villains let the shark chomp off his leg, and they leave him with a note that says, "He Disagreed With Something That Ate Him." The same shark later kills a corrupt drug enforcement agent who falls into the tank during a fight with James Bond (Timothy Dalton). The villain in *Police Academy 5* threatens to use a hostage as "shark bait." *Blood and Wine* portrays a popular sport that feeds on sharks. The film opens on a south Florida beach with two friends fishing for sharks at night, and after they catch one, they sell it. *Any Given Sunday* exploits the shark theme in a different way. The film recounts the troubles of a professional football team (the Miami Sharks) that plays in Shark Stadium.

10. Felix Leiter (David Hedison) being tortured by a shark in *Licence to Kill* (1989). By permission of Photofest.

Like Florida's coastal waters and beaches, the state's interior can be portrayed in idyllic terms or as an inferno. Filmmakers generally view the landscape of central and north Florida through the lens first used in *The Yearling,* with dense woodlands of trees covered in Spanish moss that allow only filtered sunlight to shine through. This setting reappears in *Gal Young 'Un* (1979), directed by Victor Nuñez and based on another story by Marjorie Kinnan Rawlings. The small-budget independent film depicts central Florida during the 1930s and 1940s. The forests are dominated by pine trees with occasional dogwoods in bloom and a few palm trees. The sun's rays scarcely penetrate the foliage. A creek, bordered by cypress trees, runs through the woods. The only signs of civilization are some dirt roads and isolated wooden buildings with tin roofs. The sounds of nature are ever present with chirping birds during the day and cicadas at night. A later film, *Cross Creek* (1983), relates the story of Marjorie Kinnan Rawlings's arrival and early years in the area. Directed by Martin Ritt, the film has a now familiar setting of woods with the addition of a beautiful lake that has cypress knees poking out of the water. Rawlings's property boasts an orange grove that she brings back into production despite a freeze that threatens her crop.

More recent films set in Florida's rural interior show an area caught in a time warp. *Ulee's Gold* (1997), *Night Orchid* (1997), *Trans* (1998), *Trash* (1999), and *First of May* (2000) all suggest that little has changed since the days of Marjorie Kinnan Rawlings. The natural environment still includes moss-laden trees, as well as rivers and swamps with protruding cypress knees. Orange groves also appear in several of these films. Rural Florida is dated and rotting, consisting of dirt roads and small towns with old gas stations, "cracker" houses, shacks, and trailers. What may have been picturesque in *The Yearling* has now become backward, especially with the complete lack of air conditioning in all these films depicting contemporary rural Florida.

Despite the decaying built landscape of Florida's interior, the natural environment can still provide an idyllic escape. *Striptease* (1996) includes a brief scene showing a Miami cop (Armand Assante) sitting on the porch of an isolated log cabin next to a lake with birds chirping in the background. "Is this really on the same planet as Miami?" he wonders. *Sunshine State* (2002) features a long scene in which two characters escape the conflicts of a beach community by canoeing down a peaceful north Florida river that is unspoiled by development. Significantly most of these films dealing with small towns and rural areas of Florida are made by independent filmmakers working with small budgets.

11. A river scene from *Sunshine State* (2002).

Hollywood has shown little interest in Florida's interior, except for the Everglades. All that Florida represents in terms of both natural beauty and mortal danger surfaces in cinematic portraits of the Everglades. Described as "a river of grass" by Marjory Stoneman Douglas, "the mysterious Everglades" have remained a place of mystery to everyone who does not understand them, she wrote in 1947.[7] For filmmakers the Everglades may reflect Florida's striking beauty when photographed from the air, especially at sunset, but at ground level the vast, swampy marshes and dark, moss-drenched stands of trees harbor evil threats, especially to white men who venture into the Indian enclave. Films portray this region of south Florida as inhabited by snakes, panthers, bears, and, most importantly, man-eating alligators. Although other critters appear in some movies set in the Everglades, gators dominate scenes of the Glades, evoking a nightmarish vision of hell on earth.

Several early films focus on the threat from alligators in Florida. In the silent film *Her Father's Gold* (1916), a reporter (Harris Gordon) goes to Florida to investigate a man-eating alligator and falls in love with a woman (Barbara Gilroy) whose money is stolen. All ends happily when they find the stash and the thief is eaten by the alligator. In *Playthings of Desire* (1934) the half-eaten body of a murder victim is discovered in an alligator-infested swamp.

Films made in the 1950s use the Everglades as background for nineteenth-century period pieces. In effect they are Florida "westerns" with white frontiersmen battling untamed Seminoles. In *Distant Drums* (1951),

Shark River (1953), *Naked in the Sun* (1957), and *Yellowneck* the Indian menace is made all the worse by the "beautiful, weird, and deadly" territory,
as the narrator explains at the beginning of *Distant Drums*. Starring Gary
Cooper as a U.S. Army captain, *Distant Drums* depicts Florida in 1840.
Chasing Seminoles through the Everglades, the U.S. troops also face panthers, snakes, and a gator that pulls one of the men under and drowns
him. In *Shark River* a white man is bitten by a poisonous snake. *Yellowneck*
has the Indians pick off escaping Confederate soldiers who also face attacks by alligators and snakes. One soldier dies after falling into quicksand, a novel plot device for the Everglades, but one that is repeated in
Lure of the Swamp (1957), a contemporary story of the Everglades, which
shows several villains sinking to their deaths in quicksand.

A more nuanced view emerges in *Wind Across the Everglades* (1958),
directed by Nicholas Ray and written by Budd Schulberg. Set at the turn
of the twentieth century when "a new frontier [was] opening in south
Florida," the film presents the area as "a wonderland of wildlife" that is
threatened by outlaws who slaughter birds for feather plumes to adorn
women's hats. The film stars Christopher Plummer as naturalist Walt
Murdock, a federal agent who goes to the Everglades to "save the birds
from extinction." There he encounters the outlaw leader (Burl Ives),
known as Cottonmouth because he always carries a cottonmouth snake.
Aside from dangerous swamp people and poisonous snakes, the Everglades are full of killer alligators, as well as raccoons, deer, and wild pigs.
Poling through the river of grass and taking pictures, Murdock initially
delights in the unspoiled beauty of the remote frontier, but the environment, which attracts evil men, leads the hero to refer eventually to "these
stinking Glades." Cottonmouth is finally killed by snakes after falling into
the water during a fight with Murdock, and the film ends with birds flying
overhead, reflecting a serene natural environment.

Contemporary views of the Everglades still present them as otherworldly. *Johnny Tiger* (1966) deals with cultural conflicts on a Seminole
reservation in the "primitive jungle" of the Everglades. The film portrays
the Everglades as a natural paradise, untouched by civilization. The only
environmental threat comes from a forest fire that is set by children
playing. The Everglades also look beautiful and unspoiled in *Joe Panther*
(1976), which has long scenes showing Seminoles moving through the
swamps filled with exotic wildlife. The continued isolation of the Everglades attracts a former government agent, played by Chuck Norris, who
briefly retires there in *Invasion U.S.A.* (1985).

Beginning in the 1980s the Everglades become a cinematic Hades, a

12. An airboat used in a chase scene through the Everglades in *The Mean Season* (1985).

haven for criminals and other deadly beasts. In *The Mean Season*, a serial killer escapes to "the Glades," where he is pursued in an airboat. Similar chase scenes figure in a number of films, including *Police Academy 5*, *Plato's Run* (1997), and *Wild Things*. In addition to "swamp trash," the Everglades are home to alligators, which appear often in *Wild Things*, poking their heads menacingly out of the swamp waters. Some are also kept at an alligator farm and wrestled in shows for tourists. In *Wild Things 2* (2004) one of the coconspirators is killed and thrown into swamp waters teaming with alligators. *Band of the Hand* (1986) features an Indian who uses the Everglades to teach survival techniques to five juvenile delinquents from Miami. In this "jungle" they face a variety of natural enemies, including a rattlesnake that bites one of them, a wild boar that turns on them, and a bear that attacks in the night. Strangely no alligators appear in the movie. Even if they do not attack, alligators are routinely used as part of the establishing shot for most films with views of the Everglades, including *Thunder and Lightning* (1974), *Porky's* (1981), *Plato's Run*, and *Held for Ransom*. In *Smokey and the Bandit II* (1980), cars crossing Alligator Alley through the Everglades swerve to avoid gators on the road, leading one character to comment, "I like this place—all the gators and snakes and stuff."

More commonly in movies, alligators attack, even in comedies. In both *Gone Fishin'* and *Police Academy 5*, leading characters successfully fight off marauding alligators. Dramas use these creatures to eliminate villains, as in *Just Cause* (1995), *Held for Ransom*, and *Adaptation* (2002). Nevertheless the primary threat in these films comes from people in the Everglades, not from the habitat, which is used to create an ominous setting. "Buried deep in the Florida Everglades is a secret that can save an innocent man or let a killer kill again," declares the tagline for *Just Cause*. A reviewer pointed out that the descent of the film's star, Sean Connery, "into the Everglades is depicted as if it were a jaunt into Hades."[8] Another critic noted that "the Florida Everglades throb with menace."[9] In *Held for Ransom*, a villain played by Dennis Hopper graphically describes the threat to high school students he holds captive in the Everglades. "If you walk out of here, there's no place for you to walk, unless you can walk on water and then the closest town is twenty-five miles away. You know outside here are the hungriest fuckin' alligators," he says, as the film cuts to alligators in a feeding frenzy. "They got this little feedin' mechanism. It's triggered by the sound of movement, especially splashin' around in the swamp." In the film's conclusion, Hopper's character dies in the jaws of an alligator.

In reality, alligators rarely attack people, but since 1948, Florida has recorded 340 attacks and seventeen deaths by alligators.[10] Most commonly the confrontations occur outside the Everglades in locations where urban sprawl encroaches on the natural habitat of Florida wildlife. In these areas alligators are frequently sighted, and if perceived as a threat by state authorities, they are relocated or killed.

The Academy Award-winning film *Adaptation* presents a nuanced view of the Everglades, showing it as home to both beauty and beast. While alligators lurk beneath the surface, rare orchids flourish overhead. *Ad-*

13. A scene from *Police Academy 5: Assignment Miami Beach* (1988). By permission of Photofest.

14. A view of the Everglades in *Just Cause* (1995).

aptation starts with scenes in California and New York, and then moves to Florida with an establishing shot that shows a sign for Fakahatchee Strand State Preserve, a state park in the Everglades. The camera follows John Laroche (Chris Cooper) and three Seminole Indians as they wade in chest-high water, shaded by trees and thick vegetation. A brief view of two huge alligators splashing in the waters reveals the potential danger to the men collecting endangered plants, including the exquisite ghost orchid. When they walk out of the swamp with bags filled with presumably illegal booty, a wildlife officer challenges them. In their defense, Laroche cites court decisions that exempt the Seminoles from laws protecting such species.

Nevertheless the incident leads to an arrest and a news story that captures the attention of a writer for the *New Yorker*, Susan Orlean (Meryl Streep), who decides to investigate. In interviews with Orlean, Laroche explains that he expects to make money off rare ghost orchids by removing some from the state preserve, cultivating them, and making them available for sale. As a result, "Laroche and nature win," he emphasizes. After researching the lure of orchids, Orlean concludes, "Orchids are the sexiest flowers on earth. The name derives from the Latin *orchis*, which means testicle." In a later interview Laroche reinforces this romantic view of nature by pointing out that every orchid "has a special relationship with the insect that pollinates it. There's a certain orchid exactly like a certain insect. So the insect is drawn to this flower, its double, its soul mate, and wants nothing more than to make love to it." As Orlean continues her research, the film shows images of magnificent orchids, more of which grow wild in the Everglades than anywhere else in North America.

Finally, half way through *Adaptation*, Susan Orlean gets John Laroche to take her into the Everglades to see a ghost orchid. The two make their way into the swamp, wading through waist-deep water, punctuated by trees and plants pushing skyward. When they get lost, Laroche tries to use the sun to find the right direction, but not enough sunlight penetrates the dense foliage. After Laroche leads Orlean to a ghost orchid and out of the swamp, he reveals the flower's ultimate secret—a hallucinogenic drug can be extracted from it. The addictive drug ensnares them both, reinforcing the view that the same plant in Florida can provide beauty and danger. Ultimately Florida's environment proves deadly in *Adaptation*, which ends in the Everglades with an alligator killing Laroche. In this way the film reveals graphically that death threatens anyone who tries to harness the undeniable beauty of the Everglades. Indeed an earlier scene in the film shows that Laroche had already experienced the wrath of Florida's environment. In one of his interviews with Orlean, he explains briefly how he lost his south Florida nursery: "Hurricane Andrew came along and just swooped down like an angel of God and just wiped out everything I had."

Any ambivalence about the beneficence of nature in Florida is missing in horror movies that seek only to scare viewers. The premise of *Alligator* (1980) is based on an urban myth. In a screenplay credited to John Sayles, this horror film tells the story of a little girl from Chicago who visits Florida with her parents and watches a man almost ripped apart by an alligator in a wrestling match. As the man is pulled away from the huge reptile, the show's announcer says, "Well now, we promised you a gator wrestling, folks, and sometimes the gators win." Interested in science, the girl then buys a baby alligator from a Seminole and returns home, where her father flushes it down the toilet. Predictably it thrives in Chicago's sewers, growing to unbelievable proportions (bigger than a car!) and feeding off human flesh. Thus the threat of Florida's most feared creature apparently reaches beyond the Sunshine State.

Other horror movies also portray threats lurking in Florida's environment. *Revenge of the Creature* (1955) is probably the first horror film set in Florida. A sequel to *Creature from the Black Lagoon* (1954), which was set in South America, *Revenge* features the same monster, Gill Man, who is now captured and put on display at a tourist attraction near Daytona Beach. Gill Man, of course, escapes, fleeing to Jacksonville, in a forgettable movie that will perhaps only be remembered as the first film with Clint Eastwood, who has a bit part.

Other films in the "nature's revenge cycle," as one critic called it, copy

15. This poster for *Revenge of the Creature* (1955) shows Gill Man but distorts the setting of the movie by locating it in a big city. By permission of Photofest.

the formula first used by Alfred Hitchcock in *The Birds* (1963). The convention includes people "at siege from nature in an isolated setting; flora and fauna on the rampage; [with] no explanation offered for what is happening . . . ; and the downbeat ending with nature triumphant and seen as humanity's natural successor."[11] Filmed and set in Florida, *Frogs* (1972) portrays a millionaire patriarch (Ray Milland) who hates nature and orders the poisoning of bothersome croaking frogs around his isolated estate. In retaliation the frogs organize nature's revenge and instigate attacks on the entire family by a host of other creatures including snakes, tarantulas, turtles, leeches, and lizards. The noisy, slimy frogs never actually kill anyone, but at the end of the movie, they romp over the bodies of the corpses. *Empire of the Ants* (1977) has these creatures mutate as a result of radioactive waste that washes ashore on an island off the Florida coast. Giant ants take over the island and turn some residents into slaves while killing off visitors. *Big Trouble*, based on Dave Barry's first novel, portrays another natural threat in Florida. One of the film's subplots shows a Bufo toad menacing Miami residents with its hallucinogenic spit.

Some of the best films about Florida appeal to more than the eyes of viewers by also evoking the sound and smell of the environment. The most pervasive sounds are undoubtedly chirping birds during the day and cicadas at night, and they can be heard prominently in films about rural Florida like *Cross Creek* and *Ulee's Gold*. The sound of cicadas adds to the tension of nighttime scenes in *Body Heat*. The soundtrack for *Sunshine State* includes not only seagulls and cicadas but also the rhythmic sound of waves breaking on the beach. In the absence of "smell-o- vision," one of the few cinematic references to natural odors occurs in *Stranger Than Paradise* when a newly arrived tourist (Eszter Balint) in north Florida comments, "The water smells funny." This allusion is probably lost on viewers who have not experienced the pungent odor of sulfur in Florida's water.

Florida's natural environment has long attracted adventurers, tourists, new residents, and filmmakers, some of whom have discovered an overheated Hades rather than a picturesque paradise. Cinematic portrayals of nature in the Sunshine State tend to extreme views. On the one hand Florida's semitropical climate represents a dreamland of healthful sunshine, shimmering waters, and sandy beaches. On the other hand the state's weather also raises a nightmare vision of blistering heat, sweltering humidity, and killer hurricanes. Florida's animal world offers similar extremes, depending on whether the camera and story line focus on the graceful beauty of dolphins and exotic birds or on the menace of sharks and alligators. Perceptions of the state's geography also alternate between the sunlit coastline that attracts tourists and the dark interior that harbors deadly threats. Indeed, these conflicting visions of the environment sometimes appear in the same film, as in *Adaptation* and *Wild Things*. Even early classics like *The Yearling* and *Flipper* portray both extremes of Florida's environment, but their images and messages are overwhelmingly positive.

By the 1980s a decided shift occurred in views of Florida's natural environment as both comedies and dramas reflected a growing disillusion and changing definitions of paradise. Whereas dreams of rejuvenation in the sun once brought tourists and migrants to Florida in films like *The Big Street* and *Midnight Cowboy*, the same environment now turns visitors off. "Man, it's so hot and humid here," a Californian says of south Florida in *2 Fast 2 Furious* (2003). The state's biggest attractions are increasingly manufactured, symbolized by Disney World, but efforts to improve upon nature have also brought mixed reactions that are explored by filmmakers.

Chapter 2

"The people down here seem to despise natural beauty. They think they're not going to feel secure until they get the asphalt in every direction."
A Flash of Green (1984)

"Nature is overrated."
"Yes, but we'll miss it when it's gone."
Sunshine State (2002)

Manufacturing Paradise

The Built Environment

Like nature itself, Florida's manufactured environment offers both the promise of paradise and the potential for hell on earth. The growth of cities, interstate highways, and theme parks may be viewed as either a blessing or a curse. Whatever the debatable results of construction projects from the first railroads to high-tech theme parks, they share in common not only the lure of money but also "the desire to improve Florida," as a state guidebook put it in the 1930s. Like other observers, filmmakers remain conflicted about whether "man's subduing efforts" have made the state better or worse.[1]

Some surviving structures in Florida date back to the Spanish colonial period and appear in films. The Castillo de San Marcos, the seventeenth-century fortress in St. Augustine, provides a backdrop in *A Florida Enchantment* (1914), *Distant Drums* (1951), and *Illegally Yours* (1988), but aside from a few exceptions like this, films set in Florida show buildings that generally date from the late nineteenth or twentieth century. Period

16. The Marx Brothers in a publicity shot for *The Cocoanuts* (1929). By permission of Photofest.

dramas about pre-twentieth-century life tend to portray a frontier wilderness, largely devoid of permanent buildings.

As early as the 1920s Florida's reputation for shady land deals cast a shadow over cinematic views of development in the state. *The New Klondike* (1926), a silent film based on a story by Ring Lardner, makes fun of contemporary attempts to transform the environment into some kind of residential paradise. The story line combines baseball spring training and land speculation near Miami. The New York baseball team's owner, manager, and players all try to profit from get-rich-quick schemes pushed by Florida "real estate sharpshooters," who promise "man-made islands of sand and coral, pumped up from the sea." When such property turns out to be an overgrown swamp filled with cypress knees, duped buyers simply resell it to unsuspecting newcomers. As one huckster says, "Dollars put in Florida real estate multiply like flies in a Greek restaurant." In short, the film portrays "the mad rush of the New Klondike" in the mid-1920s.

The Marx Brothers also satirized the Florida land boom in *The Cocoanuts* (1929), their first feature-length film and one of the first talkies. The story by George S. Kaufman features Groucho Marx as the owner of the

Hotel de Cocoanut, which is going bankrupt for lack of business in the undeveloped town of Cocoanut Beach in south Florida. Although filmed on a stage in New York City, the movie is a series of running jokes about Florida development, which Groucho sees as the only hope for salvaging his hotel business. One problem is that a hill stands in the way of construction, as pointed out by Bob Adams (Oscar Shaw), a budding architect who shows a drawing of the area to his girlfriend Polly (Mary Eaton). With the two looking at the hill on Bob's plans, she asks, "Could it be cut down?" "Too expensive," he explains. "John W. Berryman was here to see it last month. You know Berryman practically made Palm Beach and Miami, but he said he wouldn't touch this. Now when a man like that passes on a place, no one wants it." However, Bob has plans to overcome the environmental obstacle. "Without cutting down the hill or having it get in the way, I made the hill fit in with the architectural scheme," he says proudly to Polly.

Groucho Marx's character has plans too, but they rely on flimflam and double talk. "Now whether you like it or not, I'm going to tell you about Florida real estate," he says to Polly's rich mother (Margaret Dumont). "Do you know property values have increased 1929 since one thousand percent?" he asks in his nonsensical patter. "Do you know that this is the biggest development since Sophie Tucker? Do you know Florida is the show spot of America, and Cocoanut Beach is the black spot of Florida?" Showing her a map, Groucho continues, "Here is Cocoanut Manor—forty-two hours from Times Square by railroad. . . . Why, it's the most exclusive district in Florida. Nobody lives there."

In a later scene Groucho holds an auction to sell lots in Cocoanut Manor. "This is the heart of the residential district," he tells the crowd of potential buyers. "Every lot is a stone's throw from the station. As soon as they throw enough stones, we're gonna build a station. Eight hundred wonderful residences will be built right here," he claims. Moreover, "You can have any kind of home you want. You can even have stucco. Oh, you can get stuck-o. Now is the time to buy while the new boom is on." In his final pitch, he says, "And don't forget the guarantee—my personal guarantee. If these lots don't double in value in a year, I don't know what you can do about it."

Despite Groucho's presumably empty promises, the film ends with Bob Adams announcing to everyone that his "architectural plans for the development" have been accepted by the builder John W. Berryman. Bob's hopes may spring eternal and help get him married to Polly, but the Florida land boom had already gone bust by the time *The Cocoanuts* was made. Thus Groucho's jokes about real estate scams undoubtedly hit home with contemporary audiences.

The plot of *The Barefoot Mailman* (1951) alludes to real estate hustles that began long before the 1920s. In a drama set in south Florida during the 1890s, Robert Cummings plays a con man who floats a scheme to bilk local investors with rumors about the imminent arrival of the railroad. When his scam is revealed, he is forced to flee empty-handed.

With swindlers failing to deliver on their promises to ordinary people, films made prior to the 1960s suggest that Florida's development was geared to building a playground for the rich and powerful. *Girl Missing* (1933), *Moon Over Miami* (1941), *Palm Beach Story* (1942), *The Big Street* (1942), and *Some Like It Hot* (1959) all feature south Florida's luxurious hotels and chic night clubs, frequented by well-to-do people wearing tuxedos and evening gowns.

The age of Florida tourism for the masses is a recent phenomenon. Prior to the 1960s, middle-class tourists who visited the Sunshine State went for the natural environment of sun and beaches, and many brought their housing with them. After World War I cheaper automobiles and new highways made the state more accessible, and "tin can tourists" (a reference to their eating out of tin cans) arrived in their cars, pulling trailers behind them like snails with their homes on their backs. Except for paved roads and a place to park, these visitors required little infrastructure. *The New Klondike* has an aerial view of the long, winding road leading to Miami. The rest of south Florida remained largely undeveloped, especially as imagined in the movies. When a character in *Palm Beach Story* suggests driving to Ft. Myers in the early 1940s, she adds, "There's nothing there, but the ride might be nice."

As tourism expanded after World War II, so too did highway construction. Prior to the limited-access interstates, miles of two-lane roads stretched the length of the state, opening south Florida and the Keys to increasing numbers of visitors, who arrived by car and bus, as in *Key Largo* (1948) and *Midnight Cowboy* (1969). *Where the Boys Are* (1960) and *Night Moves* (1975) reinforce the perception that prior to the 1980s, these largely deserted routes were lined primarily with palm trees. Panoramic views show Florida's sparsely populated coastline.

The state welcomed tourists and their money with open arms, a point explicitly made in movies. Indeed, in some films the establishing shot for the Sunshine State features the roadside sign "Welcome to Florida." *Clambake* (1967), *Ruby in Paradise* (1993), and *Gone Fishin'* (1997) use the

17. Jack Lemmon (*left*), Tony Curtis, and Marilyn Monroe in *Some Like It Hot* (1959), which was filmed in California, but set along the beach in Miami. By permission of Photofest.

sign to show that their principal characters have arrived at their destination, where in each film the story actually begins.

By the 1980s this cinematic paradise becomes a nightmare of interstates and overpasses that blot the Florida landscape and overflow with traffic. *Honky Tonk Freeway* (1981), a comedy directed by John Schlesinger, suggests that Floridians cannot live with or without freeways. The film opens with a brilliant orange sunset over palm trees. Suddenly, an explosion rips through the trees, and huge earthmoving machines come into view, crushing everything in their path to build a road. Despite this apparent menace, residents of the fictional town of Ticlaw, Florida, decide that their small community cannot survive unless it gets an on/off-ramp for access to the new interstate. The movie ends with a massive crash of trucks and cars that turns a rhino loose on the freeway. In a similar nightmarish vision, a monstrous traffic jam releases a bunch of goats on a Miami highway in *Big Trouble* (2002). Another film set in south Florida, *2 Fast 2 Furious* (2003), features a car chase on I-95 that leads to a series of pileups. In *Ernest Saves Christmas* (1988), the star (Jim Varney) is a bumbling Orlando taxi driver who causes a number of accidents on the local interstate. The state's roads offer a different kind of menace in *Monster* (2003), which tells the real-life story of a killer, Aileen Wuornos (Charlize Theron), who prowls the highways of central Florida seeking victims. The dark mood of the film is established in the opening scene that shows Wuornos sitting at night under an interstate overpass with rain falling. Like a number of recent films, *Monster* suggests that the road to paradise passes through hell.

Drawbridges are the most distinctive characteristic of Florida roadways. Although these bridges can be found in other states, their sheer number in Florida and their potential for dramatic footage make them an ideal setting for chase scenes. In *The Longest Yard* (1974), *The Mean Season* (1985), and *Just Cause* (1995), criminals flee across drawbridges that are lifting up, forcing the hero to jump or drive across the opening gap. A drawbridge in downtown Tampa stymies the police chasing criminals in *Cop and a Half* (1993). In *Two Much* (1995), Melanie Griffith and Antonio

18. A scene from *Honky Tonk Freeway* (1981). By permission of Photofest.

19. A Tampa drawbridge used in a chase scene in *The Punisher* (2004).

Banderas safely escape across an open drawbridge in Miami while the car of mobsters chasing them teeters on the edge before falling into the water. *The Punisher* (2004) also includes a scene of the star (A. Russell Andrews) driving a car across a Tampa bridge that is opening up. *In the Shadows* (2001), a story about a stunt coordinator (James Caan), shows in some detail the making of a movie scene with a car jumping across the opening of a Miami drawbridge. The dramatic sequence emphasizes the potential danger posed by these Florida landmarks.

However visitors may have traveled to Florida, they needed a place to stay once they arrived, and the prosperity of the period after 1945 sparked a wave of motel construction along Florida's beaches. Largely nondescript, two-story buildings with a pool, the new motels became a destination for increasing numbers of college students and middle-class families in the 1960s. Films from the period, such as *Where the Boys Are* and *Girl Happy* (1965), show students crowded around motel pools, where much of the action occurs. Thirty years later *Black Spring Break* (1998) changes the cast but keeps the same motel setting. Miami Beach appealed to a very different clientele with the opening of the Fontainebleau Hotel in 1954. Attracting Presidents and celebrities, this gigantic, 1,200-room landmark so symbolized the excess of Miami Beach that it appears in several films from the 1960s, including *The Bellboy* (1960), which stars Jerry Lewis as one of the hotel's employees. The Fontainebleau also hosted conventions like the one attended by the screwball cops who seek "surf, sun, and fun" in *Police Academy 5: Assignment Miami Beach* (1988).

Florida's beach accommodations change noticeably over time in the movies. For ordinary tourists arriving in ever greater numbers, inex-

20. Elvis Presley in *Girl Happy* (1965). By permission of Photofest.

pensive motels become part of the Florida nightmare. By the 1980s aging postwar motels are rundown and seedy as portrayed in *Spring Break* (1983) and *Stranger Than Paradise* (1984). A motel owner (Elaine Stritch) in *Cocoon: The Return* (1988) calls her place a "dump." *Blood and Wine* (1997) features two crooks (Jack Nicholson and Michael Caine) who stay at a cheap motel in Miami, leading one to observe: "This is not an oceanfront suite. . . . Did you notice that? There are no flowers and champagne."

In fact, palatial waterfront hotels also deteriorated with time, but some were refurbished, making them more attractive and more expensive than ever. Although not always mentioned by name, the Don CeSar and the Vinoy in St. Petersburg provide settings for several recent films, such as *HEALTH* (1980), directed by Robert Altman, and *The Break* (1995). Built in the 1920s and known as "the Pink Palace," the Don CeSar fell into ruins after World War II, but it has been reinvented as a luxury four-star "resort hotel" that retains the outlandish Moorish exterior of the original building. "It looks like a fantasy castle," a New York visitor (Gretchen Mol) declares while observing the Don CeSar's facade at night in *Forever Mine* (1999). "It's real," a hotel employee (Joseph Fiennes) responds.

Movies have reinforced Florida's reputation for extravagant housing for the wealthy. The pattern was set by *Citizen Kane* (1941), the classic film directed by Orson Welles, which places Xanadu, Charles Foster Kane's castlelike residence, "down south . . . on the deserts of the Gulf Coast." Despite the clear use of a Florida location, most viewers probably assume Kane lives in California, given that his character is inspired by William Randolph Hearst. However, the fact that Welles relocated the setting to Florida suggests that in the 1940s the state still retained its image as a retreat for rich Americans. More recent films reinforce this view of Florida's past. Some like *Cocoon* (1985) and *Body Heat* (1981) use actual Spanish-style mansions that date from the early twentieth century. The significance of these sometimes decaying homes is emphasized by a contract killer (William Forsythe) in *Big City Blues* (1999), a film noir set in Miami. In a scene at an abandoned Spanish-style mansion, Forsythe's character explains to his partner (Burt Reynolds): "This place is like eight thousand square feet. It was built in 1927 by this gangster guy who worked for the Capone mob or something like that. . . . Look at the marble detailing. This guy had it all flown in from Italy. It's like a Sistine Chapel waitin' to happen."

Well-known historic homes also occasionally appear in films although they are not identified by name. Cà d'Zan, the Venetian-style mansion

21. The set of Xanadu, Charles Foster Kane's palatial Florida home, in *Citizen Kane* (1941). By permission of Wisconsin Center for Film and Theater Research.

built by John and Mable Ringling along Sarasota Bay, is pictured in *Great Expectations* (1998) in a state of decay before its recent restoration. Vizcaya, located on the shore of Miami's Biscayne Bay and modeled after an Italian Renaissance palace, is used as a setting in several films, including *Tony Rome* (1967) and *Any Given Sunday* (1999). The latter movie also imitates life by having the quarterback (Dennis Quaid) for a Miami football team living in a waterfront mansion that is actually the home of Dan Marino, the former quarterback for the Miami Dolphins. More commonly, palatial mansions along the water are home to movie villains, especially drug lords in south Florida, as in *Scarface* (1983), *The Specialist* (1994), and *2 Fast 2 Furious*. Despite their wealth, gangsters do not always have good taste, a point made by Sharon Stone's character in *The Specialist*. She looks around a mobster's house and says, "The next time you order a hit, you might consider taking out your decorator." Many of these lavish homes feature Spanish-style Mediterranean architecture, but a few films, such as *Blue City* (1986) and *Held for Ransom* (2000), show wealthy people in south Florida living in huge southern-style houses with pillars, making them look like plantations from the Old South.

Other Floridians depicted in movies seem to live largely in primitive or dilapidated housing. From *The Yearling* (1946) through *Just Cause*, wood cabins and shacks provide shelter for most rural Floridians. *Smokey and the Bandit II* (1980) plays up this image by portraying a gas station in the Everglades as a ramshackle log cabin, where the attendant listens to bluegrass music on an ancient Victrola. The next step in housing seems to be so-called mobile homes (or "manufactured housing"), which are cramped and apparently deteriorate quickly. While some stand alone and isolated in *Striptease* (1996) and *Wilder Napalm* (1993), most mobile homes are pictured as crowded into shabby trailer parks and home to poor whites in films such as *The Mean Season*, *2 Fast 2 Furious*, and *Sunshine State*. In two rare exceptions, *Folks!* (1992) depicts retirees living in a pleasant trailer park, and *China Moon* (1994) shows the detective played by Ed Harris living in a mobile home that is modest, but clean and tidy.

The stark contrast between the lifestyles of Florida's rich and poor drives much of the plot of *Wild Things* (1998). As the opening credits flash across the screen, the movie gives a sweeping overview of south Florida's environment. Beginning with aerial shots of the Everglades showing an airboat skimming over the river of grass and alligators poking their head out of the water, the camera races across treetops toward the built environment, revealing first suburban sprawl with a strip mall and rows of middle-class homes. The skyscrapers of downtown Miami quickly come

22. Aging house trailers in *Wild Things* (1998).

into view and then the coastline and mansions on waterways north of
the city. Finally, as the film's credits end, the camera zooms in on tennis
courts at an upscale high school on the coast, and *Wild Things* opens with
a scene in the school's auditorium. After school lets out, the film shows
how differently the main characters live. A rich student (Denise Richards)
goes home to a two-story, Mediterranean-style, waterfront mansion behind a high wall with an electric gate. Suzie (Neve Campbell) lives with
poor whites ("swamp trash") in the nearby Everglades, where homes are
old, dilapidated trailers and unpainted shacks.

The middle ground between these residential extremes is occupied by
middle-class suburbanites, but their housing figures less prominently in
Florida films. Moreover, as depicted in films like *Bully* (2001), their physi-
cal surroundings are more generically American and less typically Floridian. The noticeable exception is the Florida bungalow with its jalousie
("Miami") windows, which can be seen in *Miami Exposé* (1956) and *A
Flash of Green*, both set in the 1950s. Designed as glass slats to open like
Venetian blinds, these windows provided ventilation prior to air condi-
tioning, but are now prohibited by building codes for new construction.
The other distinguishing characteristic of Florida's middle-class housing
is its proximity to water, at least as portrayed in movies. *Traces of Red*

23. Frank Sinatra at the home of Richard Conte (*right*), who plays a Miami Beach police lieutenant, in *Tony Rome* (1967). By permission of Photofest.

(1992), *Plato's Run* (1997), and *Tony Rome* show virtually every character in south Florida living along some body of water—the ocean, a canal, or the intercoastal waterway. In some cases people actually live on the water in houseboats that are depicted in *Lady in Cement* (1968), *Blood and Wine*, and *2 Fast 2 Furious*.

Finally, like other Americans, Floridians bring water to their homes by building swimming pools that are pictured in films as both a boon and a curse. Initially, in black-and-white films like *Miami Exposé*, private swimming pools serve as a marker of wealth, privilege, and excess, given their rarity and high prices. In *The Big Street* Lucille Ball plays a dispirited New Yorker who imagines living at a Palm Beach estate with a "swimming pool, forty acres, servants running all over the joint, champagne for breakfast." With time, of course, pools became more accessible, first to tourists staying at Florida motels and then to ordinary homeowners. Early films in color, especially beach movies like *Where the Boys Are*, portray swimming pools as a spot for fun and romance. Water is also viewed as a source of rejuvenation, which turns into eternal life in *Cocoon*, when a group of retirees in St. Petersburg discovers magical powers of healing in a swimming pool. A different kind of aquatic opportunity is offered in *Ride* (1998), when struggling rappers travel from Harlem to Miami to film a music video that is shot in the private pool of a hip-hop impresario (Luther Campbell).

Despite such promises of recreation and re-creation, the reality of pools can be much less fulfilling, even deadly. As the Florida dream turns into a nightmare, pools are used by filmmakers to reflect the change. In *Revenge of the Nerds II: Nerds in Paradise* (1987), the young tourists can only find rooms in Ft. Lauderdale at a dilapidated hotel with a pool that has filthy brown water. Private pools also prove a mixed blessing since they can give instant relief from Florida's stifling heat, but they require maintenance and pose the ever-present danger of drowning. *Bad Boys II* (2003) has a subplot about a Miami cop (Martin Lawrence) who has an above-ground pool that provides a refuge from the pressures of work, but it keeps breaking, dumping all its water into the canal abutting his house.

Swimming pools can clearly serve many cinematic purposes. Explaining his film *Swimming Pool* (2003), which is set in France, director and screenwriter François Ozon points out that pools, unlike the ocean, are "manageable and controlled" bodies of water. Moreover, he sees a pool "like a movie-screen against which images are projected and into which a character penetrates."[2] This space of contained water can provoke fear

24. Will Smith (*left*) and Martin Lawrence in a pool in *Bad Boys II* (2003). By permission of Photofest.

(the deep end for a nonswimmer), stimulate eroticism or romance, and strip inhibitions.

Movies set in Florida use pools in a variety of ways. *Radio Inside* (1994) tells the story of Mike (Dylan Walsh), a young man who decides to become a lifeguard at a Miami pool in order to face his demons about his father drowning in a lake. He then becomes despondent, thinking that a boy he has been teaching to swim has drowned in the pool, and Mike wanders, nude and dazed, into the ocean, but emerges, having failed at suicide. In *HEALTH*, fear of the water is played for laughs when one of the characters stages his drowning in a hotel pool—twice. In *Cat Chaser* (1989), Miami criminals push someone who can't swim into the pool at their boss's mansion and let him drown. *Wild Things* uses the swimming pool of a jet-set heiress as a place of fun, eroticism, and danger for her teenage daughter Kelly and her friends. One pool scene at night captures these conflicting feelings when in a fit of rage Kelly attacks her girlfriend Suzie, pushes her into the pool, and holds her head under water. Suzie fights her way to the surface, gasping for air. As she breaks into tears, Kelly kisses her, and the two disrobe in the pool and embrace. Thus, emotions can change quickly in swimming pools.

Like its hotels and much of its housing, Florida's restaurants appear distinctive in films, but not because of their food. Except for passing references to ethnic dishes served by Greeks in Tarpon Springs in *Down Under the Sea* (1936) and by Cubans in *Scarface*, films focus principally on the decor of Florida restaurants, especially aquariums that figure in *Where the Boys Are* and *Honky Tonk Freeway*. Both *Off and Running* (1991) and *Analyze This!* (1999) show aquariums with women playing the role of mermaids in Miami bars. *Miami Blues* (1990) and *Adaptation* (2002) have scenes in Miami restaurants, where women perform water ballet for the diners. *The Right Stuff* (1983) features a bar in Cocoa Beach decorated with mermaids. Some restaurants are presented as gaudy tourist traps, like the one in *Summer Rental* (1985), whose owner (Rip Torn) dresses like a pirate and serves reheated frozen food.

Bars and clubs play a significant role in creating a Florida atmosphere in movies. Some portray bars that are stereotypically American, and not particularly Floridian, such as the biker bar in *Monster* and strip clubs in *Girl Missing*, *Lady in Cement*, *Striptease*, and, of course, *Porky's* (1981). Clubs in *Porky's Revenge* (1985) and *Donnie Brasco* (1997) offer gambling, but like nude dancing, this is not especially Floridian. The state's most famous bar is undoubtedly Sloppy Joe's in Key West, and it is used for a scene in *A Murder of Crows* (2001). What characterizes many bars in the

25. Barbara Nichols performing an underwater ballet in *Where the Boys Are* (1960). By permission of Photofest.

state is their dockside or beach location, as emphasized by many films from *Beneath the 12-Mile Reef* (1953) to *Heartbreakers* (2001). The Florida beach bar has become such a fixture of the imagination that in *City By the Sea* (2002) a New Yorker (James Franco) dreams of going to Key West to work in "one of those beach bars; you know, palm trees, right on the fuckin' sand." Restaurants, bars, and motels can provide a backdrop for Florida movies, but visitors do not go to the Sunshine State just to eat, drink, and sleep.

Tourists flock to Florida to play, and the natural environment no longer suffices as a lure. Theme parks and other manufactured attractions now draw millions of guests. The construction of such venues began modestly and initially exploited the state's association with nature, or at least popular perceptions of nature. One of the first films about the state, *A Florida Enchantment*, has a shot of the entrance to "the Fountain of Youth," an attraction in St. Augustine, as it looked in 1914. The same attraction reappears decades later in *Illegally Yours*. Several old theme parks provide backdrops for movies of the 1940s and 1950s. In addition to *Moon Over Miami*, *A Hole in the Head* (1959), a musical with Frank Sinatra, has scenes shot at Cypress Gardens, which is also the locale for much of the action in *Easy to Love* (1953), starring Esther Williams. Marineland gets

26. Cypress Gardens is featured in *Easy to Love* (1953). By permission of Photofest.

prominent billing in *Revenge of the Creature* (1955) as the attraction that displays the monster Gill Man. More recently, *Analyze This!* has a couple (Billy Crystal and Lisa Kudrow) visit Miami's Seaquarium to watch a killer whale show. *Sunshine State* features a subplot about a former mermaid (Edie Falco) who returns to Weeki-Wachee for a visit and talks about the difficulties of performing there as a mermaid.

All of these older tourist sites were eclipsed, and several put out of business, by Disney World, which opened in 1971. Despite its drawing power, Disney World is almost never shown in movies, perhaps because of access problems. A lone exception is *Marvin's Room* (1996), which portrays a dying woman (Diane Keaton) visiting the Orlando attraction with her family. More commonly in film, Disney World gives people something to dream about. *Curdled* (1996) depicts a woman (Angela Jones) living amidst murder and mayhem in Miami and recalling fondly a visit to Disney World: "Everybody there is having a good time." In *Girl, Interrupted* (1999), Angelina Jolie plays a woman in a mental institution who dreams of going to Florida and working in Disney World as Snow White.

Disney's unseen presence in movies is also reflected in the visible decline of other attractions that cannot compete. *The New Kids* (1985) features "Santa's Funland," a dilapidated attraction that has nonoperating rides and a petting zoo. Although located far from Orlando in the middle of nowhere near Homestead in south Florida, the park provides its owner (Eddie Jones) with dreams of a revival, bringing hundreds of visitors with "money in both hands." As he explains it, "with Disney World and Epcot a couple of hours north, this will be the perfect place for people to stomp and romp—a little appetizer."

Compared with Disney World and other mega-attractions in the Orlando area, smaller venues in the state appear prosaic, even outdated, in movies. Spring training for professional baseball has long figured in films, and the fields of play look increasingly like part of small-town Florida. As early as silent films like *The New Klondike*, the state's association with spring training provided a story line. *Take Me Out to the Ball Game* (1949), a musical directed by Busby Berkeley and set in the early twentieth century, features Gene Kelly and Frank Sinatra as ballplayers in Florida for spring training. *Strategic Air Command* (1955) tells the story of a major league pitcher (Jimmy Stewart) who plays spring training games in St. Petersburg and then returns to the Air Force. Florida's association with spring training and its lack of a major league team until the 1990s provide a Chicago cop (Gregory Hines) with an amusing line in *Running Scared* (1986). In a list of complaints about the state, Hines's character says,

"The only baseball they got down there is spring training." This, of course, changed with the arrival of the Florida Marlins in 1993 and the Tampa Bay Devil Rays in 1998. *The Rookie* (2002) tells the true story of Jimmy Morris (Dennis Quaid) who becomes one of the oldest rookie pitchers in the major leagues when he joins the Devil Rays. The film does not show any major league games in Florida, and its scenes of Morris playing minor league games at a small park in Orlando reinforce the perception of Florida sports teams as bush-league operations.

The state's best known sports stadium is undoubtedly Miami's Orange Bowl, which provides a setting for several films. In *Black Sunday* (1977), directed by John Frankenheimer, the stadium is the site of a Super Bowl targeted by terrorists. Actually shot during the Cowboys–Steelers Super Bowl of 1976, the film features real announcers, players, and fans. *Ace Ventura: Pet Detective* (1994) also includes shots of the Orange Bowl in a story about a private detective (Jim Carrey) who is hired to find the Miami Dolphins' mascot, which is stolen just before the Super Bowl. *Any Given Sunday* uses the Orange Bowl, but renames it Shark Stadium, where a fictional Miami football team plays. The Orange Bowl proves to be a multipurpose facility when it becomes a detention center for Cuban refugees in *The Perez Family* (1995).

Animals—native and otherwise—are commonly exploited for tourism in Florida. Greyhound racing thrives throughout the state, as emphasized in a number of film references. Although a dozen other states have a dog track or two, Florida has sixteen, and their lure is clearly gambling, not canines. In *Blue City*, a gangster (Scott Wilson) in the Keys owns a night club and a dog track that both feature gambling. Other films like *A Hole in the Head*, *Held for Ransom*, *The Break*, and *Sunshine State* have shots of dog tracks to illustrate plots about Floridians who lose money betting on the dogs. While *Stranger Than Paradise* has ordinary tourists gambling at the dog track, *Donnie Brasco* and *Cutaway* (2000) portray the tracks as Florida sites that attract gangsters. In *Ocean's 11* (2001), when a crime syndicate recruits a retired thief (Carl Reiner), they find him at Derby Lane, the dog track in St. Petersburg. The common theme in all these films is that dog tracks are a place to lose money in Florida.

Whether in the form of dog tracks with gambling, aquariums with mermaids, or restaurants with pirates serving frozen food, films reinforce the image of a Florida environment dotted with gaudy tourist traps. *Honky Tonk Freeway* satirizes the extremes to which Florida towns will go to lure tourists and their money. Worried that they are being bypassed by hordes of out-of-state visitors, businessmen in the fictional town of Ticlaw paint everything pink and put up road signs along a nearby interstate promoting free gasoline and a water-skiing elephant at the local "safari park." *Summer Rental* and *Gone Fishin'* also poke fun at the false advertising for Florida tourist attractions that do not live up to their promises. In *Blue City*, when the hero (Judd Nelson) returns to his hometown in the Keys after a five-year absence, he concludes that "this town is really turning into a dump—fast food, tourist bullshit, cheap hotels."

A different kind of development has swept rural Florida. Prisons and other state institutions increasingly dot Florida's otherwise sparsely populated interior. Indeed, they are one of the only signs of modernization in rural Florida. "There's prisons all over this county," says a local resident in *Night Orchid* (1997), which is set in central Florida's Sumter County. *Chattahoochee* (1989) and *Out of Sight* (1998) reinforce the fact that many state hospitals and prisons are in the middle of nowhere.

Despite its many ugly aspects, Florida's built environment includes one shining star that retains its luster. The Kennedy Space Center evokes images of rockets red glare at sunrise over Florida's east coast. Although Jules Verne first imagined a manned rocket leaving "Tampa Town" in his 1865 novel *From the Earth to the Moon*, the reality of space travel did not arrive in Florida until 1961. In that year the country's first manned space flight lifted off from Cape Canaveral, but only after a series of failed rocket tests vividly depicted in *The Right Stuff*. Snapshots of the life of astronauts in and around Cape Canaveral appear in *The Right Stuff*, *Apollo 13* (1995), and *The Race to Space* (2001). Military installations are also an important feature of the Florida landscape, but they are rarely shown in movies. One exception is *Strategic Air Command*, which has the hero, played by Jimmy Stewart, fly in and out of Tampa's MacDill Air Force Base, where the movie was actually shot with the cooperation of military officials.

Massive development since World War II has radically changed the look of the Sunshine State, where ever taller buildings reach skyward and block out the sun. Some movies shot on location just after the war vividly portray old(er) Florida, which now appears caught in a time warp in films from the 1940s and 1950s. Sarasota, for example, has a decidedly small-town skyline as depicted in *The Greatest Show on Earth* (1952) before high rises dotted the urban landscape.

Clearly, changes in the state's environment can be viewed differently. Golfers, for example, may salivate at the number of luxurious courses that are open all year, while environmentalists may decry the desecration of the landscape and the depletion of scarce water resources for irrigation. Over the years Hollywood has touched on some of this debate about the impact of development in Florida. As early as the 1920s, films begin noting the empty promises of real estate salesmen. The collapse of the speculative boom of the 1920s destroyed many such dreams, but the long period of prosperity after World War II revived them.

The physical results of urban growth are most apparent in the changing skyline of Miami. Bird's-eye views from the 1950s appear as establishing shots for *Miami Story* (1954), *Miami Exposé*, and *The Bellboy*, featuring the newly opened Fontainebleau Hotel, but little else to break the horizon. Miami was transformed by an earth-shaking building boom in the 1980s that gave the city its "shimmering skyline," that has become iconic, as one writer has noted. He pointed out that unlike Manhattan's skyline, which is "angular, sharp," Miami's seems to be "vaporizing in the heat," producing the impression that "you can see those buildings vibrating, oscillating."[3] This new skyline is captured in dozens of films. Whether photographed in bright sunlight (*Up Close and Personal*), at sunset (*Out of Time*) or even at night (*Any Given Sunday*), aerial views of Miami are

27. Downtown Sarasota served as a location for *The Greatest Show on Earth* (1952), directed by Cecil B. DeMille, and the marquee of the Ritz Theater (to the left of Penney's) billed *Samson and Delilah* (1949) as "CECIL B. DE MILLE'S MASTERPIECE." By permission of Photofest.

28. The Miami skyline in *Out of Time* (2003).

unmistakable and reflect its overheated atmosphere and pulsating life-
style.

On the ground, Miami has grown into a city of identifiable neighborhoods. First and foremost is Miami Beach that has gone from a seedy,
rundown destination for retirees seeking cheap housing to a trendy,
neon-lit enclave of restored Art Deco buildings. The shabby reputation of
Miami Beach in the 1960s is depicted in the two films starring Frank Sinatra as the private eye Tony Rome. In addition to shots of strip clubs, *Tony
Rome* has the female lead (Jill St. John) refer to Miami Beach as "twenty
miles of sand looking for a city; twenty miles of pure jerks." The old Miami
Beach briefly appears in *Black Sunday*, which was made in the mid-1970s,
and the area looks tranquil with modest hotels, aging retirees, and no
tourists. Made several years later, *Eyes of a Stranger* shows little change
in Miami Beach with its dingy buildings and adult entertainment. Beginning in the mid-1980s, Michael Mann's TV series *Miami Vice* portrayed
the reversal of fortune, depicting a vibrant, youth-oriented wonderland.
Hollywood soon followed suit. The establishing shot for *Married to the
Mob* (1988) shows newly restored Art Deco buildings and the renovated
Eden Roc Hotel. The impact of gentrification provides the story line for
The Crew (2000), a film about retirees in South Beach who try to pre-
vent their modest rooming house from being sold out from under them.
"South Beach is in transition from eighty-two year-olds to youth," a land-
lord explains.

The results of the transition fill movies from the 1990s. Nighttime
shots of neon-lit Art Deco buildings suggest coolness and become the
dominant image in *Radio Inside*, *The Blackout* (1997), *There's Something
about Mary* (1998), and *Bad Boys* (1995). These films also emphasize the

downside of this environment that includes night spots that are the set-ting for drugs and murder as with "Club Hell" in *Bad Boys*. Nevertheless a positive glow emanates from the new Miami. As Roger Ebert noted in a review of *Miami Rhapsody* (1995), the film uses the city's "tropical colors and Art Deco architecture to create a pulsing backdrop, and there's the sense that the characters are just a little warmer, faster and more lustful here than they might be up north."[4] The opening sequence of *All About the Benjamins* (2002), starring Ice Cube, "offers a south Florida montage even faster and shinier than Michael Mann's mid-1980s exercise in early postmodern visual cool," observed a reviewer for the *New York Times*.

A different kind of pulse beats in Miami's Little Havana, and it too at-tracts filmmakers. Even *Scarface*, one of the first films to focus on Cuban criminals in Miami, paints a largely positive portrait of the surround-ings of "good" immigrants living in modest homes and working in diners that serve Cuban food. In *The Perez Family*, when a newly arrived Cuban (Alfred Molina) hears someone in Little Havana propose a toast to "Next year in Havana," he interjects, "Look around, my friend, Cuba is here." Businesses with Spanish names, men in guayaveras playing dominoes, and dance clubs with Cuban music all attest to the island's influence on Miami, as depicted in films such as *Blood and Wine*, *Point of Impact* (1993), and *Up Close and Personal* (1996). Indeed, Miami's Little Havana has be-come so large and so colorful that it overshadows the city's other ethnic neighborhoods in films. One of the few films set in Liberty City, a pre-dominantly African-American area, is *A Miami Tail* (2003), a little-known movie that apparently went straight to video. *2 Fast 2 Furious* has a rare, and brief, scene in Miami's Little Haiti.

Explicit critiques of development in Florida are mounted largely in independent films and Hollywood comedies. Real estate con artists are a recurring subplot in movies, but the major fault of such hucksters is their failure to deliver on promises rather than their destruction of the natural environment. Nostalgia for the disappearing manufactured environment of old Florida marks the opening scene of *Body Heat*, which shows Ned Racine (William Hurt) looking out at the night sky with flames rising in the distance. "The Seawater Inn," he says under his breath. "My family used to eat there twenty-five years ago. Now somebody's torched it to clear the lot. . . . My history is burning up out there." The film's plot also suggests that the threat to old, small-town Florida comes from conniv-ing outsiders. Significantly, Matty, the film's femme fatale who manipu-lates Ned, is a northern transplant. Her husband, Edmund, is an investor

29. Al Pacino (*left*) in *Scarface* (1983), working at a Little Havana diner when he first arrives in Miami. By permission of Photofest.

speculating in real estate and a graduate of the Columbia Law School in New York. In contrast Ned is a provincial attorney who went to Florida State University (a "good school," remarks Edmund condescendingly).

One of the first (and best) films with a plot about the destruction of Florida's natural environment is *A Flash of Green*. Directed by Victor Nuñez and based on a novel by John D. MacDonald, the 1984 film is set in the 1950s in a fictional city on Florida's west coast that resembles Ft. Myers where the film was shot. The plot focuses on a local newspaper reporter, Jimmy Wing (Ed Harris), who learns that a county commissioner, Elmo Bliss (Richard Jordan), is working with developers to fill in the city's bay and create an island for housing. "Maybe I'm a dreamer," Commissioner Bliss tells Wing. "We're going to build an island out there. Fill it with streets and homes. We're going to manufacture a paradise." Reinforcing the idea that man can improve upon nature, an advertisement for the project calls it "A Planned Community styled for the best of tropical life." Most of the city's residents, rich and poor, back the scheme, convinced that "the bay fill is just what the county needs." Money, or at least the dream of money, assures unquestioning support, even from fishermen. "The people down here seem to despise natural beauty," observes a newcomer. "They think they're not going to feel secure until they get the asphalt in every direction."

30. Ed Harris at the site of the waterfront development project in *A Flash of Green* (1985). By permission of Photofest.

Opposition to this "hideous development" comes from a small group of locals, some of them recent arrivals. They organize "Save Our Bay" (SOB) to mount an educational campaign prior to a vote on the project by county commissioners. In addition to showing the natural beauty of the tree-lined and largely deserted beaches of pristine white sand, the film gives voice to an opponent who explains the critical role of bays in Florida's ecology. Filling in the bay "would be like spitting in the face of God," declares one expert. Despite the political weakness of these opponents, Commissioner Bliss pulls out all the stops to assure official approval of the project. By the time the county commissioners actually vote, the outcome is such a foregone conclusion that the film does not even cover it. However, the obvious contradiction of trying to improve upon nature by destroying it, is brought home in the final scene of *A Flash of Green*. Jimmy Wing approaches a high fence that blocks access to the beach, where he sees a huge dredge illuminated by powerful lights in the night. He encounters a uniformed security guard who looks at the otherworldly sight and says, "Kinda pretty, ain't it?"

Other films from the 1980s use humor to expose the shortsightedness of developers. In *Caddyshack* (1980), Rodney Dangerfield plays Al Czervik, a loudmouthed boor who has made millions from real estate and now wants to join Bushwood Country Club, an elite enclave. While playing golf at the club, Czervik points with pride to a sign on adjacent land that proclaims The Very Latest Czervik Condominiums. " Not bad," he says. "I'll have two thousand more units in the next two years. Hey, I'll bet they'd love a great shopping mall right here. Condos over there. Plenty of parking. I'll tell you, country clubs and cemeteries—biggest wastes of prime real estate." As part of a man-versus-nature subplot, *Caddyshack* has the club's groundskeeper (Bill Murray) in deadly pursuit of a gopher that is tearing up the golf course and ruining the good life. Unable to catch or kill the pesky critter, the groundskeeper concludes that gophers are tunneling in from Czervik's construction site, where their habitat is being destroyed.

Caddyshack II (1988) has a similar story line with Jackie Mason playing Jack Hartounian, a millionaire developer who wants to build apartments

31. Bill Murray and his nemesis in *Caddyshack* (1980). By permission of Wisconsin Center for Film and Theater Research.

next to the golf course to provide "decent housing for working people." In addition to poking fun at Florida developers, the sequel also targets their opponents by emphasizing their upper-class bias. Led by Cynthia Young (Dina Merrill), the snooty wife of the president of Bushwood Country Club, the Historical Preservation Society tries to block Hartounian's project by organizing protests with signs that say Heritage NOT Housing. The group gets a court injunction to block destruction of a dilapidated garage that Hartounian describes as "an old dump," but Cynthia Young demurs. "This building is over seventy years old—it's part of our heritage," she says. "Stop the bullshit, lady," Hartounian responds. "You just can't stand working people living in this neighborhood." After Hartounian is finally rejected for membership in the country club, he buys the club and turns it into an amusement park for "the general public." This cynical view of the motives of developers and preservationists leaves room for several interpretations, but *Honky Tonk Freeway* offers no such ambiguity. The movie shows Florida's natural environment under assault by greedy businessmen and crooked politicians who are paving the state with highways that are crammed with traffic.

All the themes relating to Florida's environment are brilliantly explored by John Sayles in *Sunshine State*, which he wrote, directed, and edited. A reviewer for the *New York Times* called it "the most far-reaching civics lesson ever crammed into a 2-hour-21-minute film." Set on a fictional island called Plantation Island, the film was shot on Amelia Island, which is located along Florida's Atlantic coast, north of Jacksonville. The complicated plot examines the impact of tourism, land development, political shenanigans, and history on Floridians of different ages, classes, races, and genders. The central story line focuses on the efforts of outside developers, in league with corrupt real estate agents and politicians, to buy up property for megacomplexes of shopping centers and luxury homes. They encounter resistance from Marly (Edie Falco), who runs a motel/restaurant for her retired parents, and from African-American residents, who live in a historically black neighborhood that is clearly modeled after American Beach on Amelia Island. The lives of the many characters in *Sunshine State* eventually intersect and reveal the divisions that economic growth brings to families, neighbors, and friends. The film depicts developers plotting their takeover with military precision. As one of the outside agents (Miguel Ferrer) eyes Marly's property through binoculars, he says to his partner (Peter Lang): "Headquarters says that's where we establish our beachhead, then spread out and take the rest of it. . . . Right here is the soft underbelly of the island. . . . Point of weakest defense. You make the frontal assault, and I go behind the lines."

Yet the film's view of development is ambiguous. Marly's aging motel may not be worth saving, and she is attracted to a well-meaning landscape architect, Jack Meadows (Timothy Hutton), who works for the developer of Plantation Estates. Jack explains to Marly that his inspiration comes from Frederick Law Olmstead, the designer of New York's Central Park. "You take this land that's wild and inaccessible, and you refine it some," he says. "You showcase the natural beauty, you accentuate the topography, you create space for everybody—rich, poor, in-between—where they can come together and appreciate it." When Marly questions the access of ordinary people to what developers create, Jack admits, "Well, the populist part of it has fallen away."

While exposing the machinations of big corporations and their local allies, *Sunshine State* also presents glowing portraits of Florida's lush natural environment that remains largely untouched. The island boasts what one African-American resident (Bill Cobbs) describes as "the prettiest beach on the Atlantic coast." Views of it show little development except for aging homes set behind sand dunes covered with sea oats. The blue water stretches to the horizon and sends waves that break on the beach, providing a soothing sound that can often be heard in the background. On the mainland lies a river of unspoiled beauty where Marly goes canoeing with Jack. Filtered sunlight shimmers off the water that is bordered by dense woods and trees dripping with Spanish moss. Toward the end of this blissful scene, Marly explains how it was threatened by developers. "They were planning on building all along here," she says. "One of those assisted-living deals. Would have done it too if the Feds hadn't snapped it up first." Yet the film's dialogue reminds viewers that Florida's environment also includes mosquitoes and hurricanes.

A foursome of golfers appears throughout the film and comments on the battle between preservation and development. According to Sayles in his commentary on the DVD edition of the film, these aging golfers act like Greek gods on Mount Olympus, looking down on earth with "insider knowledge." One, named Murray Silver (Alan King), is apparently an experienced developer, and he describes how Florida was once worse than a swamp with alligators and mosquitoes. "Almost overnight, out of the muck and the mangroves, we created this," he says as he points to the manicured golf course and calls it "Nature on a leash." Later the golfers discuss global warming and the melting of the polar icecap. One notes that "every day another species goes extinct," leading the cynical Murray to scoff, "Nature is overrated." "Yes," counters another golfer (Eliot Asinof), "but we'll miss it when it's gone."

Mixed feelings about literally selling out to developers is shown in Marly's changing attitude. She and her father (Ralph Waite) initially refer to developers and their agents as "buzzards," but she's clearly tired of running the aging motel/restaurant. Finally she talks to her father about selling, and he tells her to go ahead and "get the best price." Her mother, Delia (Jane Alexander), plays hardball with the developer's agent and asks about plans for the site. "We prefer not to destroy anything when we come into an area," the agent responds, "whether it be an ecosystem or a small business person." Delia skeptically suggests that development will transform "our little beachfront into one of those cash-generating monstrosities that grace the coastal areas further to the south." She then demands not just a good price for the property but also a percentage of future profits on whatever is built.

The film ends with groundbreaking to clear the land for Plantation Estates, complete with television cameras, protesters chanting "Stop Plantation Estates," and police holding them back. As a Native-American construction worker slowly drives an earthmover forward, he immediately digs up human skulls and an arrowhead, all to the horror of businessmen who are watching. The discovery marks an end to this project, but *Sunshine State* leaves no doubt that development will continue. Nevertheless questions remain about what form growth will take and who will control it.

Cinematic portrayals of Florida's environment contain their share of goofs. Some of these result from conscious plot devices, but many are just errors of fact. Filmmakers understandably relocate sites to fit story lines. For example *China Moon* and *Forever Mine* move the Don CeSar Hotel from St. Pete Beach to Miami, but more amusing and confusing are the films that suggest Florida has mountains and other unlikely features. Early movies shot elsewhere are especially prone to misrepresent the Florida landscape. *Girl Missing*, a film from the 1930s, is set in Palm Beach, and the action is largely indoors. However, the few outdoor shots show mountains in the background, as does *Juke Girl* (1942), which was made in California. *Some Like It Hot* is perhaps the best known film to use California sets to tell a Florida story, and the result is a horizon in south Florida that features a mountain range. In *Clambake* Elvis Presley unwittingly draws attention to a location goof when he takes his love interest (Shelley Fabares) for a drive along the water, supposedly near Miami.

With big hills in the background, he points proudly to a large oil rig on the beach and says he owns many even larger ones. One of the few recent movies with an equally silly depiction of Florida's environment is *Point of Impact*, which was filmed entirely in South Africa and shows wooded foothills bordering Miami. Since most films are now shot on location, such obvious goofs are rare. However, after the production of *Scarface* was moved to California as a result of growing opposition in Miami to the film's portrayal of Cuban immigrants, a scene showing Tony Montana riding to the detention center in downtown Miami has the Los Angeles city hall in the background.

Despite these few obvious mistakes, it is not factual errors in films but their interpretations that make cinematic portrayals of Florida's environment so significant. As with portrayals of the natural environment, images of the state's built environment vary widely in films, and over time, they have become increasingly negative. Beginning with silent films, early depictions of Florida buildings often show a dreamland for the wealthy, dominated by luxurious hotels and private mansions. Even in films of the 1940s, ordinary people penetrate this world only by pretending to have money and position, as in *Moon Over Miami*. At the other extreme, films from that period like *The Yearling* show struggling Floridians living in rustic cabins with few amenities.

The economic boom after World War II opened the Sunshine State to the middle-class. Improved highways with motels strung like pearls alongside them brought tourists searching for cheap vacations and college students looking for a good time. The advent of air conditioning and suburban sprawl also attracted middle-class migrants and retirees, who took up residence in bungalows near the water and mobile home parks. Swimming pools began popping up everywhere.

Florida's most distinctive structures in the movies are largely designed for tourists. Amusement parks, dog tracks, tacky restaurants, and beach bars all serve visitors who are increasingly disappointed by the rundown accommodations and the ubiquitous congestion, as in movies like *Summer Rental*. Even once stately Mediterranean-style mansions from the 1920s are now old and rotting in films such as *Great Expectations*. Indeed, many aspects of Florida's natural and built environments have gone from dream to nightmare on the big screen.

Movies have consistently represented real estate agents and developers as the villains responsible for destroying Florida's natural paradise. At best these greedy hucksters fail to fulfill their promises, and at worst they ruin the environment by attempting to manufacture paradise. Even a film like *Sunshine State* that suggests not everything in Florida may be worth saving takes a largely critical view of developers and their efforts to put "nature on a leash."

One exception to generally negative depictions of growth is Miami. Many recent films present the city's new skyline of shimmering skyscrapers in glowing, sun-bathed aerial shots. The city's lure is further enhanced by the visual coolness of nighttime scenes of Miami Beach and its Art Deco buildings. The characters and story lines in films like *Bad Boys* may be degenerate, but the physical setting is not, at least not in the eyes of filmmakers and presumably their audiences.

Indeed, despite increasingly negative portrayals of Florida's natural and constructed environments in recent movies, the promise of rebirth or rejuvenation in some kind of paradise continues to attract visitors and new residents, as well as the filmmakers who portray them on the big screen.

Part II

Plots

The narratives of feature films set entirely or partly in Florida encompass all conventional genres—crime, drama, comedy, westerns, adventure, thrillers, musicals, and fantasies—as well as subgenres that blur or intertwine these formulaic approaches to storytelling. Plots for Florida films, nevertheless, cluster around three distinct general themes—re-creation, tourism, and crime.

The consistency of these themes about people who live in or travel to Florida reflects historic notions about what the state represents to filmmakers and their audiences. Some story lines portray the state as an untamed wilderness ripe for transformation, while others critique the human and environmental costs of these changes. In many plots Florida offers the possibility of rejuvenation or a chance to start life over again, and these dreams meet with widely varying degrees of fulfillment. Similarly, as a site for sheer enjoyment, relaxation, and escape, the Sunshine State has brought tourists both pleasure and disappointment in movies. Despite the state's association with starting over and tourism, the most common story line about Florida focuses on crime in all its various forms.

Over the years, movie plots reflect disparate, changing, and even conflicting views of what Florida means. The genres and subgenres used to tell stories often reveal dominant political, social, and economic notions of their periods. Westerns and war stories, for example, have been more popular in some decades than in others. Romance dramas have enjoyed more consistent popularity, but expectations about how the story unfolds and concludes have changed along with social conditions. Similarly, the nature of crimes depicted in movies and the identity of perpetrators reflect both new conditions and changing perceptions about criminal behavior. Over time, stories about gangsters in Florida have shifted from bootlegging by local crackers to drug running by Latino immigrants.

Whatever the genre, plots about Florida focus on residents, migrants, and visitors, whose stories usually revolve around starting over, tourism, or crime. Their experiences bring, of course, differing results in the movies, but most often the Sunshine State fails to deliver on its promises.

Chapter 3

"No doctors. . . . Florida—you get me to Florida."

Midnight Cowboy (1969)

"The word . . . is that you dudes are onto some kind of rejuvenation."

Cocoon (1985)

Re-Creation
Starting Over in Paradise

The search for a new life has brought waves of people to Florida for centuries. In 1513 Ponce de León became the first recorded European traveler to arrive, looking for rejuvenation through the Fountain of Youth. Like many others after him, he may have been disappointed by the reality, but the perception of Florida as a place to start over, to begin again, persists to this day, built on centuries of experiences—real and imagined. Surviving images from French expeditions in the 1560s portray a paradise with unbounded possibilities, including the chance of starting over, "of re-creating the self," according to the authors of a recent collection of impressions of Florida.[1] The eighteenth century brought a new group of migrants, as Indians from neighboring colonies moved into northern Florida. Known as Seminoles, "a term identifying them as separatists or 'runaways' from the Creek federation," these Indians were joined in Florida by runaway slaves seeking freedom from their English masters. Attracted to Florida by "land emptied by warfare and disease, both Indians and blacks saw in the territory the possibility of renewal, a place for rebuilding their shattered communities," as two scholars have pointed out. Along with early European travelers, Indians and runaway slaves set a pattern for subsequent visitors, migrants, refugees, and retirees, who have pictured Florida as a place "for renewal, re-creation, rejuvenation, and regeneration."[2]

This theme of starting over has captured the attention of countless filmmakers who have invoked the dream of re-creation in Florida. Indeed, they have portrayed a surprising number of different ways that people have tried to reinvent themselves in the Sunshine State. Cinematic portrayals of starting over have emphasized varying degrees of success, ranging from the setbacks suffered by ex-cons to the eternal life achieved by retirees in *Cocoon*. However, no matter what the goal or the results, renewal remains a dominant vision of the state almost five hundred years after Ponce de León's frustrated search for the Fountain of Youth. The dream that such a source actually exists in Florida provides the plot for *The Fat Spy* (1966), a comedy about the greedy competition between two cosmetics manufacturers (Phyllis Diller and Jack E. Leonard) who scour the state looking for an ingredient that will guarantee eternal youth.

The most romantic image of Florida in movies portrays it as a place for outsiders to find love or to rekindle it. Love on the rebound first appears in silent films like *The Daughter of MacGregor* (1916), which tells the story of an English woman who flees to Florida after a sad love affair, and there she is eventually reunited with her lost love. *Second Honeymoon* (1937) is set in Miami, where a divorced couple (Loretta Young and Tyrone Power) run into each other and rekindle their romance, leading her to leave her new husband and remarry her first husband. Clearly, Florida has a special magic, which continues to cast its spell in movies. In another comedy, *Fun on a Weekend* (1949), Eddie Bracken and Priscilla Lane play a penniless pair who meet on a Florida beach and manage to live the good life by passing themselves off as a wealthy couple. Although the pretense collapses, they fall in love, which, of course, is more important.

One of the first movies about Florida took the theme of reinvention to a bizarre extreme. *A Florida Enchantment*, a 1914 silent film, tells the story of Lillian Tavers (Edith Storey), a young heiress from New York, who visits her aunt in St. Augustine and discovers a letter from 1813 with "a secret for all women who suffer." The secret, contained in a box that washed ashore a century earlier, turns out to be seeds, "which changed men into women and vice versa." Unhappy with her fiancé, Lillian decides to swallow one of the seeds, and she immediately effects a masculine strut. By the following morning, "the metamorphosis," as the film calls it, is com-

32. Lucille Ball on the dance floor with Henry Fonda in the final scene of *The Big Street* (1942). By permission of Photofest.

plete. Lillian has sprouted a beard, which she shaves, and in a further effort to disguise her transformation into a man, she continues to dress as a woman. However, unable to suppress her masculine behavior, she kisses women on the lips and smokes in public. Finally Lillian embraces her new self, becomes "Lawrence," cuts her hair, dresses as a man, and courts women. Florida, it seems, possesses the power to make anything possible. *A Florida Enchantment* ends with Lillian waking from "a horrible dream," a decidedly negative description, considering the exuberance and freedom Lillian clearly enjoyed in her imagined rebirth as Lawrence.

The transformations sought in subsequent Florida films have been more prosaic than sex changes, but often just as illusory. Indeed numerous films portray dreams of physical regeneration that remain unfulfilled in Florida. *The Big Street* (1942), directed by Irving Reis and based on a story by Damon Runyan, stars Lucille Ball in a dramatic role as Gloria Lyons, a self-centered performer in a New York club who is paralyzed in an accident. Condemned to a wheelchair, she allows a fawning busboy, nicknamed "Pinks" (Henry Fonda), to care for her, and he caters to her every wish. When she says that she wants to go to Florida where it's warm, the penniless Pinks decides to push her there in a wheelchair. After finding rides along the way, the pair finally arrives in Miami, where the gold-digging Gloria tries to link up with a rich man she knew in New York, but he will have nothing to do with her when he sees that she's paralyzed. Living in a fantasy world, Gloria only gradually faces the reality of her condition, and then with her "illusion shattered," she falls into despair. Pinks tries to keep her dreams alive by stealing an expensive dress for what Gloria hopes will be her return to the stage, but the police arrest Pinks, and Gloria dies in his arms, declaring she is "happy for the first time" in her life. With its stated message that "love is the most important thing," *The Big Street* suggests that Florida may provide spiritual rejuvenation, even if it lacks miracle cures for physical impairments.

Several films from the 1940s and 1950s reinforce this theme. *Night Unto Night* (1949), directed by Don Siegel, tells the story of a scientist (Ronald Reagan) suffering from epilepsy who moves to Florida, where his condition deteriorates into suicidal tendencies. However, as in *The Big Street*, love provides a temporary form of salvation, when a widow (Viveca Lindfors) professes her love and convinces the scientist not to kill himself. *Interrupted Melody* (1955) keeps alive the hope of spiritual rejuvenation by recounting the true story of Marjorie Lawrence (Eleanor Parker), an Australian-born opera singer who is stricken with polio. Confined to a wheelchair, she gives up hope of ever singing professionally again, but her husband (Glen Ford) takes her to Florida, where she regains her confidence and returns to international prominence as a singer. In *Meet Me After the Show* (1951), a musical comedy starring Betty Grable, a singer in New York develops amnesia and ends up working in a club in Miami, where she regains her memory.

The theme of spiritual renewal in Florida drives the plot of *Radio Inside* (1994). Written and directed by Jeffrey Bell, this independent film follows Matthew (William McNamara) from Indiana, where he has just graduated from college, to Miami Beach, where his brother Michael (Dylan Walsh) lives with his girlfriend (Elizabeth Shue). The film's title refers to Matthew's psychological problems, which include guilt over his father's drowning death and music he hears inside his head. Although a love triangle further complicates his state of mind, Matthew finds Florida a place to start over and achieve some inner peace.

Florida's promise of physical, economic, and personal rebirth proves especially alluring to New Yorkers in several major films that contrast the Empire State and the Sunshine State. John Schlesinger's celebrated film *Midnight Cowboy*, which won Academy Awards for both best director and best picture, takes place largely in New York City, but the dream of life in Florida preoccupies Enrico Salvatore ("Ratzo") Rizzo, played by Dustin

33. "Ratso" Rizzo (Dustin Hoffman) surrounded by Florida posters in *Midnight Cowboy* (1969). By permission of Photofest.

Hoffman. Saddled with a nickname that seems all too appropriate, Ratzo is a sickly, New York lowlife, who literally limps through the dark, cold streets surrounding Times Square. He survives through petty theft that brings him into contact with Joe Buck (Jon Voigt), a struggling hustler newly arrived from Texas. Unable to support himself by living off women willing to pay for his sexual services, Joe moves in with Ratzo, who is squatting in a shabby room in an abandoned building. The first shot of the dilapidated room shows a FLORIDA travel poster with a picture of a fisherman in a boat. Subsequent scenes reveal that Ratzo's only wall decorations are related to Florida—a picture of a family looking at a huge orange grove and signs advertising orange juice. The subliminal message is soon spelled out by Ratzo who tries to explain the bounties of Florida to his new friend. Still convinced that he can find a rich woman to keep him in New York, Joe shows little interest in the reputed charms of Florida, but Ratzo persists in extolling the state.

After stealing a coconut from a fruit stand, Ratzo tells Joe, "The two basic items necessary to sustain life are sunshine and coconut milk," and Florida has "got a terrific amount of coconut trees." Even better, according to Ratzo, there are "more ladies in Miami than in any resort area in the country." Declaring "we gotta get outa here," Ratzo says to Joe, "Miami Beach, that's where you could score. Anybody can score there—even you."

In a later scene when Joe tries to hustle a woman in a New York hotel, Ratzo stands outside on the cold street and imagines himself sitting on a Florida beach with the sun reflecting off the water. In his imagination, Ratzo jumps up and runs along the beach, having lost his limp. As the daydream continues, Ratzo pictures himself as some kind of Don Juan at the Diplomat Hotel in Miami Beach. With Joe as his sidekick, Ratzo imagines old ladies in swimsuits and fur stoles pursuing him.

Florida's contrast with New York City is reinforced in a scene where Ratzo and Joe listen to a portable radio in their cold, unheated room. The radio announcer declares that the temperature is "now twenty-eight degrees and the weatherman says it's going down tonight. . . . We can expect a few snow flurries later on." The camera focuses on water freezing as it drips out of a faucet in the room, and when Ratzo and Joe bounce up and down, trying to get warm, a jingle comes over the radio: "Orange juice on ice is nice. . . . Break away from old habits, take a word of advice, serve real Florida orange juice."

34. "Ratso" Rizzo (Dustin Hoffman) as he imagines himself transformed in *Midnight Cowboy* (1969), hustling women at a hotel in Miami. By permission of Photofest.

With winter weather worsening and Ratzo's health declining to the point where he can no longer walk, Joe decides to get a doctor, but Ratzo stops him. "No doctors. . . . Florida—you get me to Florida. . . . Just get me on a bus." Joe then steals the money for two bus tickets to Miami, and the pair embarks on the thirty-one-hour trip. Suffering from a fever and sweating profusely, Ratzo passes the time by talking about what starting over in Florida will mean. His reinvention will begin with his name, "Because I mean like what's the whole point of this trip anyway? . . . I mean, can you see this guy running around the beach all suntanned, and he's goin' in swimmin' and somebody yells, 'Hey Ratzo' . . . Sounds like crap. I'm 'Ricco' all the time, okay? We're goin' to tell all these new people my name's Ricco."

The pair's rebirth begins once the bus crosses into Florida. At a stop in a small town, Joe buys new clothes at a discount store and throws away his boots, cowboy shirt, and treasured leather jacket with fringes. He gets himself a conservative sport shirt and finds a bright print shirt with palm trees for Ratzo, who then sheds the black clothes he has worn throughout the film. Even Joe begins dreaming about a new life as the bus approaches Miami. "Hey, you know Rats—Ricco, I mean. I got this whole thing figured out. When we get to Miami, . . . I'm going to get some sort of job because, hell, I ain't no kinda hustler. . . . Some sorta outdoors' work." At that point, Joe realizes that Ratzo has died while sitting in the bus, only a few minutes from Miami. The film ends with a shot of Ratzo in Joe's arms, as seen through the bus window. Reflected on the window are Miami buildings flashing by like a mirage.

The illusion of starting over in Florida serves as a subplot in other films featuring New Yorkers. *Requiem for a Dream* (2000), directed by Darren Aronofsky, depicts the disastrous and depressing cycle of decline experienced by a young pair of heroin-addicted New Yorkers who, like Ratzo Rizzo and Joe Buck, dream of finding success in Florida. After failing to score any heroin to use and peddle in New York, Harry (Jared Leto) and his pal Tyrone (Marlon Wayans) head to Florida. Their decision is prompted by missing out on a shipment of drugs that arrives in New York in a semitrailer, emblazoned with the words FLORIDA ORANGES. As the truck filled with drugs speeds away, Ty says, "They're goin' right back to Florida, sittin' their ass in that hot-ass sun, while we're sittin' here ass-deep in some mother-fuckin' snow." Harry suggests the two go "down there" to score some heroin. Like the pair of losers in *Midnight Cowboy*, Harry and Ty never fulfill their Florida dream. Their car trip is interrupted when Harry's arm becomes so infected from shooting up heroin that

Ty has to take him to a hospital. There a physician calls the police, and the film ends with Harry in the hospital and Ty in jail, somewhere between New York and Florida.

Another drug addict never even leaves the New York area in *City by the Sea* (2002), but he too dreams of starting over in Florida. After killing a dealer in a drug-induced haze, Joey LaMarca (James Franco) tells his mother, "If I can get away, maybe I could just clean up. I don't know—go some place like Key West." Joey then tries unsuccessfully to get "some travelin' money" to go "down there" to Key West. His former girlfriend (Eliza Dushku) later explains to his father (Robert DeNiro), "Whenever he gets rabid, he's gonna fly away to Florida, like it's some magic country."

Even New Yorkers who actually make it to Florida often find their dreams dashed. Perhaps the most fully explored attempt at reinvention appears in *Donnie Brasco* (1997). Based on a true story, the film recounts the exploits of Donnie (Johnny Depp), an undercover FBI agent who infiltrates a gang of small-time New York mobsters. Donnie befriends "Lefty" Ruggiero (Al Pacino), an aging mafioso. Never able to rise in the crime world, despite having supposedly "clipped" twenty-six guys, Lefty is now burdened by cancer, and he takes Donnie under his wing, allowing the undercover agent to lure him and his fellow hoods to Florida as part of an FBI sting operation. When Donnie first raises the subject of Florida by suggesting that "it's fuckin' wide open down there," one of the mobsters chimes in, "The whole economy's movin' down there. They call it the Sunbelt." Another gang member points out that the problem in New York "is that you got three thousand wise guys all chasin' the same nickel."

After some initial doubts, Lefty sees Florida as his last chance to make it big. Taken to a rundown club that he calls "a fuckin' dump," Lefty quickly imagines the south Florida lounge as a way out of his dead-end life in New York. "Thirty years I'm bustin' my hump," he tells Donnie. "What do I get? Even a dog gets a warm piece of the sidewalk. I oughta show somethin' for what I did. . . . This ain't New York down here. . . . Down here a guy like me could sit down with the boss. . . . Get out from under. Be a free agent again." Reality, of course, catches up with Lefty, destroying his dream. On opening night at the refurbished club, which features illegal gambling, local police stage a raid, smash the interior, and arrest Lefty and the other New York mobsters. It turns out that the local Mafia boss, Santo Trafficante (Val Avery), tipped off the police because the club threatened his grip on Florida. *Donnie Brasco* reinforces the image of Florida as a place of unfulfilled dreams. Despite its promise of regeneration, the state often brings disillusion, especially to outsiders trying to start over.

Marjorie Kinnan Rawlings provides a real-life success story of a New Yorker who reinvents herself in Florida. As recounted in the film *Cross Creek* (1983), Rawlings (Mary Steenburgen) leaves her husband and moves from New York to rural Florida in 1928 to devote herself to writing. Based on her Florida experiences, she later wrote *The Yearling*, which won a Pulitzer Prize in 1939. Few fictional characters find this kind of fulfillment in Florida, although the 1998 film *Ride* suggests that a group of struggling hip-hop singers from Harlem achieves success by going to Miami to make a music video.

In addition to portraying many New Yorkers who dream of rebirth in Florida, movies show that the same illusion also attracts outsiders from other states. *Hard Choices* (1985) largely transpires in Tennessee, but it tells the story of a teenager (Gary McLeery) who goes to jail for his involvement in a robbery/murder. With the help of a sympathetic social worker (Margaret Klench), he escapes, and the two fugitives flee to Florida, where police catch up with them, smashing the dream of starting over in paradise. In *Miami Blues* (1990) Florida does not fulfill the dreams of Frederick J. ("Junior") Frenger Jr. (Alec Baldwin), an ex-con from California trying to start over in Miami. While continuing his life of crime in south Florida, Junior meets Susie Waggoner (Jennifer Jason Leigh), a dumber-than-dumb hooker from Lake Okeechobee, who hopes

35. Alec Baldwin and Jennifer Jason Leigh (*far right*) at their Coral Gables home in *Miami Blues* (1990). By permission of Photofest.

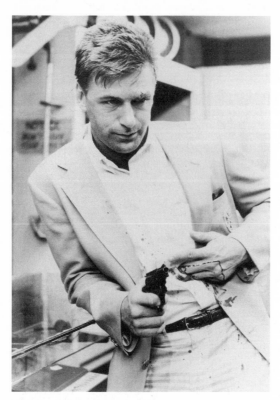

36. Alec Baldwin, mortally wounded by police, in the last scene of *Miami Blues* (1990). By permission of Photofest.

to improve herself by taking business courses at Miami-Dade Community College. Explaining why she turned to prostitution, she tells Junior, "I got a job at a Burger World up in Hollywood, and I was going to save up and get my own franchise, but Pablo offered me this job [as a hooker]. Well, it pays a whole lot better." In search of the American dream, Susie and Junior rent a house with a white picket fence in Coral Gables. However, Junior cannot escape his criminal past, and he winds up killed by police.

Another ex-con from California tries his luck in Florida in *Out of Sight* (1998). Based on the novel by Elmore Leonard, the film uses flashbacks to tell the story of Jack Foley (George Clooney), a convicted bank robber who moves to Miami after getting out of prison in California. In a futile attempt to start over in Florida, Foley takes a legitimate job, which he soon quits because it proves too menial. The film opens with him walking out of a Miami office building, pulling off his tie, and sauntering across the street to rob a Sun Trust Bank. In a smart heist that relies on his guile, Foley gets away with no problem, except that his old car will not start, and he is arrested in the parking lot of the bank. Sent to prison in Belle

Glade, he then escapes and flees to Detroit, where most of the film is set. Unlike Junior in *Miami Blues*, Foley survives his brief stay in Florida, but like many cinematic criminals trying to start over in the Sunshine State, he fails.

The Greatest Show on Earth (1952) has a subplot about a wanted man failing to escape his past in Florida. Featuring the Barnum & Bailey name and filmed in the Sarasota area in the 1950s, Cecil B. DeMille's three-ring circus has Jimmy Stewart playing a clown, who is actually a physician on the run from the law for the "mercy" killing of his dying wife. Despite his makeover, his cover is blown when he performs difficult surgery on the injured circus manager after a train wreck.

Even Floridians are often frustrated in their attempts to start over. In *Stick* (1985) Burt Reynolds plays Earnest ("Stick") Stickley, who tries to go straight after his release from a Florida prison. However, in this movie version of an Elmore Leonard novel, the Miami environment of drugs and murder quickly sets Stick on a path of revenge after the death of a friend, who is bumped off while delivering drug money. Despite his eventual success in dispatching the villains, Stick seems doomed to a life outside the law because of his own melancholy and his dismal Florida surroundings.

These films all reinforce the message that Florida holds promise of personal regeneration, but it rarely delivers. Moreover, when some kind of rebirth does occur in Florida, the setting usually does not explain the change. For example *The Rookie* (2002) traces the true-life story of Jimmy Morris (Dennis Quaid) who becomes the oldest rookie in forty years to play in a major league baseball game when he pitches for the Tampa Bay Devil Rays. After years of coaching high school baseball in a small Texas town because of an injury that keeps him from playing, Morris discovers in his thirties that he can still throw the ball ninety-seven miles an hour. He tries out with the Devil Rays and gets a contract. After playing with their minor league team in Orlando, he is called up to the majors, but the film shows him pitching in only one game for the Devil Rays—an away game against the Texas Rangers. Thus, Florida provides only a brief backdrop for Morris's rejuvenation.

A recent example of someone successfully starting over in Florida provides the story line for the leading character in *2 Fast 2 Furious* (2003). Brian O'Connor (Paul Walker), a former Los Angeles policeman, moves to Miami after he is thrown off the force in L.A. for helping a friend avoid criminal charges. Facing possible indictment himself, O'Connor agrees to go undercover for U.S. Customs to bust a Latino drug lord in Miami. His

37. Gregory Hines (*left*) and Billy Crystal on a Key West beach in *Running Scared* (1986). By permission of Photofest.

success in dispatching the bad guys gets O'Connor's record in L.A. wiped clean, and he decides to stay in Miami.

The dream of starting over in Florida is not confined to criminals or aging baseball players. Indeed, the theme appears as a prominent subplot in many films. *Running Scared* (1986) tells the story of two Chicago cops, Danny Costanzo (Billy Crystal) and Ray Hughes (Gregory Hines), who take a vacation after they are almost killed on duty. A trip to Key West gives them the idea of quitting the force, taking their pensions, and opening a bar in Key West. However, they soon decide that they prefer the excitement of Chicago to the boredom and humidity of the Florida Keys. Back in the windy city, they reflect on how bad Florida is in reality. "Hell, they don't even have thick pizzas," Danny says. "A lot of old people down there, too," Ray adds. "You go down there, you get old and die."

Key West provides a chance to start over for Lawson Russell (Cuba Gooding Jr.) in *A Murder of Crows* (1999). After he is disbarred in Louisiana for making the moral (but professionally unethical) choice of exposing a client as a murderer, Russell leaves New Orleans. "I'm going to go down to Key West," he tells a friend. "My father kept a house there. Hell, I might even write a novel. I'm as smart as John Grisham." In a convoluted plot, Russell's career as a novelist is undone by his decidedly unethical decision to put his name on someone else's book manuscript. After returning to New Orleans, where he tracks down a murderer, Russell then goes back to Key West at the end of the film to begin a second attempt at starting over in paradise.

Films about outsiders seeking the road to easy money in Florida often portray the proverbial gold digger. This theme is especially prominent in older movies like *Moon Over Miami* (1941) and *Palm Beach Story* (1942) that feature women looking for rich men but finding that love triumphs over money. In *Moon Over Miami*, sisters Kay (Betty Grable) and Barbara (Carole Landis) decide to forsake Texas in order to find rich husbands in Miami. Although initially presented as gold diggers, the sisters are redeemed in the end because they marry for love (in conformity with 1940s' moral standards). Nevertheless the film clearly shows Miami as a good hunting ground for gold diggers. According to a hotel employee, "Some people come down [here] to chisel—as gold diggers—and not all of them are women."

In *The Palm Beach Story*, Gerry Jeffers (Claudette Colbert) is a bored New Yorker who has fallen out of love with her unsuccessful husband (Joel McCrea). Deciding to start over in Florida, Gerry cons her way onto a train bound for Palm Beach. En route she meets a rich man, John D. Hackensacker III (Rudy Vallee), whom she uses to get her husband back

38. Rudy Vallee and Claudette Colbert in *The Palm Beach Story* (1942). By permission of Photofest.

39. Joe E. Brown plays a millionaire attracted to Jack Lemmon, who arrives at a Florida hotel disguised as a woman, in *Some Like It Hot* (1959). By permission of Photofest.

on his feet. After her husband follows Gerry to Florida, where he finds success, she returns to him. Like *Moon Over Miami*, this movie concludes with the triumph of love and marriage, but it presents south Florida as a haven of the rich and a place of opportunity for those who want to become wealthy.

Some Like It Hot (1959) echoes these themes. When Joe (Tony Curtis) and Jerry (Jack Lemmon) flee Chicago after witnessing the 1929 St. Valentine's Day massacre, the two musicians join an all-girl band by cross-dressing as Josephine and Daphne. On the way to a three-week stand in Miami with "Sweet Sue and Her Society Syncopaters," the pair befriends the band's singer Sugar (Marilyn Monroe), who says she is glad they are going to Florida because the state has "millionaires, lots of them. They all go south for the winter like birds." As band members arrive at the Seminole-Ritz Hotel in Miami, they see the porch lined with aging millionaires, all dressed alike, sitting in rocking chairs, and reading the

Wall Street Journal. Joe/Josephine remarks to Sugar, "Well, there they are. More millionaires than you can shake a stick at." After establishing the plot of gold-digging by Sugar, *Some Like It Hot* follows the cinematic formula of the period and has Sugar fall in love with Joe. Although he initially pretends to be a Shell Oil heir, Joe manages to keep Sugar's affection even after his pretense collapses.

The gold-digger theme is revived in *Heartbreakers* (2001). The film stars Sigourney Weaver and Jennifer Love Hewitt as a mother/daughter team of con artists who target a Palm Beach billionaire (Gene Hackman). Reminiscent of earlier comedy romances, Hewitt's character falls in love with a rich bar owner (Jason Lee), suggesting that women can find both love and money in south Florida.

Hollywood's Florida also attracts struggling people who are willing to work their way up and come to the state because of its heralded opportunities. *Juke Girl* (1942) shows Steve Talbot (Ronald Reagan) and a friend from the rural Midwest traveling to Florida to work as migrant laborers in the fields during the early 1940s. Steve, an honest man who constantly fights for the rights of the downtrodden, befriends a south Florida farmer who is exploited by a local wholesaler engaged in pushing down the price of tomatoes. Steve is joined in his battle by a juke-joint singer (Ann Sheridan) who falls in love with him because of his defense of the oppressed. The film has this pair of lovers ultimately succeed in their moral crusade against cutthroat businessmen.

Another morality tale from the 1940s, *Sixteen Fathoms Deep* (1948), also features an outsider seeking work in Florida. Ray Douglas (Lloyd Bridges) is an ex-Navy diver who hears that there are jobs available in Tarpon Springs. Like Ronald Reagan's character in *Juke Girl*, Ray discovers that a Florida industry is controlled by an evil businessman. In this case it is the sponge industry that is dominated by Mr. Demitri (Lon Chaney Jr.), a greedy wholesaler who will use any means to keep sponge-divers dependent. However, the forces of good ultimately triumph. In an interesting twist that attests to the state's actual opportunities, *Sixteen Fathoms Deep* helped launch a Florida career for Lloyd Bridges himself, since it became the basis for his long-running television show *Sea Hunt*.

The dream of finding success in Florida provides the plot for *Lucky Me* (1954), a musical comedy. The film stars Doris Day as a Pollyanna singer seeking a "stage career" in Miami, and Robert Cummings as a songwriter and playwright trying to get backing for a Broadway show. Thanks to the money of a millionaire, everyone gets lucky, and Florida launches them on their way.

40. Elvis Presley in a scene that is set on a Florida beach in *Follow That Dream* (1962). By permission of Photofest.

Films often portray struggling southerners seeking rebirth in Florida. *Follow That Dream* (1962) appropriates the illusion of starting over in its title. The movie stars Elvis Presley as Toby Kwimper, a disabled Army veteran from Georgia, who relocates to the Florida panhandle with his family in hopes of finding a better life. The film's premise is that Florida law allows squatters to become legal homesteaders if they can stake out an unclaimed parcel of land and keep a roof over their heads for six months. Toby's family sets up a fishing and tackle business on a spot along the Gulf Coast and then successfully defends it against the law and gangsters. This uplifting musical has a Florida judge deliver the film's message: "The spirit of the pioneer is still functioning today. It's what has made this country great."

During the years after World War II, Hollywood clearly saw Florida as America's new frontier, and that dream persists. In the ironically titled film *Ruby in Paradise* (1993), directed by Victor Nuñez, Ashley Judd plays an independent woman from Tennessee who flees a domineering husband and moves to Panama City, where she finds a job in a beach shop. Although she has only modest expectations for herself and Florida's opportunities, Ruby is consistently disappointed, a fate she shares with other young, working-class women in the film. Florida is not a paradise, but after a series of setbacks, Ruby becomes assistant manager of a souvenir shop, which sells trays decorated with beautiful sunsets and the slogan Day in Paradise—the words that fill the film's final frame.

While many films like *Follow That Dream* and *Ruby in Paradise* picture common people finding modest success in Florida, the state has also produced Horatio Alger characters in movies. *Tony Rome* (1967) features a subplot about a Miami construction magnate, who "holds a mortgage on Florida" and lives in the waterfront mansion Vizcaya (though it is not identified by name). Explaining his rise to success, he says: "I started out as a common bricklayer. Twenty million dollars later, they said I had no class, so I bought some." The film *Up Close and Personal* (1996) also presents something of a female version of Horatio Alger. Loosely based on the real-life story of Jessica Savitch, the film shows how Tally Atwater (Michelle Pfeiffer) breaks into television with no previous experience by sending out a demo tape to dozens of stations and only getting a response from a Miami outlet. An outsider who knows nothing about television or Florida, Tally is mentored by Warren Justice (Robert Redford), the news director at WMIA. Beginning as a gofer, Tally moves up quickly from weather girl to reporter to co-anchor to a big-time job in Philadelphia. For people with potential and drive, Florida can be a place of enormous opportunity, some films suggest.

The state's reputation for economic opportunity has always attracted immigrants from overseas, but Hollywood did not focus on this theme until the 1980s. Prior to that only Greeks who migrated to Tarpon Springs serve as subjects in dramas like *Sixteen Fathoms Deep* and *Beneath the 12-Mile Reef* (1953). After 1959 Castro's rise to power sparked an exodus of Cubans to Florida, but these predominantly white, well-to-do refugees scarcely registered on Hollywood's radar. Miami remains largely an enclave of native-born whites in films through the 1970s. In fact one of the few movies from the 1960s that deals with Cubans arriving in Miami is *Popi* (1969). The comedy stars Alan Arkin as a Puerto Rican living in New York City who devises an unsuccessful scheme to pass off his two sons as Cuban refugees so that they can take advantage of various relief programs to get ahead.

Hollywood discovered the subject of Cuban immigration after the Mariel boatlift of 1980 brought over one hundred thousand Cubans to south Florida. The cinematic template for the portrayal of these largely working-class refugees is established by Brian De Palma in *Scarface* (1983).

41. The last scene in *Scarface* (1983), showing the dead body of Tony Montana (Al Pacino) floating in his fountain, which has a statue bearing the slogan *The World Is Yours*.

The film opens with U.S. immigration officials suspiciously questioning Tony Montana (Al Pacino) about his background. He spits back, "I'm Tony Montana, a political prisoner from Cuba. And I want my fuckin' human rights. Just like the president Jimmy Carter says."

For Tony starting over in Miami means the opportunity to get rich by using his ruthlessness to exploit the local drug scene. "This is paradise," he tells another Cuban refugee. "I'm telling you, I should have come here ten years ago. I'd "a been a fuckin' millionaire by this time." Tony quickly rises to become a millionaire drug lord, but he is brought down by his own cocaine addiction and competitors who prove just as ruthless. Killed in one of Hollywood's longest and bloodiest shootouts, Tony falls from a balcony in his mansion into a reflecting pool with a statue of several figures holding aloft a globe with the words *The World Is Yours*, a motto taken from the original *Scarface* film. As with so many other movie characters before him, Tony's dreams of making it in Florida turn into a deadly nightmare of failure.

Tony Montana may be the most (in)famous cinematic Cuban trying to start over in Florida, but Hollywood has featured other refugees who are more sympathetic and ultimately more successful. In *The Perez Family* (1995), the Mariel boatlift brings together Dorita Perez (Marisa Tomei), a onetime cane cutter, and Juan Raul Perez (Alfred Molina), a longtime political prisoner. Although unrelated, the pair uses their common last name to create a pretend family in an effort to expedite their release from a Miami detention center. Dorita's rebirth (and reinvention) begins when she arrives on a boat from Cuba and assumes an American persona, declaring in a distinctly Spanish accent that her name is "Dottie." When challenged by a skeptical immigration agent, she says, "I'm a new woman here." She and her invented "family" initially face a variety of disappointments, leading Dottie to ask, "Why did we come to this terrible country?" However, she and her pretend husband ultimately fall in love and find happiness in Miami, countering the predominant Hollywood scenario of Florida as the land of unfulfilled dreams. In *Miami Rhapsody* (1995), Antonio Banderas plays a Cuban immigrant who has an affair with a rich Miami woman (Mia Farrow). "He came over on the boatlift," Farrow explains to her disbelieving daughter (Sarah Jessica Parker). "He was in jail in Cuba. I don't know what for. He wouldn't tell me." It turns out that he was imprisoned for car theft, but in Miami he does quite well as a male nurse and lover.

Other films celebrate the success of Cubans finding political freedom in south Florida. "That's why my family left Cuba—because Castro turned Communist," a Miami high school student comments offhandedly in *The Substitute* (1996). Gabriela (Jennifer Lopez), the nanny in *Blood and Wine* (1997), explains her flight from Cuba: "It took me a week. Fifteen of us on a very small boat. . . . Even when we were coming over, the sea was so beautiful. I never wanted to sleep. I was happy." She still has family in Cuba, and she proudly declares, "I'm going to bring them, one by one if I have to." While disease and botched crimes strike down the other lead characters in *Blood and Wine*, including a transplanted New Yorker (Jack Nicholson), the film ends with Gabriela as a struggling survivor in Florida.

In addition to Cuba, Russia is the other principal source of contemporary immigrants starting over in Florida movies. Aside from its communist background, Russia is like Cuba in that its major export appears to be criminals, according to several films. *Big Trouble* (2002), based on a novel by Dave Barry, shows contemporary south Florida plagued by villains, including Russian arms dealers who run a bar in Miami. *Bad Boys II* (2003) also portrays Russian criminals who have moved to Miami, where they operate dance clubs and deal drugs, but they are dispatched by a Cuban-American drug lord, whose ruthlessness rivals that of Tony Montana.

Florida provides political refuge not only for Cubans but also for other Latin Americans. In *Cat Chaser* (1989), the former head of the secret police in Trujillo's Dominican Republic starts over in Miami, but his past catches up with him, and he is killed. Once again rebirth in Florida proves impossible, especially for criminals.

42. The indoor pool, where retirees are rejuvenated, in *Cocoon* (1985). By permission of Photofest.

The ultimate Hollywood rendition of the search for the Fountain of Youth appears in *Cocoon*, Ron Howard's paean to retirees and their quest for eternal life. A strange combination of science fiction and comedy, the film tells the story of four space travelers, led by Walter (Brian Dennehy), who arrive in St. Petersburg from the planet Antarea. Their mission is to rescue twenty Antareans who thousands of years earlier were stranded on earth, where they have survived in cocoons now lying at the bottom of the Gulf of Mexico. Disguised as humans, Walter and his crew of rescuers slowly remove the cocoons from the Gulf and place them temporarily in a swimming pool at a waterfront mansion that they rent next to a retirement home. A trio of residents from the home—Art Selwyn (Don Ameche), Ben Luckett (Wilford Brimley), and Joe Finley (Hume Cronyn)—have been secretly using the mansion's pool, and they now discover that its waters, containing the cocoons, have magical powers. When they first swim in the pool with the cocoons resting on the bottom, they immediately feel rejuvenated, and they frolic in the water like kids. In perhaps the ultimate test of regeneration, they each get an erection, and Art sings, "I'm in the mood for love." Even more important, Joe finds out that his cancer goes into remission, which his physician describes as "a miracle." Recognizing the power of the pool water, the retirees take their wives for a swim, and they experience the same revival of youthfulness that gives them the energy to go dancing and bowling. Back at the retirement home, one of the residents says to them, "The word on the corridor is that you dudes are onto some kind of rejuvenation."

Only a crotchety friend, Bernie Lefkowitz (Jack Gilford), questions the wisdom of turning back the clock. "Nature has dealt us our hand of cards, and we played them," he says. "Now at the end of the game, suddenly you're lookin' to reshuffle the deck." Bernie later argues that his suspicion about fooling mother nature is confirmed when Joe's wife Alma (Jessica Tandy) leaves him. "Old is right," Bernie declares. "I don't want to be young again. Your life is a mess because of the Fountain of Youth. I don't care how healthy you think you are. . . . You can keep the goddamned Fountain of Youth."

After the powers of the magical waters evaporate, the retirees face a choice when the space traveler Walter offers to take them back to Antarea, where they could have eternal life. Even though it means leaving behind their grandson, Ben and his wife Mary (Maureen Stapleton) decide to go because, as Ben says, "we'll never be sick, we won't get any older, and we won't ever die." When Mary has second thoughts that they might be "cheating nature," Ben responds, "The way nature's been treating us, I don't mind cheating her a little." As the movie ends, the trio of couples, including Joe and Alma, leave with the Antareans.

Thus Ponce de León's dream is finally realized in a movie fantasy almost five hundred years after the quest began. One message of *Cocoon*, however, is that permanent rejuvenation can only be achieved by leaving Florida and the planet earth. The film also clearly raises doubts about the desirability of eternal life. For a variety of reasons, *Cocoon* was enormously popular, even among film critics who listed it as one of the year's top ten movies. It also won Don Ameche an Academy Award for best supporting actor. One dissenter, however, called the film "a naive wish fulfillment fantasy of rejuvenation," and he attributed the critical acclaim to reviewers "most akin to the age group" featured in a film "that spoke directly to their lives."[3]

The popularity of *Cocoon* undoubtedly explains the making of a sequel, *Cocoon: The Return* (1988). Although not directed by Ron Howard, the follow-up film features most of the original cast. The trio of couples who depart for Antarea at the conclusion of the original film return to earth in the sequel for a visit as part of another rescue mission. In St. Petersburg the couples reconnect with relatives and friends, reviving memories and doubts about the value of eternal life on another planet. "People shouldn't outlive their children," Mary says to her husband Ben, and adds, "I don't want to leave here." After Joe's cancer returns and he dies, Alma also decides to stay. Only one couple chooses eternal life and returns to Antarea. For the others life is worth living on earth with family and friends, even if it means eventually dying. *The Return* also emphasizes that rejuvenation can take various forms. Alma stays in St. Petersburg because she finds a job working with children, and Bernie finally accepts his wife's death and begins dating another woman.

Whether imagined as a Fountain of Youth or some other kind of rebirth, re-creation has long defined Florida's appeal, especially to outsiders. Films have portrayed the persistence of this longing, even as they have exposed its illusory aspects. *Human Stain* (2003), based on a novel by Philip Roth, takes place in a New England college town, but Florida figures in the dialogue when a working-class woman (Nicole Kidman) explains what she did after she was abused by her stepfather and no one would believe her. "That's when I split. I went to Florida. Did a little of this and that. . . . You know, a girl like me can always get by—no possessions, travel light." She says nothing more about her experiences in Florida, but the escape clearly did not bring much reward since she winds up working as a janitor in New England. The dream of reinventing oneself may bring people to Florida, but as pictured in movies, the reality usually proves harsh. Perceived as a paradise where people can find rebirth, the state does not deliver salvation in most films. On the contrary, the Florida dream can turn into a nightmare.

One of the most recent and complex tales of disillusion is told in *Adaptation* (2002). Based on Susan Orlean's book *The Orchid Thief* and with a screenplay by Charlie Kaufman, the film injects both Orlean (Meryl Streep) and Kaufman himself (Nicolas Cage) into the story of John Laroche (Chris Cooper). After Laroche is charged with taking a rare ghost orchid from a state preserve near Miami, Susan Orlean travels from her home in New York to interview him for an article. Gradually she becomes fixated with a quest for something larger that she recognizes might be unattainable. "I wanted to want something as much as people wanted these plants, but that isn't part of my constitution," she reflects in a voice-over, while images show her in her dark New York apartment. "I suppose I do have one unembarrassed passion. I want to know what it feels like to care about something passionately."

Echoing the common theme of a New Yorker seeking to break with the past and start a new life in Florida, *Adaptation* has Orlean return to the state. In her search for the ghost orchid and perhaps passion, Orlean

43. Chris Cooper examining a ghost orchid in *Adaptation* (2002). By permission of Photofest.

becomes increasingly entranced by the toothless, shaggy-haired Laroche. When she discovers that he has been a collector of various things from turtles to Dutch mirrors since the age of ten, Orlean marvels at his ability to move from one passion to another. "Laroche's finishes were downright absolute," she notes. "He just moved on. I sometimes wished I could do the same." After explaining his repeatedly starting over with new collections, Laroche points out why he is now so interested in plants. "Because they're so mutable," he observes. "Adaptation is a profound process. It means you figure out how to thrive in the world." Looking to change her own life, Susan retorts that "it's easier for plants. I mean, they have no memory. You know they just move on. . . . But for a person—adapting is almost shameful. It's like running away."

For Susan Orlean Florida's ghost orchid turns out to provide an unexpected escape. After Laroche leads her through a swamp to find the rare plant, he reveals the flower's secret power—a hallucinogenic drug can be extracted from it, and Seminoles use it "to get stoned." After becoming addicted to the drug and searching for a new life in Florida, Susan moves in with Laroche and his collection of ghost orchids. However, her dream of rebirth spirals out of control, ending with his death and her arrest. "It's over," she sobs in her last scene, as she sits on the edge of a swamp. "I did everything wrong. I want my life back. I want it back before it all got fucked up. I want to be a baby again. I want to be new." Thus *Adaptation* demonstrates that starting over in Florida can bring changes for the worse. Paradise can turn into hell, at least on the big screen.

Monster (2003) is another recent film that reinforces the idea that outsiders seeking rebirth in Florida find only disappointment. Aileen Wuornos (Charlize Theron) explains that she moved to the state as a young teenager after she was raped by a family friend in Michigan and was rejected by her siblings for turning to prostitution to survive. "They threw me out in the snow, screaming how I'm a whore and they're so embarrassed and they hate me and all that," she tells a friend. "I just took off and never went back." Later as a seasoned prostitute working the streets of central Florida, Wuornos meets Selby (Christina Ricci) who is another refugee from the Midwest. Explaining her own reasons for leaving Ohio, Selby says: "This girl in my church—she told everyone that I tried to kiss her, so my parents basically disowned me. And I decided to come down here and try to figure some things out." After arriving in Florida, Selby broke her arm and couldn't find a job, so she thinks about returning home to Ohio. However, once she starts a relationship with Wuornos, the pair dreams of moving to the Florida Keys to start over again. "Some day I'm going to take you to some real top-notch places in the Keys," Wuornos says. "I've always wanted to go to the Keys," Selby responds. "I always wanted to have a house on the beach, you know? But I haven't even been to the beach since I've been here." Continuing to dream about the life neither has found in Florida, Wuornos promises to buy her partner a house on the beach, but try as she might, Wuornos cannot break out of the cycle of hooking, robbery, and murder that leads to her execution.

Most people fare better in Florida than Aileen Wuornos, but few characters in films find the renewal or rebirth they seek in the Sunshine State. Despite the disappointment (and worse) suffered by many outsiders who try to start over in Florida, the promise of a re-creation continues to motivate dreamers in movies, as well as in real life. In fact one scholar has argued that there is a "peculiarity in American character that encourages us to see moving as a solution to most of our problems." In his book *Restless Nation: Starting Over in America*, James M. Jasper points out that this urge first brought European explorers to America, and it has propelled Americans to relocate throughout their history. As he notes, "Americans move in order to do better economically, to get in touch with the higher things in life, including their own souls, to adjust or flee family ties, to pursue physical health, to escape what constrains them." Moreover, he contends, "This restlessness is especially characteristic of men."[4]

All of these goals explain why characters move to Florida in films, but romance also clearly figures in the transformations people undergo in the state. Whether couples actually move to Florida in search of romance, they often find it in the movies. South Florida in particular provides the ideal setting for love, even for outsiders who travel there for other reasons, including the pursuit of money. The state's seemingly magical power to bring couples together dominates comedies, musicals, and dramas made in the 1940s, and it remains a common theme in such recent films as *Random Hearts* (1999), *Heartbreakers*, and *Adaptation*.

Despite Hollywood's repeated use of the love-conquers-all plot, movies generally emphasize other ways of seeking rebirth in Florida. The desire for physical or spiritual rejuvenation serves as a motive in some films like *Cocoon* and *Interrupted Melody*, but plots overwhelmingly highlight the search for either economic advancement or escape from constraints as the primary considerations that attract people to Florida. Con artists and gold diggers are recurrent characters in movies over the last century. In addition to various hustlers and criminals, ordinary people are also lured to the state in search of economic opportunity, as in *Juke Girl* and *Follow That Dream*. Just as commonly in films, characters imagine Florida as a place to reinvent themselves and escape familial, political, legal, or social restraints elsewhere. This desire finds expression in comedies, dramas, and action movies. Many migrants, notably Cubans, move to Florida for both political and economic reasons, a point made in *Scarface* and *The Perez Family*.

In many ways Florida represents a frontier, filled with opportunities, from the earliest silent films to the present. Migrants from other parts of the United States and from overseas are drawn to the state because of its reputation for offering outsiders a chance to re-create themselves. Whether defined in spiritual, physical, economic, or political terms, the promise of rebirth lures people to Florida in the movies. According to this plot device, it is the opportunity for change and growth, not the climate, that attracts characters to the Sunshine State. The exotic, semitropical environment may cause some of the heat in films, but other considerations usually provide the principal motivation for relocating.

Whatever the particular reason for moving to Florida, films demonstrate that women, as well as men, share the dream of starting over. Significantly films based on real-life stories often feature women seeking some kind of new life in Florida, as in *Interrupted Melody*, *Cross Creek*, and *Monster*. Moreover, in all the but the last film, these women often fulfill their dreams in Florida. Nevertheless most films demonstrate that the hope of rebirth in Florida proves illusive or impossible. Aside from sparking love, which frequently arrives unexpectedly, Florida usually fails to deliver on promises of a new and better life in films. Significantly, the ultimate achievement of eternal life depicted in *Cocoon* lies elsewhere, and even that fantasy fails to satisfy all of the film's characters. No matter what the particular goal or its outcome, the desire for re-creation drives the plots of many Florida movies.

Chapter 4

"It's beautiful down there. White beaches and girls in bikinis, Cape Canaveral, Miami Beach."

Stranger Than Paradise (1984)

"I've been in this town thirty years! And every summer you renters come down and think you can take over the whole town! . . . The red-beaked, seer-suckered, summer renter!"

Summer Rental (1985)

Tourism

Strangers in Paradise

Other than problems with girth, Elvis Presley and John Candy wouldn't seem to have much in common. But both actors starred in Florida vacation films, and both played characters who won the flagging admiration of their families by winning a regatta in a refurbished boat, Elvis in *Clambake* (1967) and Candy in *Summer Rental*. And both were transformed by their Florida trips.

The last of three movies starring Elvis and set in Florida, *Clambake* finds him aimlessly driving from Texas through Florida, trying to figure out if he wants to go into his daddy's oil business. Finally he ends up working in a four-star Miami hotel where wealthy white vacationers lounge in a bar decorated like a harem and sip drinks served by Arab-costumed Anglos. Elvis takes time out of his job as a ski instructor to develop an oil-based speedboat coating. In the regatta he challenges an even brasher, more self-absorbed playboy (Bill Bixby), tests out the new hull finish, gets the girl, and establishes his own career.

44. Elvis Presley in *Clambake* (1967). By permission of Photofest.

Twenty years later the hero and the setting change significantly in *Summer Rental*. Candy plays a burned-out air traffic controller whose boss arranges a forced vacation on Florida's Gulf Coast. The rental turns out to be a rundown motel adjacent to a busy public-access path to the beach. Within the first few days, Candy wrestles with Florida's notoriously similar addresses ("That's Beach *Road*, not Beach *Lane*"), bad plumbing, sunburn, crowded beaches, a sprained knee, rain, flies, fuzzy television reception, and difficulties finding good Florida seafood. After being humiliated by his temporary landlord and losing the respect of his son, Candy decides to enter the Citrus Cove Regatta to prove to himself and his family that he is not a complete loser. In contrast to the all-white cast in *Clambake*, wealthy and working-class African-Americans, Asians, and Latinos appear throughout *Summer Rental*, and unlike *Clambake*, it was actually filmed on location. The changed depiction of traveler experiences between 1967 and 1985 may in part reflect film trends that took root in the 1960s—to develop plots that portray realistic characters with whom audiences could identify. Elvis had enough money to stay in the four-star hotel in *Clambake*, but chose to disguise himself as working-class and live simply, while hanging out with the rich. Middle-class Candy had no such option, and his visit created more obstacles than opportunities, until the regatta.

Also released in 1984, the independent film *Stranger Than Paradise* presents another perspective of Florida tourism as less than idyllic. Here three working-class young adults drift toward Florida via New York and Cleveland. Although they impulsively search for different experiences in their lives, they fail to find them, even in Florida. The two gamblers and a frustrated Hungarian woman visit the northeast Florida coast in the gray and windy dead-of-winter, when the sun doesn't shine and there are no bikini-clad tourists. Their seedy motel has no landscaping, pool, television, or anything else to recommend it. And the visitors continue to be bored and lost. The guys go off to gamble at the racetrack while the woman stays alone, restless in the room. Despite its largely negative view, *Stranger Than Paradise* captures certain realities of Florida tourism. After an exhausting marathon car trip from the North, the trio arrives tired, stiff, and dirty. Their car is littered with snack remnants and coated with road dirt. In contrast, when Elvis and other tourists arrive by car in earlier movies, they are relaxed and neat—even in cars without air conditioning. Their drives are leisurely, with few cars on the road and, of course, no construction.

45. John Candy on a crowded beach in *Summer Rental* (1985). By permission of Photofest.

The Florida tourist first became a subject in films during the silent era. In films like *Palm Beach Girl* (1926) and *The Joy Girl* (1927), the focus is on wealthy south Florida vacationers, who arrive as cars and roads facilitated the boom in real estate and tourism. During the 1930s it was more difficult to attract tourists to the state. The few films made about the subject during the Depression reflected a common theme that continued throughout the century: women vacation in Florida to find wealthy men.

For decades the conflicts faced by female characters in films were internal and interpersonal, focusing on how to find a husband. The gold-digging women of film were lured to the state by the presence of wealthy men, but Florida also provided an ideal setting for them to find romance. The natural environment of swaying palm trees, wave-lapped beaches, soft moonlight, and breezes has often been associated in literature and song with a sensuous atmosphere of possibilities. An early example of gold-digging women is *Footloose Widows* (1926). In this plot two New York models take their borrowed expensive clothes and head to a luxury hotel in Florida to pose as wealthy widows. Flo (Louise Fazenda) targets "The Senator" (Neely Edwards), while Marian (Jacqueline Logan) looks for purported millionaire Mr. Smith (Jason Robards). Both succeed at snaring their prey. Bette Davis carries out a similar strategy to catch a husband in *The Golden Arrow* (1936), pretending to be a wealthy heiress in Florida. Female opportunists are not always covert, of course. The plot for *Girl Missing* (1933) is about a secretary brought to Palm Beach with her boss. She and a friend get drawn into a murder mystery involving another gold digger.

Sometimes men also help women find wealthy husbands. In *Everything's on Ice* (1939), Joe Barton (Edgar Kennedy) and Irene (Irene Dare) are fast-talked into letting friend Felix Miller (Roscoe Karns) take their daughter Jane (Lynne Roberts) to Miami and promote her as an ice skater. To trap a millionaire for Jane, Felix poses as a millionaire, but targets a man who is also posing as a millionaire. Meanwhile Jane falls for a "regular guy" who turns out be a millionaire. This kind of double-switch appears frequently in films.

To some extent the gold-digger tourist theme reflects conflicts about changes taking place in women's roles during the 1920s and 1930s. While women gained more political rights and entered the paid work force, both women and men debated the consequences of these changes. In the age of the "new woman," films seem to suggest that women had become more aggressive and devious. Jobs were merely temporary necessities until women could find husbands who would eliminate their need to work.

However, a formula for gold-digger films often highlights the triumph of love over money. *Moon Over Miami* (1942) best exemplifies this happy ending. Here, three Texas women working in a hamburger joint head for Florida to snag a wealthy husband by posing as an heiress and her entourage. Their prey is identified and manipulated, but all three ultimately prioritize love. And since this morality is rewarded, the youngest women end up with both love and money. Another film from the same year presents a less flattering image of gold diggers. Gloria Lyons (Lucille Ball) displays opportunistic tendencies before her paralyzing accident in New York, but says she wants to get to Florida for her health in *The Big Street* (1942). Clearly, she also wants to connect with wealthy New York socialites on vacation. On the beach, "Your Highness," as Henry Fonda's character always calls her, is carefully placed beneath a beach cabana, and she immediately dismisses him ("Now, evaporate!") as she zeroes in on a rich tourist she recognizes. Ball displays no redeeming qualities in the film, which explains why she fails to find love, money, or health in Florida.

The gold-digger tourist plot has become so familiar for Florida settings that it is reprised in *Heartbreakers* (2001), this time with a mother/daugh-

46. Carole Landis, Robert Cummings, Betty Grable, and Don Ameche in *Moon Over Miami* (1941). By permission of Photofest.

47. Lucille Ball with William T. Orr on a Miami beach in *The Big Street* (1942). By permission of Wisconsin Center for Film and Theater Research.

ter con team searching for rich men. Once again, money is the initial goal, but the daughter ends up finding true love with the owner of a beach bar.

While gold-digger plots tend to focus on female predators, *Clambake* points out that some men traveled to Florida for the same reason. Here the female star (Shelley Fabares) confesses her objective to Elvis (still posing as a poor ski instructor): "You boys come down for the season—as cabana boys, ski instructors, or life guards—hoping to find a girl with money. I'm doing the same thing; trying to land a millionaire."

As a vacation destination, Florida conjures up images that filmmakers have both represented and created. First the playground mainly of the wealthy, Florida became more accessible to the middle and lower classes with expanded automobile travel. Dependent on tourism for over a hundred years, Florida businessmen and public officials have promoted the Sunshine State as a region of natural beauty, leisure, and diverse entertainment. Brochures, travelogues, and videos emphasize an environment of spaciousness. They feature young and old healthy white couples with sun-kissed glows, frolicking in the water, golfing, fishing, playing tennis, cuddling with their loves, and building sandcastles with their children on the beach. In tourist promotions the beaches are almost deserted, and the lightly traveled roads and highways snake past sunset-lit beaches.

The reality of these images for tourists has varied as much as the feature films about Florida tourism. Social class, era, and/or location can shape tourist experiences, and movie images have both reinforced and contradicted audience expectations.

Early accounts by travelers viewed Florida as a place for physical and spiritual renewal. As William Bartram wrote in 1791, "How happily situated is this retired spot of earth! What an elisium [sic] it is! . . . Our situation was like that of the primitive state of man, peaceable, contented, and sociable."[1] Travel writers contributed to the expansion of Florida tourism by their descriptions of the environment and people as exotic and mysterious.

Films set before the 1920s capture the limits imposed by upper-class clothing styles. Draped in long dresses with high collars, women typically lounge about on porches fanning themselves or take evening strolls. Men in suits and high-button collars accompany them or venture out on their own, but engage in few physical activities.

With the growth of automobile travel in the 1920s, "tin-can tourists" drove in, but filmmakers ignored these middle- and lower-class vacationers and continued to focus on upper-class tourists who traveled by rail and boat. Movies from the Twenties show the wealthy swimming, playing tennis and croquet, and mingling with the locals at winter league baseball games. Tourists targeted for real estate scams in films like *The New Klondike* (1926) and *The Cocoanuts* (1929) seldom stray far from their hotels without a developer's help.

After the Florida real estate bubble burst and the Great Depression reduced tourism, the Federal Writers' Project reevaluated the impact of early tourist promotions. The 1939 report tried to dispel the image of Florida as a vacation paradise, arguing that "attempts to romanticize Florida's playground features have resulted in an elaborate painting of the lily." The WPA guide to Florida cautioned that "coast resorts have been strung into a bejeweled necklace that sparkles on the bosom of a voluptuous sea; all is glamour and superficiality."[2]

Despite these criticisms federal, state, and local policies renewed the promotion of Florida as a tourist paradise after World War II. Federal programs for veterans' assistance and highway expansion, as well as space projects, were matched by state and city efforts to attract more visitors. Tourists arriving by car could find more attractions and accommodations along the roadways. In movies since that time, tourists have been portrayed as more active: swimming, fishing, boating, gambling, shopping, visiting attractions, and attending conventions. Sometimes they are shown enjoying themselves en masse, like the students in Spring-Break films, the Canadian shoppers in *Ruby in Paradise* (1993), and the convention guests at the Don CeSar Hotel in *HEALTH* (1979). They are also cast as the victims of crimes, either individually or in groups.

Of course, visitors to a new place must always be alert to the known and unknown dangers of entering an unfamiliar environment. Filmmakers have seen in the sun-drenched paradise of Florida the opportunity to remind viewers that no Eden exists by introducing both natural and unnatural predators into scenes or entire plots. No natural creature has been more prominent than the alligator, whose first film appearance may be in *The Gator and the Pickaninny* (1900). For more than a century, in movies about Florida tourists, the alligator threat has become a convention, the staple reminder of danger in paradise.

The idea that natural creatures can become greater threats when removed from their natural environments is at least as old as *King Kong* (1933). In the 1950s and 1960s, a proliferation of low-budget horror movies, particularly those aimed at teen drive-in audiences, used otherwise idyllic settings to heighten the contrast between leisurely indulgence and unexpected danger. Florida's contribution was Gill Man, who attacks after becoming a tourist attraction in *Revenge of the Creature* (1955).

In *Matinee* (1993), set in 1962, shock filmmaker Lawrence Woolsey (John Goodman) represents the creativity of directors and producers in the style of Ed Wood, William Castle, Roger Corman, and Alfred Hitchcock. On his way to Key West, Woolsey gets an inspiration for another film by stopping at a rural Florida gas station. Eyeing a stuffed alligator mounted on the wall, he considers a title before developing a plot: "Manogator," "Alliman," "Seagator," "Gatorgal," or "Galligator."

Unfortunately for fans of the Florida alligator, it was a shark attacking New England vacationers that introduced the blockbuster era in film with *Jaws* (1976). Since then the search has continued for a similar success in a Florida creature film. The most notorious effort is *Alligator* (1980), which capitalized on a still-popular legend about what happened to all those alligators taken north by naive tourists. Here a baby alligator taken back to

Chicago and flushed down the toilet is nourished by chemically enriched sludge, becoming a superalligator That Must Be Destroyed.

The success of *Jaws* and its sequel eventually led to a third film set in Florida. In *Jaws 3-D* a mean and hungry great white shark gets into the tank at the Atlantic Coast Sea World Park. The film has all the requisite elements of tourist terror: park visitors are trapped in a flooded viewing tunnel, and water skiers, swimmers, boaters, and park workers all get chomped. Finally the shark explodes into a bloody mess. Shark attack films might have run their course, since marine scientists have made valiant efforts to educate the public about shark behavior and species protection. Nevertheless every shark attack in Florida is widely publicized, so it is possible that another shark film might be Coming Soon to a Theater Near You.

Despite tourists' dependence on theme parks, motels, and restaurants, films about tourism from the perspective of the service industry are rare. The first was probably the Marx Brothers' *The Cocoanuts*. In this comedy Groucho tries to get money to run his bankrupt Florida hotel by making love to a rich guest and selling worthless Florida real estate. The hotel/motel operator story reappears in Frank Sinatra's leading role in *A Hole in the Head* (1959), set in Miami. The famous nonspeaking performance of Jerry Lewis in the title role of *The Bellboy* (1960) is a rare focus on the experiences of bellhops at Miami's Fontainebleau Hotel. Later, the R-rated *Screwball Hotel* (1988) unsuccessfully attempted comedy with another scenario involving Miami hotel workers.

The charter fishing boat business has also attracted filmmakers. In the drama *The Gun Runners* (1958), Audie Murphy stars as a Key West charter boat captain caught up in illegal activities in revolutionary Cuba. And in *Joe Panther* (1976) the crew working for charter boat captain Brian Keith also becomes involved with Cubans, this time smuggling them into Florida. Peter Fonda plays a slightly more successful charter captain in the comedy *92 in the Shade* (1975), and boat salesmen and tournament organizers try to deal with the bumbling fishermen in *Gone Fishin'* (1997). All these films provide a view of those who serve the tourist industry as suffering though series of crises, and all share a traditional take on the business as a difficult way to earn a living.

Vacationers who converge on the state and Floridians who depend on them are played for comedic effect in *Honky Tonk Freeway* (1981). The scenes switch back and forth between the stories of the various tourists traveling to Florida and the extraordinary efforts of local townspeople to get a highway ramp built to serve the tourist-dependent community. Neither the tourists nor the Floridians desperate for their dollars are portrayed in positive ways. *Ruby in Paradise* effectively portrays a beachside souvenir business on the Redneck Riviera of the Panhandle by focusing on a transplanted Tennessee woman with limited skills and ambition working at the shop.

With few exceptions, the tourist sector tends to provide part of the back-story in films, responding to rather than creating the climate for drama or comedy. Nowhere is this more evident than in tourist films highlighting that annual trek to Florida by college students, known as Spring Break.

Films about Spring Break first appeared in the 1960s, but they followed in a tradition of Hollywood movies geared to teenagers. Filmmakers began developing stories around high school teens and college youth in the 1930s with the Andy Hardy series, starring Mickey Rooney. Merging teen romance with light conflict, most teen-centered films appealed to families and to the growing segment of the population that was becoming differentiated as "teenagers." During the era of movie censorship, these early films aimed at teen and family audiences included overt moral messages. In the 1930s, filmmakers also responded to national hysteria regarding the supposed drug threats facing teens. Films like *Reefer Madness/Tell Your Children* (1938), *Marihuana* (1936), *Assassin of Youth* (1937), and *She Shoulda Said No* (1949) have achieved cult status for their contrived plots and extreme views of the consequences for teens indulging in one night of pot smoking. Teens in these films are in stark contrast with the Andy Hardy character that always ends up making socially acceptable choices. The only "joint" he knew about was the local soda shop.

The war-era children and first baby boomers were entering their teens in the late 1950s. At the same time, the postwar Beat Generation of writers and performers began to define the counterculture for some teens, and these characterizations entered films. Movies also began to portray the rising popularity of rock 'n roll, with *Rock Around the Clock* (1956) and many others that showcased performers that most teens would otherwise never see.

Teens of the 1950s were growing up in a culture of consumerism and an economy that targeted them because of their sheer numbers. Increasingly differentiated from the older generation by music, dress, language, and interests, teens also had more disposable income and mobility, a combination their elders apparently considered dangerous. Films from the period reflect the popular images of white middle-class teens as lacking maturity. While most teens focus on romance, the latest singing craze, and indulgence, they also display anxieties associated with growing up in the atomic age. Their parents, teachers, and law enforcement officials try to cope with their demands and problems. In 1950s' films we also glimpse the beginning of the counterculture youth, who reject consumerism and attempt to create their own style and community.

World War II-era perceptions about "zoot suiters" and the criminal tendencies of unsupervised young men defined as "juvenile delinquents" carried into the 1950s along with the growth of motorcycle clubs. Film-makers portrayed groups of young men and women in black leather jackets, motorcycling through towns as examples of the threatening aspects of teen freedom and parental neglect. The most effective foundation for this image probably came from the classic film *The Wild One* (1953). When Marlon Brando responds to the small-town soda jerk's question, "What are you rebelling against?" with "What have you got?" the exchange suggests counterculture youth is aimless and reckless. In *Rebel Without a Cause* (1955), absent and neglectful fathers and overpowering mothers are blamed for teen angst and violence in California's middle-class white families. The same year, *Blackboard Jungle* introduced audiences to urban school violence in a northern multiracial neighborhood. The predominant theme in these teen films is that the youth of the era are self-destructive, undirected, and indulgent. They desperately need the mature guidance of their elders.

At the same time, atomic-age propaganda stressed the precariousness of existence, as schools organized duck-and-cover drills for responding to a presumably imminent nuclear attack. Anxieties were exploited in B movies that subtly portray the hidden dangers and uncertainties of scientific experiments. They also dramatize Cold War messages of enemy infiltration that dominated politics. The expansion of the television industry brought the Cold War into homes, with broadcasts of the McCarthy hearings, news and "news magazine" programming, and live melodramas. In response the movie industry attempted to compete with television by taking plots, as well as techniques, into new directions. And film studios continued to target young audiences as significant consumers of the theater experience.

Part of the strategy for attracting this audience was the development of the teen star, inaugurated by James Dean. Another part of the strategy involved developing plots attractive to teen viewers, as well as using well-known stars that young people had watched on television since childhood. The televised *Mickey Mouse Club* made Annette Funicello an early and late adolescent icon who translated her popularity into beach-blanket films in the 1960s.

All across America, children learned about California's Disneyland from television. This fantasy experience, duplicated in the early 1970s in Florida's Disney World, captured the increasing desire among all age groups to escape from reality. Throughout the 1950s and 1960s, Florida and California competed for teen movie audiences.

Another television icon, Dick Clark, took over *American Bandstand* in 1956, and this first nationally broadcast dance party, combined with the expansion of radio stations and the development of the transistor radio, focused teen attention on music and dance. To succeed, teen films increasingly incorporated music and popular singers into story lines that were familiar and/or desirable. By 1959 filmmakers hit on a formula: depict teen stars behaving like teenagers—which meant dancing, drinking, and ignoring education—and let them act out their experiences in open spaces, at the beach.

The first beach-centered movie was *Gidget* (1959), starring Sandra Dee as a naive teen rejecting her stodgy parents to enter tentatively into a life of "beat" dropouts at the beach in California. That state seemed a natural choice for beach movies. Long before, body builders had staked out space in Santa Monica and Venice, and muscle-beach activities were popular entertainment. Pacific waves also drew crowds of surfing enthusiasts, and teens embraced the sport in the 1950s. They brought cars, radios, blankets, and picnics to the beach and created a culture of youthful, enthusiastic sun worship against a backdrop of sand, cliffs, and surf. *Gidget's* popularity sparked more exploration of the themes, and the beach-blanket movies of the 1960s cashed in on teen experiences and desires for freedom in the outdoors, away from responsibilities and adults. The stories featured the leading young actresses and attempted to appeal to both female and male audiences by focusing on female dilemmas and female body parts.

Florida's coastlines had already been highlighted in other films, of course, but now filmmakers saw the opportunity to use Florida beaches and Spring Break as a setting for teen films. The first of these, and perhaps the best known, is the 1960 film *Where the Boys Are*. Although loosely based on the book of the same name, the film shares limited similarities to the book. Instead the movie reflects the decision of the producers to create a plot that would both teach a moral lesson to female viewers and omit the more controversial themes in the book.

48. Jim Hutton in *Where the Boys Are* (1960). By permission of Photofest.

Glendon Swarthout, a professor at Michigan State University, wrote *Where the Boys Are* as Cuban revolutionaries were attempting to overthrow the dictatorship of Fulgencio Batista. In his book Swarthout included this rebellion, along with the Cuban exiles and U.S. college students eager to join it. This part of the plot is omitted from the film, however.

Swarthout told the story from the point of view of Merritt, as does the film, with Dorothy Hart cast in her first role. While the book's Merritt has been sexually active since high school and hooks up with Ryder, TV, and Basil, the film's Merritt is virginal and holding out for love and marriage. Merritt's film friends are not quite true to the book's characters either. In both the film and the book, the Yvette Mimieux character is determined to find an Ivy Leaguer she hopes will fall in love with her, the classic gold-digger role. In the book she is gang-raped and tries to commit suicide. The film suggests that she has been raped and beaten by her Spring Break boyfriend. Despondent as she recuperates in the hospital, she bemoans the irony of her fate: "And the boys [*boy*, in the film] weren't even really Ivy Leaguers!" Film Merritt reassures her that it is still possible for her to "find a nice guy" someday.

Swarthout wrote what was probably a more realistic portrayal of female attitudes during the beginning of the sexual revolution in the 1950s. Females *were* having sex, but would only reveal the experiences to their closest friends, if at all. In addition to conflicts about sexual liberation, females were also aware of the problems educated women faced in mapping out a career and marriage plan. Merritt and her friend Tuggle have been "cursed" with high IQ's, and they debate the advantages and disadvantages of their abilities throughout the book, problems ignored in the film. The women's lib song lyrics written by Basil and performed by Cuban exile Ramona in the book are replaced in the film by Connie Francis singing a light song about sunshine (as well as the popular theme song).

Screen adaptations often deviate from the written word, of course, but the alterations in this film are particularly significant. The messages of the film are fairly clear. Young men are interested mainly in sex while women want marriage. If females withhold sex, as Merritt did with Ryder, they might eventually find rich Ivy League husbands. But if women "put out" (in the language of the day) as one did, they threaten to ruin their lives. The myth of female virginity remains intact through this and other teen beach films of the 1960s.

49. Dolores Hart, George Hamilton, Paula Prentiss, and Jim Hutton in *Where the Boys Are* (1960). By permission of Photofest.

The novel's Merritt is much more cynical and intellectual than the film version, particularly in her discussions of double standards about sex and careers. But the characters in the film are college-educated young men and women who have no complex insights, a standard portrayal in films. Scholarly discourse is not common in movies, after all, and the filmmakers apparently understood their audiences. *Where the Boys Are* was a hit that became a classic for its Spring-Break theme.

The decision to leave out the story line about the Cuban Revolution is more understandable, given the political climate of the era. By the time the film was released, the Cuban Revolution had succeeded in overthrowing dictator Fulgencio Batista. Many young men from the United States had in fact joined the rebels in Cuba's mountains and the rebel underground to become "rebels with a cause."[3] But their activities were not widely publicized, and the U.S. government was formulating its opposition to the new government in Cuba. Clearly the film's producers felt the Cuba story line would delve into political areas best left ignored.

After the successful release of this film, California fired back with a Spring-Break film and more beach-party movies that included characterizations very familiar to viewers of *Where the Boys Are*. The formula remained focused on the female lead who withheld sex while the male lead got increasingly impatient. In the California beach films, a counterculture character was often added to the mix: the biker, played by "Eric Von Zipper" (Harvey Lembeck) as a black-leather-jacketed buffoon. He and his sidekicks invariably tried to horn in on the clean, wholesome fun of beach-blanket kids and turn it into something sleazy.

The success of these films and of *Where the Boys Are* encouraged filmmakers to return to Florida for more Spring-Break movies. Drawing on the popularity of his first Florida musical film, *Follow That Dream* (1962), Elvis Presley travels to Florida for Spring Break in *Girl Happy* (1965). The opening narration sets the stage as the camera zooms in from an aerial shot: "This is Ft. Lauderdale. This girl on the beach is 36-24-36. This beach will soon be jammed for Spring Break." Similar to the establishing shots used in *Where the Boys Are*, the camera pans a deserted beach, portending the arrival of thousands of teens, and then cuts to a snowy northern city. In this case the city is Chicago, and Elvis is not a college student, but a performer in a nightclub band. The club owner is a mobster who wants his daughter (Shelley Fabares) protected during Spring Break, so he sends Elvis and his band to Ft. Lauderdale to covertly chaperone her.

With this film a subtle but important shift occurs. From this point on, nearly all Florida beach movies are told from the point of view of males.

The target audiences for Elvis movies are both women and men, but by making men the center of the story, the plots start to move in different directions. Nevertheless men continue to be portrayed as sexual predators. One of the early songs in *Girl Happy* includes the line: "Any male who is not pursuing a female will automatically wind up in jail, courtesy of the Ft. Lauderdale Chamber of Commerce." Uncommitted sex is the objective for all men. The exception is a young man who is looking for a woman "with a mind," but even he realizes his error, and ends up with a heart-of-gold stripper.

Primarily a vehicle for Elvis songs, the movie also includes an unusual scene for Elvis. The bumbling-but-benevolent police raid a strip club and lock up all the women there, including Shelley Fabares, in a temporary detention center. Elvis tunnels his way in and leaves dressed as a female, speaking in a high-pitched voice. This is Elvis's only film appearance as a woman. Although Ft. Lauderdale had its share of Latino immigrants by 1965, the cast in this film is all white, and no Latinos appear anywhere. The only suggestion of a "Latin" presence is a young man with an accent. Contradicting the whole premise of Spring Break, when the girls meet this exchange student from Italy, one describes him as shallow: "All he ever thinks about is sex. Well, you know those Latins." Of course, in the end, Elvis gets the girl and the respect of her father, whose mob connections extend from Chicago to Florida. While the motel and beach scenes don't capture the crowded conditions of Spring Break as well as *Where the Boys Are*, the environment of drinking and frivolity is still intact.

As California's era of beach-blanket movies ended, Elvis wrapped up his last Florida beach movie, *Clambake*. Now the setting is Miami, and it is summer, not Spring Break. In the end he is seen driving along the beach, explaining to Shelley Fabares that he is actually wealthy, and he points out oil rigs along the beach. This could be a bit of foreshadowing, but other scenes in the film, like mountains in the background, make it clear that the film was made in California.

In the battle for teen beach movies, California seems to have won, not only in numbers, but also in popularity. That state had both the sets and the beach sounds, from Dick Dale and the Del Tones to Jan and Dean and the Beach Boys.[4] *The Fat Spy* (1966) starring Jayne Mansfield, Phyllis Diller, and Jack E. Leonard, demonstrates a failed attempt to associate beach music sounds with Florida. However, the movie's painfully repetitive beach songs, badly performed by frugging shoreside teens, might be a spoof on beach movies. Appropriately, the plot is about agents from cosmetics companies competing to find the source of a Fountain of Youth beauty product.

By the late 1960s the beach theme and locations were drowned out by the popularity of the Beatles and other new performers associated with urban America and Great Britain. Although the ritual of Spring Break continued in Florida, no teen beach movies were produced during the 1970s. The theme finally resurfaced in 1983 with a low-budget movie, *Spring Break,* which revived the formula, complete with music, the black-leather-jacketed biker, males hoping to "get lucky," and lots of women in even skimpier bikinis. Explicit wet T-shirt contests, banana-eating contests, other sexual games, and drunkenness now emphasize sexually interested females. Times had clearly changed, and so had the films. Following the popularity of *Animal House* (1975), *Porky's* (1981) introduced the Floridian nerdy/loser teens as antiheroes. *Spring Break* incorporated this theme with its naive male leads.

In Ft. Lauderdale two local college boys must share their small motel room with two New Yorkers. While initially frustrated that their roommates are more successful at finding sexual partners, the men finally get what they came for and more. Reflective of the new political and social environment, the women in this movie are savvy, talented, and sexual. African-Americans also appear in the film, both as Spring Breakers and as operatives working for a Senate candidate. But the only Latino in the film is Ish, a motel bellhop who is decidedly effeminate. Ish helps the motel owner and the "kids" resolve the film's conflict, the potential loss of the motel to the corrupt Senate candidate's friends. Despite its attempts to include more contemporary themes, the film lacked the box office appeal of early beach movies.

In 1984 a new version of *Where the Boys Are* was released. Panned by reviewers, the film stars Lorna Luft and Lisa Hartman, looking for romance in Ft. Lauderdale. Though unable to entice a wide audience, this was one of the last of the Spring-Break/beach films to prioritize the female point of view.

After *Porky's II* (1985) and *Revenge of the Nerds* (1984) successfully continued the theme of nerdy teens stars, *Revenge of the Nerds II: Nerds in Paradise* (1987) brought teen tourists back to Florida. In this plot five members of a midwest college frat attend a fraternity conference in Ft. Lauderdale. The beaches are filled with bikini-clad females, and the opening scenes resemble beach-movies-past, with white sands, sunny skies, and impending opportunities. But when the nerds find out they can't stay

50. A scene from the 1984 version of *Where the Boys Are*. By permission of Photofest.

at the conference hotel, the mood shifts. Their alternative is a dilapidated Third-World-looking motel run by a gaudily dressed Latina. With a thick accent, she points out the "gym," which has several uniformed soldiers lined up in front, waiting for what is clearly a prostitute. The pool has filthy brown water, and their room (the "Ricky Ricardo Suite") still has the chalk outline of a body in the middle of the floor. The presence of Cuban exiles continues through the film and includes the frat boys' discovery of a cache of arms and military supplies left by Cuban terrorists on a deserted island off the coast. Thus Swarthout's book plot finally appears in a teen beach movie, but with a notable twist. Ft. Lauderdale, the paradise for Spring Breakers, has been damaged/decayed by the presence of Cubans. The film adds a few African-American portrayals, including one of the fraternity members who is clearly gay (and referred to as an "effeminate little pansy"), and a small group of frat brothers attending the conference. But like past beach movies, the lead actors are Anglo.

Another all-Anglo cast appears in *Lauderdale* (1989). A soft-porn comedy, the movie opens with the theme music from the film *2001* as a girl emerges from the water and walks toward the beach. There, two guys—one with his face flat in the sand, grasping a beer can—discuss their goal of finding the "perfect beach bunny." They are in California, but decide to pursue a potential bunny to Ft. Lauderdale for Spring Break. What follows is a confusing plot with lots of nudity and adolescent quips: "Women. If they didn't screw, there'd be a bounty on them." The Spring-Break theme was definitely losing its cachet.

Another indication of its loss of popularity is the film *Nightmare Beach* (1988), starring John Saxon and Michael Parks. Filmed in Ft. Lauderdale and Miami, this slasher film pits a vengeful follower of a gang leader against unsuspecting teens on Spring Break. The heroes are a vacationing football player and his girlfriend. With such well-known stars, audiences probably expected more than they got, and critics panned the film.

Black Spring Break (1998) finally focuses for the first time on another popular site for Spring-Break activities—Daytona Beach. This east coast beach has long been a destination for Spring Breakers. In 1962 it drew an estimated thirty-five thousand college students, and the numbers continued to rise during the decade. For many Florida natives, its contrast with Ft. Lauderdale often made it more appealing. From the early 1960s, the Miami-Ft. Lauderdale region was well understood as home to many Cuban exiles. While some college students found the southern region more interesting and "exotic" for that reason, many others rejected this notion of cultural mixing. Daytona Beach is also more centrally located in the state, and therefore more accessible. Moreover students were aware that motel accommodations were cheaper in Daytona. The city's reputation for allowing cars on the beach was also appealing. Although there are no reliable data to support the contention, Daytona Beach may have attracted a different social class of Spring Breakers than Ft. Lauderdale. And until the beaches of Florida were forced to desegregate after 1965, Spring Break was decidedly a segregated experience.

51. A rundown Ft. Lauderdale motel in *Revenge of the Nerds II: The Nerds in Paradise* (1987).

The origins of Daytona's "Black Spring Break," or "Black College Reunion," are debatable. Some argue that it derived from "Freaknik," a spontaneously organized gathering of students from historically black colleges that began in Atlanta in the early 1980s. City officials tried to rename "Freaknik" several times to disassociate it from negative images and to channel students' energy into more organized activities. The media depicted "Freaknik" as a raucous and violent event that caused damage and business closures in central Atlanta. After the 1996 attacks at the Atlanta Olympic Park, the local government tried to discourage black Spring Breakers by setting up roadblocks that made it more difficult to get into the city. Black College Reunion in Daytona and the Kappa Beach Party in Galveston drew Atlanta Spring Breakers away, and "Freaknik" ended by 2000. The idea of black student gatherings then spread to new regions.

Others suggest that "Black College Reunion" originated in 1985, when Bethune-Cookman College in Daytona Beach notified student government associations of several historically black colleges about a career fair for potential law students. Three thousand attended this spring fair and discovered the beauty of the beach. Still another version identifies Bethune-Cookman as the initiator, but suggests that the origin was a 1984 football match-up between Bethune-Cookman and Florida A&M (both historically black colleges) after a three-year hiatus. Students from both colleges decided to celebrate by coming together on the campus of Bethune-Cookman and on the beaches of Daytona. An early organizer from the college still holds the copyright on the name.

This celebration and the role of Bethune-Cookman are significant for several reasons. Florida beaches were segregated until the late 1960s, and one of the founders of Bethune-Cookman College, Mary McLeod Bethune, had previously established "Bethune Beach," five miles south of New Smyrna, as a site for African-American beachgoers. When the governor finally ordered desegregation in 1965, the violence that ensued captured national headlines. A few miles north, in St. Augustine, blacks were escorted to the beach by state troopers, past jeering crowds of KKK members, who proceeded to launch attacks on the black community under cover of darkness. Other struggles for beach desegregation through the decade and tensions during the 1980s in south Florida left African-Americans more sensitive to their access to public space than most whites appreciated or, indeed, cared about.

In general, governments and businesses view all Spring Breakers as necessary evils. More police are hired to work longer hours handling crowds. Out-of-control students—like those who jump or fall from balconies, drink themselves to death, or engage in violence—have created financial liabilities and negative images for the cities that host them. In addition many college students are not wealthy, and they are notorious for their strategies in cutting expenses. Given a choice, most Florida motel and restaurant owners would probably rather host a family from any foreign country than college students. But Spring Break brings in large numbers of students for a short period of time, and most businesses and governments have balanced out the damages and the profits and decided that the revenues outweigh the costs. In 1998 alone, more than one hundred and ten thousand students visited Daytona for Spring Break, pumping needed dollars into the local community.

Through the late 1980s and 1990s, the Daytona City Council and residents debated the problems they believed were associated with continuing to host "Black College Reunion," even as Miller Brewing Company, Coca-Cola, Coors, McDonalds, and M&M Mars added their corporate sponsorship to events. In 1997 a segment of motorcycle enthusiasts/bikers, who also have an annual trek to Daytona Beach at a different time of the year, organized a "white-pride ride" down the main street during "Black College Reunion." Students also reported incidents of racism by hotels and other businesses, and the NAACP investigated many of these complaints. Local college students organized demonstrations against city attempts to require passes to drive on the beach, and a suit filed against a major hotel chain for discrimination suggested a difficult future for the Spring-Break event in 1999.

The tradition nevertheless continues with some difficulties, but with enormous popularity. As late as 2002, the mayor and the head of the local NAACP received bomb threats prior to the opening of activities. However, corporations are still eager to support the events. BET cable channel hosts "Spring Bling," a three-day concert during the events, and in 2000 the Disney Corporation signed on as a major sponsor of "Black College Reunion." As an opportunity for African-American students to come together, this Spring-Break experience seems similar to others, as the independent film *Black Spring Break* suggests.

Following the familiar formula, the film opens with bikini-clad girls dancing on the beach and guys throwing Frisbees. Since it is Daytona, shots of cars cruising on the beach help identify the setting. Much of the action takes place in and around motels rather than on the beach, but the story line is more important than the setting. Written, directed, and filmed by an African-American crew and starring the screenwriter Daron Fordham, *Black Spring Break* essentially lampoons characterizations of various ethnicities that have been part of other filmmakers' stock-in-trade. The main plot is about a not-too-bright football star from Howard University, who is being pressed to sign contracts offered by competing black and white agents, while his friends try to get him to do the "right thing." In contrast to the white agent who is bumbling and suffers with a nagging wife, the black agent is smoothly underhanded, using offers of hookers and other promises to get the football player to sign with him. Ultimately the football star signs up with the honest white agent for the NFL draft.

Stereotypes of blacks pervade the film and include a pushy, rude, hotel clerk who is a single mother and takes bribes. When a white man comes in looking for a room, she tells him, "Don't you see it's Black Spring Break? I don't want to hear you accusing a gang of attacking you." A limping security guard (clearly based on the high school principal character played by David Alan Grier in television's *In Living Color*) also remarks, "Haven't you all arrested enough niggers this year?" The young college women have exaggerated attitudes, and one remarks as she plans her seduction of the football player with the bright future, "I can act like a nigger when I gots to." A black rap star and his white sound mixer make an appearance, and a black drug dealer evaluates his opportunities in a hotel lobby phone call to his supplier: "This place is full of hoes and agents." Not missing the opportunity to mention the O. J. Simpson case, a hitchhiking Spring Breaker at one point gets a car to pull over after yelling at him: "Hey, give a nigger a ride! I ain't goin' to cut you up. I ain't O. J.!" The driver, an Asian, demands fifty dollars for the ride and then races off alone after collecting the money.

Male and female behavior in this film is similar to other recent Spring-Break films. The young men in this film are "players" (in modern parlance), and the young women are sexually active, but use sex as a means to a greater end. When one of the male students remarks after his arrival in Daytona, "Bitches goin' to be everywhere," his friend tries to contradict this characterization. "Why not call them 'honeys,' not 'bitches'?" The response is "Because all of them will be." Language and brief nudity earned this film an "R" rating. It was followed in 2001 with a video sequel: *Black Spring Break II*.

Although R-rated films like *Senior Week* (1987) tried to capitalize on elements from Spring-Break movies, the theme has otherwise inspired little interest by studios or independent filmmakers since the 1990s, even as notable differences took place in the Spring-Break experience. Students

52. College students on Daytona Beach in *Black Spring Break* (1998).

began to celebrate the rites of spring by traveling to new places. Mexico, Jamaica, and other foreign sites attracted college students with reasonably priced packages, unrestricted drinking, and the lure of the exotic. MTV has followed the crowds to many of these sites, as well as to Panama City and Daytona Beach, as Spring Break has become a ritual experience enjoyed by more and more students. But many of *their* experiences couldn't be captured by a fictional film that hoped for anything above an "X" rating. At the same time, the corporate sponsorship of Spring-Break activities has led to an orchestrated, staged effort at promoting spontaneity. Sponsors such as MTV, beer and food companies, clothing manufacturers, and other marketers set up contests and provide prizes, stages, and entertainers to broadcast Spring Break as a televised special. Ordinary college students can gain moments of notoriety on television if they look or behave in ways that program producers and advertisers want, and businesses earn high profits on revenues beyond the local economy. Spring-Break participants undoubtedly still want to experience many of the same freedoms and impulsiveness that their parents and grandparents did, but the staging of Spring-Break specials has removed some of that spontaneity. For many Spring Break now means attending a corporate event, organized around profitable activities with sets and backdrops that fit in with camera framing.

But just as we thought it seemed safe to say good-bye to the Spring-Break film, a new one was released in 2003. Opening to limited acclaim and disappointing box office receipts, *From Justin to Kelly* attempted to capitalize on the popularity of Justin Guarini and Kelly Clarkson, created as idols in the television series *American Idol*. The movie tries to depict a wholesome Spring-Break musical experience with popular new characters. The Florida establishing shot is reminiscent of *Where the Boys Are*, as Kelly (Kelly Clarkson) arrives in Miami from Texas, after her friends have convinced her that's where "the boys will be." These women are not on a quest for husbands, however; they just want to have fun. Falling in love is an unanticipated bonus. There are no sticky sexual entanglements, drugs, or raucous young men who get drunk and engage in outrageous acts. Aimed at audiences of all ages, this tame version of Spring Break failed to interest most viewers. Perhaps those who had actually experienced Spring Break could no longer be interested by purified film versions, especially given widely marketed "Girls Gone Wild" videos that feature young women in various stages of undress at Spring-Break sites.

With the exception of *Black Spring Break*, filmmakers have chosen only Miami-Ft. Lauderdale sites for their films. But Spring Breakers descend upon many coastal cities throughout the state. If the theme has run its course, it is because audiences are not content with story lines that digress so far from a reality with which they are very familiar. *Where the Boys Are* now seems like an amusing relic of older values, and viewers today probably have no idea how far removed from reality it was even during its time. Still the possibility always exists for a reemergence of this decades-old theme. Spring-Break promoters are now marketing packages to high school students, and more of them are joining the activities. Perhaps the next film(s) will tell the story from a different point of view or in a new Florida location. For now we are left with a legacy of films that portray images of college students *from other states* as overwhelmingly wild, sex-hungry, impulsive, and indulgent. And the Floridians who deal with them, from business owners to police and other officials, are engaged in frantic efforts to control them while not pushing so far that they might lose the profits from their visits.

Most Florida residents harbor mixed feelings about tourists. Ask anyone in the state; they've all got opinions about tourists. Usually it's a love-hate relationship. Floridians love the money tourists bring and hope they bring enough to keep residents from paying a state income tax. But they also wish there weren't so many hotels obscuring views of the beaches, so many cars causing traffic jams, and so many people eating at "our" restaurants. Former Spring Breakers living in Florida now complain about "today's teenagers" during the season. Floridians understand why outsiders visit, but wish they would just leave soon.

Except for the comedy *Gone Fishin*,' no movies focusing on Florida tourists have been made for many years. Even though Florida tourists have become more diverse and the industry has expanded, the theme itself no longer interests moviemakers. Perhaps Florida is no longer "exotic," or too many visitors have already made the trek and know what to expect from a Florida vacation. Many of the quirky roadside attractions that differentiated Florida have now closed, and tourists can have the "Florida experience" without ever leaving their chosen theme park. Interstate highways connect major centers of attraction, and visitors no longer see beyond the next fast-food exit sign.

Increasingly since the 1980s, studios and independent filmmakers are interested in what exists beyond the hype and superficiality of a marketed Florida, and they have focused on the residents of Florida, especially migrants. Often they were tourists first, who found in Florida, or hoped to find, an opportunity for a brighter future or a more peaceful life. Their failures and successes have become the major themes of Florida films.

Chapter 5

"No one tried to kill me. This is Miami.
I'm local. We only shoot the tourists!"

Fair Game (1995)

"Right now, in Florida, money is one thing.
It's drugs."

Forever Mine (1999)

Crime Stories

From piracy in the 1700s to bootlegging in the 1920s and drug trafficking in the 1980s, crime has figured prominently in Florida's history, and this has not escaped the attention of filmmakers. As the nature of illegal enterprises has changed over time, so too has its depiction in movies. Cracker rumrunners have given way to Latino drug lords in Hollywood scripts, and con artists have moved from land hustles to politics. Murder, robbery, and gambling are, of course, constant themes, even as the ethnicity of perpetrators changes. Whatever its guises, crime has found its way into every film genre, making it a staple in dramas and comedies, as well as in horror and science fiction movies, set in Florida.

Few films deal with criminal activity in Florida before the Roaring Twenties. However, two historical dramas cover early periods. *Reap the Wild Wind* (1942) relates the highly fictionalized tale of "lawless captains," who supposedly destroyed and plundered great ships passing near the Florida Keys during the 1840s. *Wind Across the Everglades* (1958) focuses on the illegal slaughter of Florida birds, a crime that in fact existed at the turn of the twentieth century because of the fashion of women wearing hats with feathers.

Although crime certainly did not suddenly appear in Florida during the 1920s, it took new forms that quickly became prominent themes in movies. The national thirst for liquor and real estate bargains helped turn Florida into a Mecca for bootleggers and con artists, who have provided story lines for numerous films like *The Confidence Man* (1924), a silent film about a Florida promoter of phony oil stocks who goes straight. The state's infamous land schemes in the Twenties become a source of comedy for the Marx Brothers in *The Cocoanuts* (1929). Con artists reappear in several films from the 1930s and 1940s, including *Hard to Handle* (1933), a comedy starring James Cagney, and *Tell It to a Star* (1945), a musical highlighting various confidence games at a south Florida hotel.

During the 1920s Prohibition also contributed to Florida's reputation for crime. The state's long coastline and proximity to Cuba and the West Indies made it a haven for rum-running by locals, as depicted in silent films like *Sweet Daddies* (1926). The Ashley Gang, real-life gangsters from south Florida, are featured in *Little Laura and Big John* (1973), a low-budget attempt to portray this couple as Florida's own Bonnie and Clyde. Indeed, the movie opens with a voice-over narrator explaining that rural America produced criminals like Bonnie Parker and Clyde Barrow. The movie then shows a map of south Florida superimposed over images of bank robberies and car chases with sounds of police sirens and gunfire, and the narrator continues:

> The John Ashley gang—still remembered in Florida today for the legacy of violence and death that it left across this land. Bank robbers, hijackers, rumrunners, highway robbers, murderers—John Ashley, along with Laura Upthegrove, known as "Queen of the Everglades," led a gang of vicious youth and rebels as wild and untamed as the swamps they hid out in. . . . John Ashley came from a typical cracker family, those families who pioneered the settling of south Florida in the 1890s and early 1900s.

Starring the miscast duo of Fabian and Karen Black, *Little Laura and Big John* follows the escapades of the Ashley Gang from 1915 to 1924, when John and Laura are killed in a police ambush that closely resembles the final shootout in *Bonnie and Clyde* (1967).

Even after the end of Prohibition in 1933, moonshining remained a southern phenomenon associated with Florida in several films. *Gal Young 'Un* (1979) highlights the illegal whiskey business in rural Florida during the 1930s and 1940s. *Thunder and Lightning* (1974) updates the running of homemade booze and shows the modernization of production and distribution. Set in the 1970s, the film opens with two old men in the Everglades, bemoaning the destruction of their whiskey still. One of the aging moonshiners observes, "Time is a changin'—ain't no time left for independents." The two men have been put out of business by a competitor, R. J. Hunnicut (Roger C. Carmel), who uses his bottling plant for soda ("Honey Dew") as a cover to produce and distribute illegal whiskey. His network reaches to New York, where he is in league with Italian-American mobsters. Despite their modern methods, R. J. and his two henchmen ("Jim Bob" and "Bubba") are stereotypical southerners with their accents, and R. J. proudly displays a Confederate flag in his office. In one scene R. J. even refers to a local resident as a "damn cracker."

Contemporary cracker crime became the bread-and-butter of Burt Reynolds in a series of movies about various southern characters. Although the action in some of his movies, notably *Smokey and the Bandit* (1977), takes place outside Florida, Reynolds himself is so closely identified with the state where he played football at Florida State University that it is difficult to separate the two. The offenses committed by Reynolds's cracker characters are clearly meant to be taken lightly, even in *The Longest Yard* (1974), which opens with Reynolds as a gigolo who beats up his "girlfriend," takes her car, and resists arrest when stopped by police. His conviction gets him sent to Citrus State Prison, a fictional Florida institution, where he draws on his years as a former MVP pro-football player to organize a team of prisoners to take on the guards.

Cracker crime became a virtual movie franchise in the series that began with *Porky's* (1981). Set in the Everglades during the 1950s, the 1981 film portrays Porky (Chuck Mitchell) as "a bad-assed redneck" who wears a Confederate flag emblem on his hat and runs a strip joint that serves underage drinkers. In the sequel, *Porky's Revenge* (1985), the action moves from the strip bar to a boat where Porky operates an illegal gambling casino, but more than anything else, he says, he wants "a young grandchild, little Porky, somebody to bounce on my knee, teach him how to hustle, beat people, go fishing, break heads, kick ass—somebody to be proud of—carry on the family name." Comments like this are clearly designed to convey the idea that cracker crime is relatively harmless, even humorous.

Prior to the 1980s serious crime depicted in films is often imported into Florida by outsiders who are passing through. When Tony Curtis and Jack Lemmon escape to Miami to evade Chicago gangsters in *Some*

Like It Hot (1959), the two cross paths with their nemesis Spats Colombo (George Raft) at a Miami hotel, only because Spats and his henchmen are in town for a mob meeting, thinly disguised as the tenth annual convention of "the Friends of Italian Opera." Like Spats, these 1920s gangsters presumably committed their crimes elsewhere.

One of the best known criminals to appear briefly in Florida was Ma Barker, whose life has become the source of myths that figure in several low-budget movies. Kate Barker and her four sons committed a series of crimes in the Midwest and West, and their notoriety earned them a place on the FBI's most-wanted list in the 1930s. Adding to her infamy as the supposed brains behind the Barker-Karpis gang, J. Edgar Hoover labeled her "a veritable beast of prey." On the run from authorities, Ma fled to Florida with her son Fred in 1935. They hid out in a cottage near Lake Wier, where FBI agents traced them and killed both in a gun battle depicted at the very end of *Ma Barker's Killer Brood* (1960). Roger Corman made a more lurid film, entitled *Bloody Mama* (1970), starring Shelley Winters and featuring Robert De Niro as one of the Barker boys.

In addition to Ma Barker, a number of fictional outsiders bring crime to Florida in movies made in the 1940s and 1950s. Perhaps the best known is Johnny Rocco (Edward G. Robinson), who is the villain featured in *Key Largo* (1948), the classic film noir directed by John Huston. Like the hurricane that crashes ashore in the film, Rocco is an outside force that passes through, only briefly threatening Florida's peaceful residents at a hotel in Key Largo, run by James Temple (Lionel Barrymore) and his daughter-in-law (Lauren Bacall). After thirty years in the United States, Rocco explains that he has been declared "an undesirable alien" and deported, "like I was a dirty Red." Exiled in Cuba, the aging Rocco travels with his gang of thugs to "the remote coral island" of Key Largo in order to sell counterfeit money to a gangster from the mainland. The film ends with Rocco killed by the reluctant hero (Humphrey Bogart) who acts in self-defense as Rocco tries to return to Cuba.

Made fourteen years after *Key Largo* and directed by John Frankenheimer, *All Fall Down* (1962) uses the Florida Keys to reveal the seedy character of Berry-Berry (Warren Beatty), who is a "drifter, and a sponger, and a parasite." The action in *All Fall Down* takes place mostly in Cleveland, but the opening scenes show Key Bonita, a fictional location with a navy base, a fishing fleet, and a bar frequented by sailors and featuring women (modestly clothed) dancing on a runway. Berry-Berry soon leaves the Keys after his arrest for beating up one of the dancers, but the brief twenty-minute sequence of Florida scenes gives the impression of a re-

53. Humphrey Bogart (*left*) and Edward G. Robinson in *Key Largo* (1948). By permission of Photofest.

mote outpost with, at worst, petty crime like prostitution. Made thirty years later, *CrissCross* (1992) has a story line that reflects how much the image of the Keys changed. Set in Key West in 1969, the film stars Goldie Hawn as a part-time topless dancer, whose young son (David Arnott) discovers that the fish he's carrying to a restaurant for a local fisherman are filled with packets of cocaine.

A real-life outsider who targeted victims in Florida gets title billing in *Murph the Surf* (1975). Based on the actual exploits of Jack Murphy (Don Stroud), the film tells the story of how this surfer became a jewel thief operating in south Florida, the Bahamas, and New York. Like the press at the time, the film romanticizes Murph and his Florida crimes, which led to the famous theft of the Star of India in Washington.

A much greater threat to the state came from organized crime. The cinematic link between Miami and the mob dates from the years after World War II, but hints of Italian-American mobsters in south Florida appear in early films. *The Guilty Generation* (1931) has a story line about a gang feud that pits Mike Palmiero (Leo Carrillo) against Tony Ricca (Boris Karloff) in a battle to gain control of the bootlegging racket in Miami. *The Chase* (1946), an early film noir, is also set in Miami and features a murderous villain, Eddie Roman (Steve Cochran), and his henchman Gino (Peter Lorre). Although the film does not emphasize their ethnicity, the names of this pair are suggestive, as is Lorre's foreign accent. *The Chase* immediately establishes Roman as a hot-tempered thug, who invites a business competitor to dinner and has him killed by an attack dog after he hesitates to sell two ships. Roman keeps his beautiful wife Lorna (Michèle Morgan) on a tight leash, and she looks to the troubled hero, Chuck Scott (Robert Cummings), for aid in fleeing to Cuba. Scott, a veteran suffering from shell shock, goes to work for Roman as a chauffeur after finding his wallet on the street. Scott readily agrees to help Lorna for one thousand dollars. Effectively employing common techniques of the noir style, *The Chase* has several unexpected twists, and the story unfolds almost entirely in scenes shot at night and often indoors with heavy shadows darkening the images. Although the film includes scenes set in Havana, its focus is the dark, dreamlike quality of Miami life, and in the end it turns out—uncharacteristically for a film noir—that love conquers all.

The presence of organized crime in south Florida was exposed by the U.S. Senate's Kefauver Committee in 1950. Public hearings were followed by two Hollywood movies with similar themes and titles—*The Miami Story* (1954) and *Miami Exposé* (1956)—and both directed by Fred F. Sears. The two films adopt a documentary style and emphasize the spread of the mob to Florida and its links to crime in Cuba. *The Miami Story* opens with aerial shots of south Florida beaches and hotels and a voice-over declaring, "In the years following World War II, organized crime grew" and "sought new headquarters in a city where they thought they'd be safer." Miami was a "vacation wonderland, a Mecca, and a place where the police force was inadequate in size." To reinforce the film's documentary style, Florida's U.S. Senator George A. Smathers then appears, sitting at his desk, to explain the problems with organized crime and what cities can do to eliminate it. The film's action begins at the Miami airport, where two men are killed while getting off a plane from Cuba. This turns out to be the handiwork of Miami mobster Tony Brill (Luther Adler), who is battling gambling operators in Havana. Despite the imprimatur of Senator Smathers, *The Miami Story* suggests that the way to deal with mobsters is vigilante action. City leaders get an ex-gangster (Barry Sullivan) to infiltrate Tony Brill's gang and destroy it. Although Brill's ethnicity is unclear and he is ultimately eliminated, the film reinforces the growing association of Miami and the mob. As a review pointed out in the *New*

54. A scene from *Miami Exposé* (1956). By permission of Photofest.

York Times, "*The Miami Story* may not precisely entice vacationers, but it does make the area picturesque and interesting."

Two years later, *Miami Exposé* echoed the same theme, using similar techniques. The opening scene features the mayor of Miami telling viewers, "The film you are about to see is about organized crime's attempt to take over the state." The next scene shows a plane in flight, and a voice-over declares that Florida is the fastest-growing state in the nation. "The end of the line is Miami, where millions are flocking in on planes, trains, and boats." The plane then explodes, establishing the dangers of Miami in a scene likely to give tourists second thoughts about flying to south Florida. Once again the ethnic background of the film's gangsters is vague, and their principal enterprise is illegal gambling, based in Havana. The story line has a Miami real estate developer promoting legalized gambling, which would undercut the mob's operation. The developer's methods include blackmail and even murder as part of his campaign to get a state law legalizing gambling. Thus, *Miami Exposé* demonstrates that crime in Florida extends far beyond criminal syndicates.

Hints of Italian-American involvement in Florida's organized crime come only in the names of a few characters in films made prior to the 1960s. Both *The Chase* and *Key Largo* have criminals with Italian names. *The Brothers Rico* (1957) went beyond names to show the Mafia with an outpost in Miami, but the film refers to this clearly Italian-American mob only as "the organization." Loosely based on a novel by the Belgian writer Georges Simenon, the film tells the story of Eddie Rico (Richard Conte), a former accountant for the mob, who has married and turned legit in Florida. His younger brothers, Gino (Paul Picerni) and Johnny (James Darren), continue to work for the mob as hit men in New York, and they become targets for elimination after Johnny starts talking to the district attorney. Unable to save the lives of his brothers, one of whom is murdered in Florida, Eddie takes vengeance on "the organization" by killing one of its bosses in self defense and then going to the New York district attorney himself. In short, his Italian-American family, which includes his mother and grandmother in New York, proves stronger than the mob, which has its tentacles in Florida, according to *The Brothers Rico*.

Films made in the 1960s increasingly point to the presence of Italian-American mobsters in Florida. When Elvis Presley encounters gangsters in *Follow That Dream* (1962), their names are Carmine and Nick. The pair run a floating gambling operation in a trailer that threatens a small fishing business set up by Elvis along the coastline on Florida's Panhandle. *The Happening* (1967) stars Anthony Quinn as Roc Delmonico, a retired mafioso living in Miami, who is kidnapped by four beach bums. They dis-

55. Richard Conte (*right*) with Larry Gates, who plays a Miami crime boss, in *The Brothers Rico* (1957). By permission of Photofest.

cover that none of Delmonico's family or mob friends is willing to pay any ransom, and the comedy has Delmonico take charge of his own kidnapping to extort the money. Even less subtle in its direct link to organized crime is *The Mafia Girls* (1967), a sexploitation movie that has a story line about a crime syndicate run by Italian-Americans in Miami Beach.

Through the 1960s those responsible for cinematic crime in postwar Florida are usually white men who appear native-born, even though some are of Italian heritage, but during the 1950s, foreign intrigue appeared on the horizon. Cuban revolutionaries, led by Fidel Castro, sought arms in Florida to sustain their guerrilla movement, and the illegal arms trade provides the plot for *The Gun Runners* (1958), directed by Don Siegel and based loosely on Ernest Hemingway's novel *To Have and Have Not*. The film stars Audie Murphy as Sam Martin, a former naval officer and Key West boat operator, who rejects the offer of two Cubans to transport arms to the revolutionaries in Cuba. Although deep in debt, Sam also initially refuses to take a couple to Havana because the island is legally off limits, but he relents and finds himself embroiled in a deadly gunrunning plot that costs him his boat and nearly his life. Clearly, according to this film, Cuban revolutionaries represented a threat to law-abiding Floridians even before Castro rose to power in 1959.

In the 1960s Frank Sinatra starred as Tony Rome, a former Miami cop who works as a private eye. With Miami increasingly identified as the cinematic center of crime in Florida, the opening shot of *Tony Rome* (1967) shows the Miami skyline from the water, where Sinatra's character lives on a boat. Despite the sun and water, the film's view of Miami and its surroundings is decidedly negative. A New York visitor (Jill St. John) refers to Miami as a "stink-pot town." The film shows the city inhabited by strippers, drug dealers, gamblers, bigamists, drunks, and killers. Nevertheless *Tony Rome* emphasizes that those responsible for Miami's criminal activities are often outsiders, mainly from New York and with no particular ethnic background. As a local club owner says to Tony, "Most people in Miami have a return ticket to somewhere."

The story line of *Lady in Cement* (1968), the sequel to *Tony Rome*, is distinctly more deadly, as the title suggests. The film opens with Tony Rome (Frank Sinatra) diving for treasure in sunken, sixteenth-century galleons; instead of treasure he discovers a nude, dead woman with her feet anchored in cement. Hired to find the murderer, Tony encounters one murder victim after another. Scenes portray the sleazy underside of Miami and Miami Beach, but except for the string of murders, local crime appears harmless, even silly. Women, wearing both tops and bottoms, dance for tips in a "go-go club," run by a gay man and his partner, who is a former pro-football player. In another scene an undercover policeman dressed as a woman keeps a strip club under surveillance. The city also has massage parlors and a funeral home with a floating crap game. As in most previous crime movies set in Florida, the bad guys are all white.

Aside from a few minor films in the 1960s, the most direct and explicit connection between Miami and the Mafia first appears in *The Godfather: Part II* (1974). Directed by Francis Ford Coppola and set in the 1950s, the film has a few scenes in Miami, where Michael Corleone (Al Pacino) goes to eliminate Hyman Roth (Lee Strasberg), a Jewish gangster clearly based on Meyer Lansky, who settled in Miami after Castro's revolution closed down gambling in Havana. Even though *The Godfather II* makes clear the presence of mafiosi in Miami, their threat to Floridians or tourists appears remote and dated in the film.

For the period the most unusual foreign threat to Floridians appears in *Black Sunday* (1977). Directed by John Frankenheimer, the film develops a plot around the Black September Movement, the Palestinian group actually responsible for the massacre of Israeli athletes at the 1972 Olympic Games in Munich. In the film's fictional plot, the terrorists target the

56. Fritz Weaver (*left*) and Robert Shaw at the Super Bowl in Miami as the Goodyear blimp, commandeered by terrorists, hovers overhead in *Black Sunday* (1977). By permission of Photofest.

Super Bowl game in Miami's Orange Bowl. With opening shots in Beirut, where Dahlia Iyad (Marthe Keller) meets with coconspirator Mohammad Fasi (Bekim Fehmiu), *Black Sunday* links the planning of the Miami attack to both the Munich killings and the cause of "the Palestinian nation." The movie follows the plotters from Beirut to Los Angeles and finally to Miami for the climactic forty minutes surrounding the Super Bowl championship. The terrorists, pursued by Major David Kabakov (Robert Shaw) of Israeli intelligence, plan to crash a bomb-laden Goodyear blimp into the Orange Bowl filled with eighty thousand spectators, including the president of the United States. The blimp, piloted by a deranged Vietnam vet (Bruce Dern), crashes into the Orange Bowl and causes a panic, but a helicopter tows the crippled blimp out to sea before it explodes.

Terrorist threats reappear in several later films, but the evildoers are almost single-handedly defeated by Chuck Norris and Arnold Schwarzenegger. *Invasion U.S.A.* (1985) pits Norris, an ex-CIA agent, against a small army of mercenaries, led by Mikhail Rostov (Richard Lynch) and his sidekick Nikko (Alexander Zale), who both speak Russian and drink Stoli vodka. The group makes an amphibious landing in Florida and plans to bring down the entire country by fomenting civil war, beginning in Miami, where they are stopped in their tracks by Norris's character acting alone as a "vigilante" (in the words of a newscaster). However, the story line, written in part by Norris and called "idiotic" by Roger Ebert, suggests that private justice as a means of turning back "the tide of terrorism sweeping the nation" is preferable to the government's alternative of "an impending suspension of constitutional rights and the imposition of total martial law."[1]

Several other action films depict south Florida as a hotbed of foreign terrorists and spies. *True Lies* (1994), a popular film starring Arnold Schwarzenegger as a secret government agent, largely takes place in Washington, D.C., and Switzerland, where he goes in search of the Crimson Jihad, a terrorist group in possession of nuclear arms. An intercontinental chase ends in the Florida Keys, where Arnold eliminates the Islamic terrorists who are threatening to blow up American cities. One of their nuclear bombs explodes off the Florida coast, but it presumably does no harm. *Deadly Rivals* (1993), a forgettable movie that went straight to video, tells the complicated story of a "brainy" professor (Andrew Stevens) from "up north," who is engaged in research related to the Strategic Defense Initiative. While attending a conference in Miami, he becomes a target of Russian spies who want to steal secrets about the antiballistic-missile system, but with the aid of the FBI, the professor defeats the interlopers.

The 1970s saw a revival of Florida noir in *Night Moves* (1975). Directed by Arthur Penn, the film employs many techniques associated with the film noir of the 1940s. Although set primarily in the Florida Keys, *Night Moves* has many night scenes and a convoluted plot that takes private-eye Harry Moseby (Gene Hackman) from California to the Keys in search of a missing teenager. The double-crossing villains are all outsiders who engage in old-fashioned crimes like smuggling and murder. The only hint of contemporary Florida life is some Cuban music on the radio and several Spanish-speaking fishermen. Overall, *Night Moves* is decidedly backward-looking in its view of Florida.

In 1981 *Body Heat* and *Absence of Malice* appeared, and despite their differences, their story lines marked the end of an era in Hollywood's vision of Florida crime. Written and directed by Lawrence Kasdan, *Body Heat* looks backward both cinematically and thematically. Loosely based on the story line of *Double Indemnity* (1944), which was directed by Billy Wilder and is considered the original film noir, Kasdan's film was immediately labeled "neo-noir" by critics. *Body Heat* is set in the fictional seaside town of Miranda Beach, north of Miami. The film's doomed antihero, Ned Racine (William Hurt), is ensnared by a spiderlike femme fatale, Matty Walker (Kathleen Turner). Matty convincingly bewitches the unsuspecting Ned into killing her millionaire husband (Richard Crenna). In addition to these plot devices, other reminders of the noir atmosphere include dark, claustrophobic scenes, often shot at night. Ned's small-town world of 1981 is still overwhelmingly white, except for the African-American detective (J. A. Preston) who heads the murder investigation. No Latinos appear in *Body Heat*, but a child describes the murder suspect (the decidedly Anglo-looking Ned!) as having "hair slicked back like a Cuban."

The increased presence of Cubans in Miami is a subplot of another 1981 movie, *Absence of Malice*, which like *Body Heat* deals with old-fashioned crimes before drugs inundated the state. The film's hero, Michael Gallagher (Paul Newman), is the son of a deceased mobster, Tommy Gallagher, who ran an import business in Miami and engaged in various criminal enterprises. In the words of one federal official, "Big Tommy handled five states' worth of liquor, did a little loan-sharking, and kept the longshoremen's union out of Miami for damn near fifteen years." After Tommy died of a stroke in 1967, his son Michael took over "Gallagher Imports." Although he never indulged in his father's now dated illegal activities,

Michael readily admits his father "was crooked." He even names his old wooden boat "Rum Runner."

Nevertheless, because of his father's reputation, Michael becomes a suspect in the disappearance of Joey Diaz, the head of Miami's longshoremen's union. Gallagher Imports employs Spanish-speaking longshoremen, who are presumably Cuban and who go on strike in the mistaken belief that Michael knows something about the disappearance of their union leader. *Absence of Malice* primarily tells the story of Michael's perfectly legal manipulation of federal prosecutors and the local press after they falsely link him to the disappearance of Diaz, but the film's view of crime is refreshingly benign. Except for the probable murder of Joey Diaz, the only crimes mentioned in the movie are bootlegging and loansharking, and neither involves Latinos. Cubans in the film are honest and hardworking, even if misguided in their strike against Gallagher Imports. The real villains in *Absence of Malice* are ruthless prosecutors and reckless newspaper reporters, all of whom are Anglos.

Although made ten years later and released in 1994, *China Moon* has direct connections to Lawrence Kasdan's *Body Heat*. The film's director, John Bailey, served as cinematographer for Kasdan on several films, including *The Big Chill* (1983) and *The Accidental Tourist* (1988). Moreover *China Moon* is set in small-town central Florida and draws on the techniques of film noir. Shot in Lakeland and Tampa, *China Moon* makes few explicit references to Florida, but the almost constant rain adds to the claustrophobic feeling of the film. Other noir touches include the femme fatale (Madeleine Stowe) who seduces a top-notch, but flawed, detective (Ed Harris) and then manipulates him into helping her dispose of her abusive husband.

At the time *Body Heat* and *Absence of Malice* were being made, another phase of foreign migration impacted Florida, supposedly bringing a crime wave in its wake. The linkage of Cuban immigration and crime is graphically fictionalized in *Scarface* (1983), written by Oliver Stone. Although based on the similarly titled 1932 classic, which drew on the life of Al Capone, De Palma's *Scarface* updates the crimes and criminals and relocates them to present-day Miami. At the beginning of the 1983 film, a rolling text explains the supposed source of the new menace.

> In May 1980, Fidel Castro opened the harbor at Mariel, Cuba, with the apparent intention of letting some of his people join their relatives in the United States. Within seventy-two hours, 3,000 U.S. boats were headed for Cuba. It soon became evident

that Castro was forcing the boat owners to carry back with them not only their relatives, but the dregs of his jails. Of the 125,000 refugees that landed in Florida, an estimated 25,000 had criminal records.

These highly questionable "facts" neglect to mention that many refugees with "criminal records" were political prisoners.

The film's opening shots use some documentary footage of the actual Mariel boatlift to establish the context and introduce the central character, Tony Montana (Al Pacino), who arrives on one of the boats. "I ain't no *puta* of a thief," says the tough-looking thug, when questioned by immigration officers. "I'm Tony Montana, a political prisoner from Cuba." This leads one suspicious official to comment: "I don't believe a word of this shit. . . . That sonofabitch Castro is shittin' all over us." Sent to a Miami detention center for processing, Tony wins his release in exchange for killing another detainee, a former Cuban official responsible for torturing to death the brother of "a rich guy in Miami [who] now wants the favor repaid." In accepting the deal for freedom and a green card, Tony reveals his viciousness, telling his sidekick Manny Rey (Steven Bauer), "it'll be a pleasure. I kill a Communist for fun, but for a green card, I'm going to carve him up real nice."

Once free in Miami, Tony and Manny go to work in a Little Havana sandwich shop, but they soon find their way into the city's underworld of drug wars that pit Cubans against Colombians, and both sides are in league with money-laundering bankers and corrupt cops. When a TV editorial uses "the rash of drug-related violence that has plagued south Florida" as an argument against legalizing drugs, Tony says to Manny: "It's those guys—the fuckin' bankers, the politicians. They are the ones that want to make coke illegal so that they can make the fuckin' money and then they get the fuckin' votes. . . . They're the bad guys!"

Tony's bravado and bloodlust quickly propel him from low-level enforcer to drug kingpin in Miami. Along the way he marries Elvira Hancock (Michelle Pfeiffer), a cocaine-addicted former girlfriend of Frank Lopez (Robert Loggia), who headed Miami's drug trade until Tony eliminated him. Upon first meeting Tony, Elvira asks, "Aren't you part of the Cuban crime wave?" To which Tony responds in a self-mocking tone, "What you talkin' crazy for? I'm a political refugee."

The linkage of Cubans and crime is so central to *Scarface* that the filmmakers apparently found it necessary to tack on a disclaimer at the very end of the film, following the final credits.

Scarface is a fictional account of the activities of a small group of ruthless criminals. The characters do not represent the Cuban/American community and it would be erroneous and unfair to suggest that they do. The vast majority of Cuban/Americans have demonstrated a dedication, vitality and enterprise that has enriched the American scene.

Following the plot of the original *Scarface*, the evil Tony ultimately destroys his sister. Attracted by his wealth, Gina (Mary Elizabeth Mastrantonio) falls into his drug-infested world, becomes addicted to cocaine, and marries his best friend Manny. Harboring vaguely incestuous feelings for his sister, Tony kills Manny, and then in the film's climax, Tony is confronted by Gina, dressed in a revealing negligee, who asks seductively, "So you want me, Tony?" She then fires a gun at Tony and wounds him, just before the two of them are murdered by rival gangsters.

Although modeled after a film that debuted fifty years earlier, Brian De Palma's *Scarface* marks a turning point in Hollywood's treatment of crime in Florida. Beginning with this film, crime becomes identified with Cuban drug dealers in Miami, and numerous subsequent movies reinforce this image. Largely (and deservedly) forgotten, these later action and crime dramas seem to feed off each other in their repetitive story lines and their derivative cinematic techniques, which draw heavily on the popular culture of the 1980s, especially MTV music videos and the TV show *Miami Vice*.

One of the first in this wave of films was *Stick* (1985), directed by Florida's own Burt Reynolds who also stars in the movie. Reynolds's character seeks revenge against an evil Cuban drug lord, Nestor (Castulo Guerra). Nestor's henchmen all speak Spanish among themselves, and Nestor controls them through the use of Santeria, the Caribbean's African-influenced religion that the film equates with "voodoo" and "black magic."

Band of the Hand (1986) also features a Cuban drug kingpin, named Nestor Quintana (James Remar). However, this Cuban villain is taken down by five juvenile delinquents, including a Cuban-American teenager, played by Anthony Quinn's son Danny, who is initially arrested for dealing drugs. As part of a supposed rehabilitation program, the five members of this racially and ethnically diverse "band of the hand" become, in effect, vigilantes who successfully eliminate Quintana and his African-American underlings.

The same far-fetched story line is used in *Only the Strong* (1993), which has an ex-Green Beret train teenage delinquents in martial arts to take on evildoers in Miami. Starring Mark Decascos, a gymnast and expert in the Brazilian martial art *capoiera*, the movie has his character Louis Stevens return to his Miami high school, which is covered inside and out with graffiti and crowded with a diverse student body of Latinos, African-Americans, West Indians, and Anglos. "Take a look around you at our current student body," explains his former social studies teacher (Geoffrey Lewis). "75 percent of them are packing weapons; 45 percent are high; 81 percent living in one-parent families." After Louis uses *capoiera* to dispatch a Jamaican drug dealer in the schoolyard, he is asked to train a dozen of the school's renegade students in martial arts to give them discipline and a way to defend themselves. The "program," of course, succeeds, allowing the gang of well-trained vigilantes to dispose of the neighborhood thugs, led by a Brazilian immigrant who also knows *capoiera*.

In the 1980s even James Bond wound up in Florida fighting Latino drug dealers. An earlier cinematic visit brought Bond briefly to Miami Beach in *Goldfinger* (1964), but his return twenty-five years later was sparked by a new threat. In *Licence to Kill* (1989), the drug lord Franz Sanchez (Robert Davi) is clearly a Latino, but his specific ethnicity is somewhat vague since he comes from a fictitious Central American country that resembles Panama. The film's implied association with Panama dictator Manuel Noriega is reinforced by Sanchez's pock-marked face. The movie also establishes a Cuban connection to drug running. In the opening scene Sanchez flies in a small private plane from Havana, which presumably provides him with a safe haven, to Key West. There Sanchez is captured (briefly) by James Bond (Timothy Dalton), who is in the Keys for the wedding of his friend, CIA agent Felix Leiter (David Hedison). Sanchez manages to escape from captivity, and he has his men seize Felix and kill his new wife. When Sanchez then flees to his Central American palace, Bond goes after him in a personal vendetta. The luxurious retreat of yet another Latino gangster prompted critic Roger Ebert to express unease "about the fashion of portraying drug smugglers in glamorous lifestyles. . . . Sure, they die in the end, but they have a lot of fun in the meantime."[2] Ebert might have added that the Hollywood villains having so much fun were usually Latino and most commonly Cuban or Cuban-American, although movies rarely distinguished between Cubans and Cuban-Americans.

Latino criminals who are not Cuban appear occasionally in films, but they usually display the same viciousness associated with Tony Montana. In *Cat Chaser* (1989), a movie based on a novel by Elmore Leonard, the villains in south Florida are Dominicans who are all depicted as brutal animals. Perhaps to counter the obvious stereotyping, the movie's voice-

57. Robert Davi plays a Latino drug lord in the James Bond film *Licence to Kill* (1989). By permission of Photofest.

over narrator observes, "The truth is we're animals, all of us." Nevertheless the film reinforces the view that Florida in particular attracts such types. Even the comedy *Cocoon* (1985) has a passing reference to "dope peddlers" making "a pickup out at sea," when the film's aging retirees see a boat land on Florida's Gulf Coast with a mysterious cargo.

In fact, by the mid-1980s, drug trafficking had largely passed out of the hands of Cuban immigrants and shifted from Florida to other states. As a result of the so-called cocaine wars of the late 1970s, Colombia-based traffickers displaced Cubans and gained control of south Florida's illicit drug trade, which at that point was the state's biggest industry, according to the Drug Enforcement Administration. The multibillion-dollar business soon attracted the attention of law enforcement, and after a federal crackdown on smuggling and money-laundering in south Florida during the 1980s, traffickers began shipping their product through other points of entry into the United States, especially by way of Mexico.[3]

Despite the new reality, crime and action movies from the 1990s still relied on the old formula of portraying Miami criminals as Cubans or Cuban-Americans. In *Point of Impact* (1993), a low-budget movie shot entirely in South Africa but set in Miami, the crime boss is Robert Largo (Michael Ironside), a Cuban-born Floridian working in league with Fidel

Castro to smuggle Soviet-made weapons into the United States for sale
to the highest bidder. All the Miami Cubans featured in the film, including whites and blacks, are ruthless, deceitful thugs, but several, including
Largo, are killed by the film's hero, Jack David (Michael Paré), a former
U.S. Customs agent. A similar image of Miami criminals is presented in
The Specialist (1994), which stars Sylvester Stallone as an ex-CIA operative
whose former partner (James Woods) now works with Miami's Cuban
crime boss Joe Leon (Rod Steiger). The movie also features Sharon Stone
as a sexy, mysterious figure whose parents were killed many years earlier
by Joe Leon's son (Eric Roberts) and two of his Latino henchmen. She
wants revenge, and Stallone's character obliges by killing the three men
responsible for her parents' death. The cinematic connection between Cubans and crime in Miami is so fixed that *Up Close and Personal* (1996) has
a cop refer to an unidentified body as "Juan Doe."

Bad Boys (1995), the enormously popular action movie starring Will
Smith and Martin Lawrence, plays against the grain. It not only features
African-Americans in the lead roles as Miami cops, but it also includes
two Cuban-Americans as fellow Miami detectives. Moreover the movie's
villain, who masterminds the theft of one hundred million dollars in
heroin from the police evidence room, is French! However, at the end of
the movie the gangster who shows up to purchase the stolen drugs is a
Latino.

58. Martin Lawrence (*left*) and Will Smith as Miami cops in *Bad Boys* (1995). By
permission of Photofest.

Another 1995 movie, *Fair Game*, relies on more familiar stereotypes about Miami. Cindy Crawford stars as Kate McQueen, a Miami divorce lawyer who takes the case of a woman married to Emilo Juantorena (Miguel Sandoval), a Cuban exile who runs a Miami bank that launders drug money. Juantorena also works with a gang of renegade Russians, headed by Colonel Ilya Kasak (Steven Berkoff), who once "ran the KGB out of Cuba." When Kate finds some hidden (and suspicious) assets during the divorce case, Juantorena orders a hit on her, but she is only nicked on the arm while jogging along the ocean in Miami Beach. "No one tried to kill me," she tells police. "This is Miami. I'm local. We only shoot the tourists!"

This throwaway line undoubtedly reflects the worldwide perception of the 1990s that south Florida was an especially dangerous place for tourists. After the drive-by killing of a German tourist on a Miami expressway in 1993 and the murder of a British visitor in north Florida, media outlets in the United States and Europe tried to outdo each other in proclaiming "the Sunshine State becomes a STATE OF TERROR" (Philadelphia *Daily News*), "Florida, Bloody Florida" (a TV special by Geraldo Rivera), "Slaughter in the Sunshine" (a British tabloid headline), and "Paradise Lost: The Sharp Decline of the Sunshine State" (a cover story by *U.S. News & World Report*). The problem with such reports was that Florida's murder rate declined 17 percent from 1990 to 1994, and only .07 percent of Florida's forty million visitors were victims of any crime at the time. Nevertheless the perception of a crime wave helps explain a temporary drop in the number of tourists arriving during the mid-1990s and the reference to shooting them in *Fair Game*.[4] Few films picked up on this theme, however, preferring instead the tired stereotype of south Florida crime as principally drug trafficking by Latinos.

In *Fled* (1996) the Miami mob is headed by a Cuban-American, Frank Montajano (Michael Nader), who is "moving Cuban organized crime into the ranks of corporate America," according to a Department of Justice official in the film's opening scene. Most of the movie's action takes place in Georgia, where Cuban gangsters working for Montajano chase a computer hacker (Stephen Baldwin) who stole millions of dollars of the mobster's ill-gotten gains, but the film's entire plot and its villains are linked to the Cuban-American mob in Miami.

Another 1996 movie, *The Substitute*, asserts a direct Cuban connection to drug smuggling. The film opens with mercenaries, led by Shale (Tom Berenger), staging an unsuccessful raid on a "drug processing plant" in Cuba. Left unemployed after the botched raid, Shale masquerades as a

Kim Dickens takes a purifying swim in the Atlantic Ocean in *Things Behind the Sun* (2001).

Michelle Pfeiffer and Robert Redford in the Florida Keys. *Up Close and Personal* (1996).

Above: The star of *Jaws 3–D* (1983), prowling at Sea World. By permission of Photofest.

Left: Felix Leiter (David Hedison) being tortured by a shark in *Licence to Kill* (1989). By permission of Photofest.

A river scene from *Sunshine State* (2002).

A view of the Everglades in *Just Cause* (1995).

This poster for *Revenge of the Creature* (1955) shows Gill Man but distorts the setting of the movie by locating it in a big city. By permission of Photofest.

A scene from *Honky Tonk Freeway* (1981). By permission of Photofest.

Will Smith (*left*) and Martin Lawrence in a pool in *Bad Boys II* (2003). By permission of Photofest.

The Miami skyline in *Out of Time* (2003).

Al Pacino (*left*) in *Scarface* (1983), working at a Little Havana diner when he first arrives in Miami. By permission of Photofest.

Alec Baldwin and Jennifer Jason Leigh (*far right*) at their Coral Gables home in *Miami Blues* (1990). By permission of Photofest.

The last scene in *Scarface* (1983), showing the dead body of Tony Montana (Al Pacino) floating in his fountain, which has a statue bearing the slogan *The World Is Yours*.

The indoor pool, where retirees are rejuvenated, in *Cocoon* (1985). By permission of Photofest.

A rundown Ft. Lauderdale motel in *Revenge of the Nerds II: The Nerds in Paradise* (1987).

College students on Daytona Beach in *Black Spring Break* (1998).

Santo Trafficante (Val Avery) and Lefty Ruggiero (Al Pacino) in *Donnie Brasco* (1997).

A crash caused by Miami street racers in *2 Fast 2 Furious* (2001).

Norman D. Golden II (*left*), Burt Reynolds, and Ralph Wilcox in *Cop and a Half* (1993). By permission of Photofest.

Jay Tavare, as a Seminole, encounters Meryl Streep in *Adaptation* (2002).

The lynch mob that terrorizes African-Americans in *Rosewood* (1997). By permission of Photofest.

C. J. Sanders as the young Ray Charles and Sharon Warren as his mother in front of their north Florida home in *Ray* (2004).

Above: Elvis Presley in a publicity shot for *Girl Happy* (1965). By permission of Photofest.

Left: Nathan Lane in *The Birdcage* (1996). By permission of Photofest.

Ashley Judd (*right*) and Allison Dean play clerks in a tourist shop in *Ruby in Paradise* (1993). By permission of Photofest.

Eddie Murphy in *The Distinguished Gentleman* (1992). By permission of Photofest.

Diane Keaton and her nephew (Leonardo DiCaprio) driving on the beach in *Marvin's Room* (1996). By permission of Photofest.

Richard Dreyfuss, Seymour Cassel, Dan Hedaya, and Burt Reynolds play retired mobsters in *The Crew* (2000). By permission of Photofest.

Jim Morris (Dennis Quaid) pitching in Orlando in *The Rookie* (2002).

Dan Marino (*center*) with his kidnapper (Sean Young) and Ace Ventura (Jim Carrey) in *Ace Ventura: Pet Detective* (1994).

Danny Glover (*top*) and Joe Pesci in *Gone Fishin'* (1997). By permission of Photofest.

59. Tom Berenger (*left*) and Ernie Hudson in *The Substitute* (1996). By permission of Photofest.

substitute teacher in a Miami high school to avenge an attack on a friend who teaches there. He discovers that the school is overrun by Latino and African-American gang members who deal drugs as part of a scheme organized by the school's black principal, Claude Rolle (Ernie Hudson). The movie's use of an African-American crime boss is unusual, but so too is the emphasis on teenage gangsters, one of whom is Juan Lucas (Marc Anthony), a Latino and presumably Cuban-American. Rolle, an ex-cop, uses school buses to transport cocaine that he stores at the school. Shale calls on his mercenary friends to eliminate the teenage villains, and the movie climaxes in a burst of violence that kills off the Latino and African-American drug dealers. In what is undoubtedly intended as a kind of epitaph for the city of Miami, one of the surviving mercenaries declares at the end of *The Substitute*, "It's definitely time to relocate."

The theme of Cuban crime resurfaces in *Plato's Run* (1997), starring Gary Busey as Plato Smith. This action movie has Plato, an ex-Navy SEAL, hired by Manuel Gomez (Salvador Levy), a Cuban crime boss in Miami, to rescue his son who is imprisoned in Cuba. Plato at first turns down the one hundred thousand dollar offer because "Gomez is scum, and I do not do business with arms dealers or gangsters." However, Plato is apparently a man of flexible principles because he quickly changes his mind when he discovers he has no money to pay his overdue rent. In a surprise double-cross, the "rescued" son turns out to be a Cuban agent who assas-

sinates his father upon arriving in Miami. Plato then finds himself running from the police and Gomez's henchmen, but he also wants revenge
against whoever set him up as part of the assassination plot. The film's
arch villain is Alexander Senarkian (Roy Scheider), an arms dealer who is,
of course, ultimately killed by Plato in a blaze of violence.

Despite the presence of a white, non-Latino villain, *Plato's Run* clearly
reinforces the view that Miami is overrun by Cubans who are duplicitous
criminals and killers. At one point, when Plato is dressed in a goofy-
looking disguise while running from the bad guys, he is stopped on a
Miami street by a roving TV reporter who sticks a microphone in his face
and asks, "Are you a tourist?" Plato responds, "No, I'm a native. I'm half
Jewish and half Seminole." The reporter then asks what is the "most serious problem confronting south Florida." Plato answers: "This is easy. It's
crime. It's definitely crime."

Cutaway (2000), another low-budget action movie, also exploits the
image of Miami as a hub of drug smuggling from the Caribbean. In this
case the two principal smugglers are Anglo (Tom Berenger) and African-
American (Dennis Rodman). Nevertheless the movie includes a scene in
which a drug shipment goes to the "Castillo twins," who are Latino (Cuban?) drug dealers living in luxury at a spectacular mansion along the
water. Cubans, it seems, are never far from the cinematic center of action
when the setting is Miami and the criminal enterprise is running drugs.

Thus it should come as no surprise that *Bad Boys II* (2003) replaces
the French villain of the original film with a Cuban-American drug kingpin, Hector Juan Carlos "Johnny" Tapia (Jordi Mollà). Tapia makes his
illicit money (one hundred million dollars!) in Miami and moves it to
Cuba, where he has built a huge compound on the coast. Will Smith and
Martin Lawrence again team up as the bad boy cops and play their parts
for laughs like Abbott and Costello, according to one reviewer.[5] Taking
them more seriously, critic Roger Ebert called the pair "egotistical monsters, concerned only with their power, their one-liners, their weapons,
their cars, their desires."[6] The film's Cuban-American villain, "the Cuban
maniac," proves more vicious than Tony Montana in *Scarface* by cutting into pieces his Russian partner (Peter Stormare), who runs a club
where the chief attraction is the free-flowing drug ecstasy. To round out
this portrayal of foreign threats to south Florida, the movie has a subplot about a gang of Haitians trying to rip off the drug dealers. During
a shoot-out, one cop dismissively refers to them as "fuckin' Haitians in
fuckin' low-ass homes with fuckin' guns." Making two Cuban-American
cops (Yul Vasquez and Jason Manuel Olazabal) the foils for ethnic jokes

about Ricky Martin concerts does little to counter the film's stereotypes. Indeed the Latino cops provide access to "the anti-Castro underground" for assistance in raiding Johnny Tapia's compound in Cuba, where the film ends with a chase featuring a Hummer ripping up the Cuban countryside. "Everybody involved in this project needs to do some community service," Roger Ebert concluded.[7]

Another recent film, *The Punisher* (2004), relies on the stereotype of Cuban-American gangsters but moves them to Tampa. Based on a Marvel comic book series, the movie tells the story of an ex-FBI agent (Thomas Jane) who becomes "the punisher." He turns into an unrelenting vigilante after his entire family is wiped out by mobsters, led by Howard Saint (John Travolta). Although Saint's ethnicity is unclear, he heads a "business [that] involves two Cubans—the Toro brothers," according to a police informant. "They control all the prostitution and gambling up and down the Gulf Coast—tons of cash. They give their dirty money to Howard Saint, who transports it in cigarette boats to his banks in the Grand Cayman, washes it, and wires it back clean as a whistle." In addition to the Toro brothers (Omar Avila and Eduardo Yáñez) with their heavy Spanish accents, Saint's ruthless wife (Laura Harring) is a Cuban-American born in Tampa's Little Cuba, a name invented by the film. Finally, gang members loading money on a cigarette boat all speak Spanish.

Once stereotypes become fixed in the imagination, they can be played for laughs, or what passes for humor in *Smokin' Stogies* (2001). The plot of this small-budget film involves Italian-American mafiosi smuggling Cuban cigars into the country through Miami, where they work with Latino gangsters who speak with heavy Spanish accents. Two are referred to as "inner-tubing Cubans," and when two others speak Spanish together, one mafioso orders them to stop speaking "Mexican." In an apparent attempt to balance the slurs, another scene has a Latino con man putting Cohiba labels on cheap cigars that he plans to pass off to the Italian-American mobsters because, he says, "These dumb wops don't know shit about Cuban cigars."

One of the few recent crime films that breaks the mold of making Florida crime primarily Cuban is *Donnie Brasco* (1997). Significantly, unlike fictional concoctions about south Florida, *Donnie Brasco* explores the real-life experiences of an undercover FBI agent (Johnny Depp) who takes the name Donnie Brasco and infiltrates an Italian-American gang in Brooklyn, headed by "Sonny Black" Napolitano (Michael Madsen). Donnie helps set up an FBI sting operation by suggesting that the New York mobsters try their luck in the Sunshine State. The problem is that Florida has its own

60. Santo Trafficante (Val Avery) and Lefty Ruggiero (Al Pacino) in *Donnie Brasco* (1997).

resident Mafia family, headed by Santo Trafficante, a real-life Tampa ma-fioso. As Donnie points out, "Santo Trafficante is the boss of Florida. He sits on the fuckin' commission." Despite Trafficante's prominence, Sonny Black sees south Florida as a great opportunity, commenting to Donnie that Trafficante "had this all to himself for fifty fuckin' years, and it's still a cow town. This could be Vegas down here. . . . This is all I want." When Sonny Black's gang opens a club with illegal gambling, Florida cops close it down the first night, and Santo Trafficante claims credit for the raid. In a telephone conversation, Trafficante brags to a fellow mobster in New York, "We busted it up. He's outa business. . . . That punk is finished down here."

Although set in the 1970s before the Mariel boatlift, *Donnie Brasco* served in the 1990s as a counterweight to the image of Cuban drug deal-ers as Florida's dominant criminal element. Several other films from the 1990s contain passing references to Mafia activity in Florida, but the perpetrators are largely outsiders who pose little threat to law-abiding citizens. In *Goodfellas* (1990), Martin Scorsese's film about New York wise guys, a brief scene has two enforcers, played by Robert De Niro and Ray Liotta, go to Tampa to collect a debt from someone who owes the mob. After threatening to "throw the bastard to the lions" at the local zoo, Liotta's character comments, "They must really feed each other to the lions down here because the guy gave the money right up." De Niro also appears in *Great Expectations* (1998) as an escaped convict and former hit man who says he was sent to jail for murdering a mafioso in Bradenton, a city south of Tampa. *Married to the Mob* (1988) transpires largely in and around New York City, but the action eventually moves to Miami because it's home to a Mafia boss who is under surveillance by the FBI.

Another comedy, *Analyze This!* (1999), makes it clear that Miami's Mafia is no laughing matter. When a local reporter (Lisa Kudrow) discovers that her financé (Billy Crystal) has a gangster, Paul Vitti (Robert De Niro), as a patient, she warns him, "I've covered the mob down here. I've seen what they can do."

Nevertheless, compared to the bloody drug wars that dominate so many recent Florida films, the crimes committed by Italian-American wise guys, such as the gambling in *Donnie Brasco*, seem archaic. *Donnie Brasco* does have one reminder of the new Florida in a brief scene showing one of the New York gangsters buying cocaine from Colombians in a Miami hotel room. In *The Crew* (2000) Italian-American mobsters retire to South Beach. Although they get involved in some illegal activities to prevent their rooming house in South Beach from being sold, these aging wise guys are a source of humor, not fear.

Many films from the late 1990s that emphasize the decadence of Miami are themselves trashy. According to a reviewer for the *New York Times*, *The Blackout* (1997), "featuring sex, drugs and Claudia Schiffer, caused a stampede when it was shown at the 1997 Cannes Film Festival." This may explain why the film did not have its U.S. premiere until two years later, even though it stars Matthew Modine and Dennis Hopper, along with the former fashion model. As the presence of these actors suggests, the film's drug abusers are all Anglos. One of them commits murder in a cocaine-induced haze, and despite its Miami setting, the movie features no Latino characters. In short, *The Blackout* is about the debauchery of rich, Anglo outsiders who flock to clubs in Miami Beach.

Blood and Wine (1997), a more critically acclaimed film, also focuses on Anglo outsiders pursuing crime in south Florida. Directed by Bob Rafelson, the film stars Jack Nicholson as a New Yorker who went to Miami to open a wine shop with his wife's money. Now facing bankruptcy, he joins up with Victor Spansky (Michael Caine), a safecracker on parole, to steal a million-dollar necklace from a palatial Miami mansion. The film's love interest brings in Gabriela (Jennifer Lopez), a Cuban immigrant who works as a nanny and lives with her extended family in a modest Little Havana bungalow. Although Gabriela takes one of the stones from the stolen necklace when it passes through her hands, she represents one of the rare Cubans with any redeeming values in a film about crime in south Florida. In another rarity, *Blood and Wine* has no references to illicit drugs.

Out of Sight (1998) also successfully plays against dominant stereotypes about crime in Florida. Directed by Steven Soderbergh, the film follows an ex-con (George Clooney) from California to Florida, where he spends just enough time to get caught robbing a bank in Miami and serve time in prison before escaping to Detroit. In the process of escaping from prison, he encounters Karen Sisco (Jennifer Lopez), a U.S. marshal, who is not only a sexy, romantic foil but also a strong, self-assured, likable Cuban-American. Indeed she is the only major character who is a Floridian in a film otherwise dominated by criminals from outside the state. Similarly one of the few honest characters in *Wild Things* (1998) is a Cuban-American detective, played by Daphne Rubin-Vega, who ultimately manages to unravel the complicated plot.

The noticeably noir atmosphere of *Blood and Wine*—steamy locations with desperate, bumbling crooks who hang out in sleazy bars and aging hotels—marked a minirevival of this style in Florida crime films. As Roger Ebert has perceptively observed, "Florida is the ideal state for *film noir*. . . . *Noir* is founded on atmosphere, and Florida has it: tacky theme bars on the beach, humid nights, ceiling fans, losers dazed by greed, the sense of dead bodies rotting out back in the Everglades."[8] Other recent films that invoke some of the noir style include *Wild Things*, *Palmetto* (1998), and *Big City Blues* (1999).

Palmetto and *Wild Things* share a lot in common, including convoluted plots and deceptive double-crossing. At their worst, these crime movies become "a parade of *film noir* clichés and caricatures," as one reviewer complained in the case of *Palmetto*.[9] Janet Maslin of the *New York Times* called *Wild Things* "a Florida *noir* heyday" with "far-fetched quintuple-crossing." Whatever their artistic merits, *Palmetto* and *Wild Things* portray flawed, white antiheroes, played by Woody Harrelson and Matt Dillon, living in small Florida towns and ensnared by the machinations of sexy women. The principal crime in both of these films is murder, motivated by sex and greed—all plot devices reminiscent of classic noir films, as is the whiteness of the leading characters. *Wild Things 2* (2004) merely duplicates much of the original story line with different actors, and it went straight to video without passing through movie theaters. However one interesting addition in the remake is a Cuban-American hit man who is identified as working for "the Cuban Mafia" in Miami.

Big City Blues updates the film noir by moving it from small-town Florida to Miami, adding drug dealing to the familiar list of old-fashioned crimes, and infusing some black humor into its nonsensical plot about two contract killers (Burt Reynolds and William Forsythe). Leaving no doubt about its cinematic inspiration, *Big City Blues* opens with Burt Reynolds's character in a movie theater watching an old black-and-white French film.

61. Denzel Washington with Sanaa Lathan, who plays the femme fatale in *Out of Time* (2003). By permission of Photofest.

The rest of *Big City Blues* unfolds during that night without a single scene in daylight. In another retro aspect the film has an almost entirely Anglo cast of characters, except for an African-American drag queen, played by Giancarlo Esposito. The plot suggests that crime is pervasive in Miami. In one scene police with drawn guns arrive at a hotel across the street from Wolfie's, the famous Miami Beach deli. Taking cover in the deli, two diners duck under a table. In disbelief their waitress says: "You two must not be from around here. . . . Because most folks who eat here are regulars. If they ducked under the table every time something like *that* happened, they'd never get a chance to sit on the chairs. I mean, something like this happens twice a week, minimum."

Forever Mine, written and directed by Paul Schrader, is a noir romance that begins with lush beach scenes set in Miami and then moves to the New York area where most of the dark action transpires. The Florida scenes are flashbacks to 1973 and feature two Latino employees ("cabana boys") at a posh beach resort who get involved in the drug trade. "Right now, in Florida, money is one thing," says Javier Cesti (Vincent Laresca). "It's drugs." His friend, Manuel Esquema (Joseph Fiennes), initially rejects this route, but after seducing a woman from New York (Gretchen Mol) whose husband (Ray Liotta) has him shot, Esquema changes his name and becomes an avenging hit man, making money through the drug wars. Once again the Florida setting establishes both the romantic mood and the connection between Latinos and drugs.

Out of Time (2003) is another film noir set in Florida, and it adds the innovative touch of casting an African-American (Sanaa Lathan) as the double-dealing femme fatale. Her target is her secret lover, the police chief of a small town in the Keys, played by Denzel Washington. She gets him to turn over $485 thousand in impounded drug money, supposedly for expensive cancer treatments that she says she needs to survive. Like any good film noir, *Out of Time* takes a number of unexpected twists and turns, involving arson and murder, but in perhaps its most unusual twist, the film has a happy ending.

Adaptation (2002) is an imaginative and fascinating film that has elements of Florida noir in its complicated plot. The film focuses on a Florida con man, John Laroche, played by Chris Cooper in a performance that won him an Academy Award for best supporting actor. Described as "bizarre and provincial," Laroche is a cagey cracker with long, stringy hair and missing teeth. His scam is using Seminole Indians as a cover to take protected ghost orchids from a state preserve. Aside from its beauty and rarity, the ghost orchid produces a hallucinogenic drug that reduces the film's star (Meryl Streep) to addiction and an improbable romance with Laroche. Her obvious decline reaches the point where she contemplates murder to keep her new life a secret. The film's overlapping plots and blurring of the line between reality and imagination give it a complexity that makes it much more than a drama about criminals in Florida. But it also brings cracker crime up to the present with an unforgettable Florida character in the person of John Laroche, who finally resorts to murder.

Cuban-Americans should probably consider themselves lucky to be excluded from Florida crime films about serial killers. Movies that feature serial murders in Florida are *Eyes of a Stranger*, *The Mean Season* (1985), *Traces of Red* (1992), *Curdled* (1996), and *Monster* (2003). Except for *Monster*, all are set in south Florida—three in Miami and one in Palm Beach—and cast Anglo men as the killers. All of the victims are white women, except in *The Mean Season* (1985), which has a villain who murders several elderly couples, picked at random. *Just Cause* (1995) also has a subplot about a condemned serial killer, played by Ed Harris, who makes us believe that this psychopath probably deserves electrocution.

The cumulative effect of slasher movies on south Florida's image is reflected in *Curdled*. The film features a TV show entitled "Miami D.O.A.," which is devoted to documenting murders in the city. During the show an advertisement for a company called Post Forensic Cleaning Service declares: "Miami: Over fifty thousand violent crimes a year. Have you or someone you know been the victim of a sudden, random, violent crime? You've dealt with the fear; you've dealt with the pain. Now, how do you deal with the aftermath? The unique challenge of violent crime cleanup is our specialty." In a passing comment, one character in the film compares decadent Miami with upbeat Orlando, where everybody has a good time.

Monster destroys this image of tranquil central Florida, just as it fractures stereotypes about serial killers. The film is based on the actual killing spree of Aileen Wuornos, who confessed to murdering six men and was executed in 2002 after ten years on Florida's death row. Some critics complained that *Monster* portrays Wuornos (Charlize Theron) as a victim more than an aggressor. Forced to live on the streets after the death of her father, she turned to prostitution at the age of thirteen. As the film's narrator, Wuornos initially explains her resort to prostitution as a choice she may have been forced into by circumstances, but a choice nevertheless. By the end of the film, however, she seems to have little choice in her fate. The first man she kills is a "John" who beats and rapes her. When she then tries to go "straight," no one will hire her, and she resumes the murder-robbery attacks on men who pick her up for sex and become threatening. In a final scene before her arrest, an acquaintance (Bruce Dern) suggests that his experiences as a Vietnam vet prove people have no control over fate—it's all circumstances. "Circumstance—that's it exactly," Wuornos agrees. "You know it's like I feel I never had a choice." Regardless of who or what is to blame, the string of roadside murders certainly reveals a dark and dangerous side of life in central Florida.

Other recent films also remind viewers that murder in Florida is not restricted to the Miami area. *Just Cause* defied a number of dominant images about crime in Florida. Set in Ochopee, a small town east of Naples in Collier County, the movie tells the story of Paul Armstrong (Sean Connery), a Harvard law professor and opponent of capital punishment, who agrees to work pro bono to investigate the case of a death-row inmate, Bobby Earl (Blair Underwood). Earl, an African-American from rural Ochopee, was convicted eight years earlier and sentenced to death for the kidnapping, rape, and murder of a young white girl. Armstrong's investigation suggests that Earl was railroaded by a forced confession and a botched defense. Flashbacks reveal that after his arrest Earl was savagely beaten by Tanny Brown (Laurence Fishburne), a local black cop. "Tanny Brown's one of those niggers who likes being a big fish in a small pond," Earl explains after Armstrong expresses surprise that Brown is African-

American. "See this is the New South," Earl continues, "and now they've got black cops to come and torment your black ass. It's called affirmative action." Lines like this led a reviewer for the *Los Angeles Times* to label *Just Cause* "a sweet slice of reactionary-ism."[10] The film's complicated plot twists ultimately follow Bobby Earl from death row to a murder spree in which he seeks revenge against those he sees as responsible for his fate. He finally kidnaps Armstrong's wife and daughter, but he falls into the jaws of an alligator after he is stabbed by Tanny Brown, who acts in self defense and thereby eliminates one of the few African-American killers in Florida films.

While Hollywood generally equates crime with south Florida, especially Miami, cinematic glimpses of illegal activities elsewhere in the state appear in independent films. In *A Flash of Green* (1984), director Victor Nuñez exposes rapacious land developers who seemingly go to any extreme to profit from the destruction of Florida's natural environment. "They have a way of getting nasty, especially when money is involved," says Jimmy Wing (Ed Harris), a newspaper reporter in the film's fictional city on Florida's Gulf Coast. The film's villain is a county commissioner (Richard Jordan), who endorses illegal measures to assure passage of a plan to fill in the local bay and build expensive homes. In a particularly vicious (and distinctly southern) attack, local rednecks flog one opponent of the project. Significantly, *A Flash of Green* goes back in time to revive an image of cracker crime in the 1950s, but these Floridians are decidedly contemporary in their pursuit of land development at the expense of the environment.

Other recent independent films focus on teenage crime in rural and small-town Florida. *Ulee's Gold* (1997), another work directed by Victor Nuñez, depicts contemporary crime in north Florida, where nasty, violent young men are robbers. White, working-class teenagers in north Florida also pursue crime in *Trash* (1999), an independent film that shows small-town high school boys seeking escape in crimes that escalate from robbery to murder.

Trans (1998) shifts the locale to southwest Florida, showing black and white teenagers who escape from a juvenile detention center. Described by a reviewer in the *New York Times* as "a sensitive evocation of youthful turmoil," *Trans* is the first film by Julian Goldberger. It focuses on Ryan Kazinski (Ryan Daugherty), a white, sixteen-year-old escapee who makes his way to his hometown of Ft. Myers and spends most of the film trying to flee the area. Unlike the teenage criminals in other films about Florida,

Ryan commits acts that appear petty and even incidental to what is basically a moving character study.

Another revealing treatment of Florida crime can be found in *Night Orchid* (1997), a little known independent film made by a faculty member and students at Valencia Community College. Despite its reliance on paranormal visions, which take the lead character back in time, *Night Orchid* is more than a ghost story. Filmed in rural areas north of Orlando, the film does an admirable job of evoking small-town central Florida, dominated by orange groves, packing plants, and a buried history of violence and murder. "Every town's got its secrets," observes one local. "Things they don't want nobody to hear." The film's flashbacks tell the story of the killing of a white woman thirty years earlier, for which a black man was tried, found not guilty, and then nearly lynched. Having escaped detection at the time, the real murderer (a white woman) goes on a killing spree in the present in an unsuccessful attempt to keep the truth hidden. Along with *A Flash of Green*, *Night Orchid* goes back in time to portray Florida locales and criminal acts rarely seen in Hollywood movies.

Crime and punishment in contemporary rural Florida is the subject of *Dunsmore* (2003), an independent film with an insightful script and strong acting. The opening scene shows the town bully (W. Earl Brown) gunned down in a volley of shotgun blasts by unknown assailants. Talk about a possible vigilante killing brings a state investigator (Kadeem Hardison), an African-American from the attorney general's office, who looks into whether the murder involved any civil rights violations. Through the use of flashbacks, residents of Dunsmore describe their encounters with the murder victim, who had brutalized people for years and finally killed the town's minister. Although the film rarely refers explicitly to race, it clearly raises the issue by having an African-American investigate the possible "lynching" of a white man.

Several marginal (and forgettable) movies rely on worn stereotypes about Florida crackers in stories about rural crime. *The New Kids* (1985) has two teenagers go live with relatives in a rural south Florida town like Homestead, where the movie was shot. In the local high school, Abby (Lori Laughlin) and her brother Loren (Shannon Presby) run up against "rednecks" (as the film's credits refer to them) who drive pick-up trucks, sport names like "Joe Bob," talk with heavy southern accents, drink beer, spit frequently, and raise pit bulls. Their leader (James Spader), a drug pusher, turns on "the new kids" after Abby refuses to date him. He and his armed thugs kidnap Abby and try to rape her, but she escapes. In the bloody denouement, all the cracker criminals are killed by various means, including a decapitation, a pit bull, and a fire. In *Held for Ransom* (2000), which went straight to video, Dennis Hopper plays a demented cracker who teams up with his redneck wife (Debi Mazar) in a murder-kidnapping plot set in the Everglades.

Middle-class teenagers in suburban south Florida become vicious killers in *Bully* (2001). Based on a true story, the film graphically depicts the brutal murder of a sociopath by his "friends," who otherwise spend their time getting high and engaging in bizarre sexual activities. Directed by Larry Clark, the photographer who previously made *Kids* (1995) about teenagers in New York, *Bully* does little to explain why these young Floridians behave the way they do, except to emphasize that their parents do not have a clue. In any case the film says little about Florida, and the story could be set in any American suburb.

More silly in its portrayal of young people in south Florida is *2 Fast 2 Furious* (2003). Nominally a sequel to *The Fast and the Furious* (2001), *2 Fast* relocates the action from the streets of Los Angeles to the streets of Miami. It also employs a new director (John Singleton) and a new cast, but it really stars the cars that race through Miami and down I-95 to Key West. (A *New York Times* reviewer even credited the cars with the movie's best performances!) To justify a starring role for the cars, the film's plot has two street racers (Paul Walker and Tyrese) go undercover for U.S. Customs to trap an Argentinean-born drug lord, whose two henchmen are Cuban-Americans. (They are referred to as "Elian and Fidel" by one of the film's heroes.) The movie's diverse cast of men and women includes street racers, who are African-American, Anglo, and Latino, and cops, who are black and Latino, but significantly, the drug-peddling villains and enforcers are all Latino.

Several recent movies about crime in Miami feature African-American casts. *All About the Benjamins* (2002) is a "hip-hop shoot-"em-up buddy comedy," in the words of a reviewer for the *New York Times*. With graphic violence and ceaseless profanity, the film tells the story of a bounty hunter named Bucum (pronounced "book "em" and played by Ice Cube), who teams up with a con man (Mick Epps) to capture a gang of jewel thieves—the only white characters in the movie. After finding twenty million dollars' worth of diamonds, the pair keeps half because it's all about the "Benjamins" (hundred-dollar bills). *A Miami Tail* (2003) is a silly attempt to update the ancient Greek play *Lysistrata* by Aristophanes. The movie has Alica Strada (Trina) organize African-American and Latina women in Miami's Liberty City to withhold sex until their boyfriends

62. A crash caused by Miami street racers in *2 Fast 2 Furious* (2001).

stop dealing drugs. Whatever their particular plots and merits, such films clearly reinforce the image of Miami as a center of criminal activity by hustlers and thieves of diverse races and ethnicities.

The corruption of public officials appears as a common theme in Florida movies. Indeed, aside from drug dealing and murder, political corruption is apparently the principal illegal activity in the state. Moreover this is one criminal act that cannot be blamed on outsiders because locals are largely responsible, even if they are occasionally tempted by the money of outsiders, as in the case of a drug enforcement agent who accepts two million dollars to let the Latino drug czar escape in *Licence to Kill*.

Corrupt public officials are sometimes portrayed as simply bizarre and provincial, especially in films playing for laughs. In *Striptease* (1996), based on the novel by Carl Hiaasen, a drug-addicted thief gets custody of his daughter because a Ft. Lauderdale judge remembers him as "a great tailback." Another judge in the film has a heart attack in a porn theater, and the movie's central politician, Congressman David Dillbeck (Burt Reynolds), is an aging, horny philanderer, who is a tool of the state's sugar interests. *Honky Tonk Freeway* (1981) presents virtually every public official as corrupt, including the governor, as well as the mayor and sheriff of the film's fictional locale. Police brutality is mocked in *The Disorderlies* (1987), which has a white cop describe a "Florida lie detector" as a three-hundred-pound man with a baseball bat. In the ironically titled film *The Distinguished Gentleman* (1992), Eddie Murphy plays a con artist who manages to get elected to Congress in north Florida after he discovers that piles of money can be illegally pocketed from campaign contributions and lobbyists. The main public official portrayed in John Sayles's film *Sunshine State* (2002) is a city councilman (Gordon Clapp) who is shown stuffing wads of cash into his pants after he sells his vote to developers.

Florida's prisons and hospitals are also often depicted as corrupt and primitive centers of abusive treatment. In *The Longest Yard* the Florida state prison is run by brutal, corrupt, racist white guards, who are a distinctly southern stereotype. *Instinct* (1999) stars Anthony Hopkins as a professor of anthropology at the University of Miami who is committed to a Florida institution for psychiatric prisoners after he kills two poachers in Africa and stops talking upon his return to the United States. The prison psychiatrist (Cuba Gooding Jr.) complains to the warden that the professor is "brutalized" by other inmates and prison guards, whose behavior is graphically illustrated. *Chattahoochee* (1989) may reinforce common images about the backwardness of southern institutions, but it is based on a true story. Set in the 1950s it recounts the experiences of Emmett Foley (Gary Oldman), the fictional name of a real-life Floridian who is committed to Chattahoochee, the state's mental institution, where he is brutalized by inmates and staff.

Police corruption, usually connected to drug dealers, is the most common offense attributed to Florida public servants in films. Brian De Palma's *Scarface* shows Miami-Dade's chief of detectives for narcotics, played by Harris Yulen, taking bribes. In return for payoffs from favored drug dealers, he provides information about the operations of rival gangsters, and he supplies cops to serve as hit men. In *The Specialist* the Cuban crime boss supposedly buys off the Miami-Dade chief of police! Both *The Substitute* and *Illtown* (1996) depict drug dealers bribing police officers. The convoluted plot of *Wild Things* casts a corrupt detective as one of many evildoers. This alleged pattern of police corruption leads the Miami divorce attorney in *Fair Game* to claim that "Florida law enforcement has set a world record in bribery and corruption." She follows this up by asking a Miami-Dade detective, "You know what they call a Florida cop in a three-piece suit? The defendant!" *Blue City* (1986) practices affirmative action in its portrayal of such behavior by casting an African-American as the corrupt and murderous chief of police, Luther Reynolds (Paul Winfield). He is in charge of a small-town department in the Keys that is described by the film's hero, Billy Turner (Judd Nelson), as "the most crooked police force in the state." Having killed Billy's father in order take his position as police chief, Reynolds ultimately overreaches himself and dies when Billy kills him in self defense.

Bumbling Florida cops provide comic relief in some movies. *Thunder and Lightning* shows sheriff's deputies smashing into one another in a high-speed chase. A similar scene is repeated—with many more police cars crashing—in *2 Fast 2 Furious*. In *A Murder of Crows* (2001) Key West

63. Norman D. Golden II (*left*), Burt Reynolds, and Ralph Wilcox in *Cop and a Half* (1993). By permission of Photofest.

police are unable to catch a visitor, played by Cuba Gooding Jr. on their own turf. *Cop and a Half* (1993), directed by Henry Winkler, features Burt Reynolds as a Tampa detective who teams up with an eight-year-old child (Norman D. Golden II) to catch a drug trafficker. *Ace Ventura: Pet Detective* (1994) has a private eye (Jim Carrey) hired to find the Miami Dolphins mascot that has been kidnapped from its tank. The perpetrator (Sean Young) turns out to be a cross-dressing escapee from a Tampa mental hospital who masquerades as a female police detective in Miami.

The assumption that police in Florida are either incompetent or corrupt may explain why so many filmmakers have their heroes take the law into their own hands to get justice. Movies with leading men who become vigilantes to dispatch the villains include *Band of the Hand, Only the Strong, Plato's Run, The Specialist, The Substitute, The New Kids,* and *The Punisher. Eyes of a Stranger* (1981) also relies on vigilante action, but with the unusual twist that it features a woman, who tracks down a serial murderer and kills him to rescue her sister. Since the vigilante heroes always succeed in eliminating the evildoers, these films clearly suggest that the end justifies the means. The hero of *The Punisher* makes this point explicit: "In certain extreme situations, the law is inadequate. In order to shame its inadequacy, it is necessary to act outside the law, to pursue natural justice. This is not vengeance. . . . No, not vengeance—punishment." Only

Invasion U.S.A. includes a counterargument, offered by a Miami police official who lectures Chuck Norris, "It's people like you who have turned this nation upside down. Nobody, but nobody, is beyond the law." However, the character played by Norris then proceeds to prove otherwise by taking the law into his own hands and disposing of a terrorist threat that even Florida's National Guard cannot handle.

In *Transporter 2* (2005) another vigilante proves he's much more effective than local and federal law enforcement in spoiling the plans of a gang of foreign mercenaries who threaten Miami. As the movie's somewhat complex plot develops, the villain turns out to be Gianni (Alessandro Gassman), a former member of Italy's Red Brigade, who is now "for hire." On the payroll of the Colombian drug cartel, he's plotting to wipe out drug enforcement officials from all over the world attending a conference in Miami. Assisted by renegade Russians, he spreads a deadly virus, but he is undone by the hero (Jason Stratham), who single-handedly manhandles dozens of Gianni's hirelings to save the day.

Beginning with silent films, all film genres have featured crime stories set in Florida. What has changed over time is, of course, the nature of crime and its perpetrators, at least as depicted by filmmakers. Reflecting significant new developments in the state and nation, Florida movies shift from a focus on period crime like bootlegging in the 1920s to drug running since the 1980s. According to Hollywood, Florida is also plagued by various con schemes from land fraud in the 1920s to political corruption in more recent years. Murder remains a continuing threat in movies, especially with south Florida's links to organized crime, increasingly featured in films since World War II. As perceptions of crime have changed, so too has the identity of criminals. Like the main characters in most films, criminals are overwhelmingly white until the 1980s, but until recently they bear special markers in Florida, where they tend to be portrayed as local crackers or outsiders with Italian-American names and often mob connections. Some of the latter are retired or aging mobsters, like Johnny Rocco in *Key Largo*, who see Florida as their last chance to make it. This theme continues in films like *Miami Blues* (1990) and *Out of Sight* with stories about outsiders unsuccessfully continuing their criminal ways in Florida.

As far back as the Marx Brothers who play con artists in *The Cocoanuts*, films about crime in Florida generally cast men as the perpetrators, but women also become lawbreakers. *Girl Missing* (1933) features several women working as con artists in Palm Beach, and one of them resorts to murder. Other deadly women appear in movies about Ma Barker and in *Little Laura and Big John* about the Ashley Gang in the 1920s. A more prosaic female criminal is played by Sigourney Weaver in *Heartbreakers* (2001), which portrays her and her daughter (Jennifer Love Hewitt) as con artists who target a rich old man in Palm Beach. Once the film noir of the 1940s pioneered the plot device of women using sex appeal to manipulate unsuspecting men into committing crimes, the popularity of Florida noir and neo-noir means that women play a prominent role in Florida crime films. The long list of movies with female villains includes *Body Heat*, *China Moon*, *Wild Things*, *Palmetto*, and *Out of Time*. The femmes fatales in these films engage in a variety of crimes, but murder is the principal one. *Monster*, of course, provides the most deadly linkage between women and murder.

The female criminals in Florida films are usually white, as are the male villains and, for that matter, the leads in most films prior to the 1990s. Nevertheless it is worth noting that when African-Americans increasingly get lead roles in Florida films, they rarely appear as criminals. Two major exceptions are *Just Cause* and *Out of Time*, but both of these also include black cops who play flawed heroes.

In terms of ethnicity the biggest cinematic shift has, of course, focused on Latinos engaged in drug running and related crimes since the 1980s. *Scarface* set the pattern, and dozens of films followed suit in portraying Cubans and Cuban-Americans as vicious drug lords.

In the Hollywood formula, drugs and Latinos equal Miami. Movies made since the 1980s generally reinforce the impression that south Florida is a crime-ridden area, overrun by Cuban gangsters and corrupt officials. Lest any viewer miss the point about Miami's decadence, one film pounded it home with vulgar explicitness. In *Miami Blues* an ex-con from California, played by Alec Baldwin, moves to Miami, where he encounters whores, gamblers, hustlers, corrupt cops, and drug dealers, leading him to conclude, "This world is a shit hole." In *Smokin' Stogies*, a mafioso who runs a pizza parlor in Miami tells his lawyer, "Everybody in this town is corrupted." Even a contemporary film set in New York, *City by the Sea* (2002), has a character refer to Florida as "the fuckin' dope capital of the world."

In *Big Trouble* (2002) stereotypes about crime in Miami are played for laughs. Based on Dave Barry's first novel, which "reads like a slapstick version of Carl Hiaasen," according to a review in the *New York Times*, the film is a comedy directed by Barry Sonnenfeld. *Big Trouble* tells the stories of a number of characters whose lives intersect. One subplot has two Italian-American hit men (Dennis Farina and Jack Kehler) go

64. Dennis Farina (*left*) and Jack Kehler as the hit men in *Big Trouble* (2002).

to Miami to rub out Arthur Herk (Stanley Tucci). An arms dealer who has double-crossed his boss, Herk is described as "one of the few Floridians who was not confused when he voted for Pat Buchanan" in the 2000 election. Several other arms merchants in Miami are Russians seeking to sell a stolen nuclear device that threatens to explode in Miami. Another subplot concerns a bumbling, totally incompetent Miami cop (Patrick Warburton) who quits the force to become a male stripper/dancer. The movie also shows the scheming of two dumb ex-cons (Tom Sizemore and Johnny Knoxville). When they see an expensive red sports car on a Miami street, they assume it is owned by "some kind of drug kingpin," who has "a helicopter, a big-ass boat, and a pad down in the Bahamas like a tax shelter." The film includes a passing reference to an "old Cuban guy" who is training pelicans to drop bombs so he can "kill Castro with a bird." All this leads the two visiting hit men to conclude that Miami is "Weirdsville, U.S.A.," and as they prepare to leave at the end of the movie, one remarks that "Miami sucks."

With recent films like *Big Trouble*, Hollywood's view of Florida crime as a source of comedy comes full circle. Starting with the Marx Brothers in the 1920s, movies have portrayed the state as a Mecca for outrageous criminals and con artists whose behavior is somehow over the top. But whether depicted as humorous or frightening, cinematic figures like Johnny Rocco, Tony Montana, and John Laroche are unforgettable as Italian-American, Cuban, and cracker criminals. However it should be noted that these three also eventually meet their demise in the Sunshine State.

Part III

Characters

In 1922 Kenneth L. Roberts published a book titled *Sun Hunting: Adventures and Observations Among the Native and Migratory Tribes of Florida, Including the Stoical Time-Killers of Palm Beach, the Gentle and Gregarious Tin-Canners of the Remote Interior, and the Vivacious and Semi-Violent Peoples of Miami and its Purlieus*. This impressive title covers many—but not all—of the kinds of characters that have been portrayed in Florida movies.

Heroes, villains, and lovers are among the specific types that have leading roles in film narratives. These characters interact with a wide range of minor figures whose actions and dialogue reinforce audience interpretations of motivation and personality. No matter what the film genre or plot, the characterizations of the men and women involved in the story reflect the dominant views of the historical period in which the film is made. For example, white movie audiences in the early decades of the twentieth century willingly accepted white screen actors who applied black color to their faces to play buffoonish African-Americans. And since the late twentieth century, film audiences have been more interested in seeing women's roles that go beyond depictions of struggles with love and motherhood.

Some characters in Florida movies are universal narrative types, while others have become more specifically identified with the state, like tourists, retirees, astronauts, and developers. This section examines the images of men and women in Florida films by looking at their identities as shaped by changing views of race, gender, ethnicity, heroism, sports, and occupation.

Chapter 6

"Imagine, prospecting on the moon!"
"Yes, but what will we do for Indians?"

Sunshine State (2002)

The First Natives

The first people to arrive on the peninsula probably made their way from the north, although some theories suggest the possibility of southern routes as well. Archaeological evidence traces their roots from east of the Mississippi to the Atlantic coast. Thriving mainly in coastal villages, where fishing and hunting sustained them, the first peninsular residents included more than a dozen groups, differentiated by language, culture, and geography. Evidence suggests migration to the St. Johns area in northeast Florida from at least 100 B.C.E., and expansion south and west over the next fifteen hundred years. Some estimates put the population at three hundred fifty thousand by the time the first Spanish conquerors arrived in 1513. Pillage, slavery expeditions, and further Spanish migration followed, with devastating effects on the native people. Exploitation, war, and disease reduced the native population to about ten thousand by the 1600s.

Despite the drama of those historical events, few films have attempted to re-create the Spanish expeditions to Florida. The 1951 movie *Hurricane Island* took great historical liberties with the story of Ponce de León's search for the Fountain of Youth in Florida. This drama focuses on Captain Carlos Montalvo (Jon Hall) and his association with Indian Princess Okahia (Jo Gilbert). Another plot thread involves Spanish efforts to overcome a large group of British buccaneers led by "lady pirate" Jan Bolton (Marie Windsor), and as a result, British challenges to Spanish territorial claims become more important than triumph over the "savage" natives.

A 1992 Mexican film, *Cabeza de Vaca*, is worth mentioning as a more recent conquest-era drama. The story draws from the bizarre memoirs of de Vaca, who was shipwrecked in Florida and wandered through the southwest in the late 1520s and early 1530s. Earlier abandoned by Captain Panfilo de Narvaez, who sailed ahead, de Vaca and a few other ragged and starving men were cast ashore on the west coast of Florida after drifting for days in the Gulf of Mexico. The film begins with the survivors rebuking both God and Spanish promises of wealth as they cling to a raft.

Washed ashore, the men believe they have arrived in *"una lugar para morir"*—a place to die. Trudging through swampy shores and moss-laden coves, they find no food or potable water, and they are captured and forced into servitude by a local tribe. The rest of the film follows de Vaca's release from his captors, his supposed travels, encounters, and displays of extraordinary healing powers, until he meets up with the Spaniards again in Mexican territory.

The Florida natives depicted in this film are understood only from the Spanish point of view. There is no attempt to suggest understandable verbal communication, and no intimation that the Spanish were able to successfully convert or conquer natives. Florida is inhospitable, not a paradise, and the natives appropriately treat each intruder as an enemy. In de Vaca we see a man who has probably gone mad, but whose experience in Florida has, nevertheless, left him "reborn," giving him new abilities and a sense of compassion toward all native people he meets. He represents the first European visitor to "go native," a theme that has appeared in many Florida films.

When de Vaca finally reunites with other Spaniards in Mexico, he is in a camp where indigenous men are held in cages and used as slave labor to build a Catholic cathedral. As he and other travelers discuss their migration from Florida to Mexico, one man claims significant sexual prowess with native women, and another says that he saw El Dorado and the Fountain of Youth. The search for these fictional sites has inspired travelers ever since.

Most Florida natives did not survive European encroachment. When the British began competing for the continent in the 1600s, moving further south from the middle Chesapeake region, some native groups fled. Migrating to Spanish-controlled Florida through the 1700s, new arrivals from the southeastern tribes of Cherokees, Creeks, Chickasaws, and Choctaws made their way to the Panhandle and into gold-poor areas neglected by the Spanish. By 1763 Britain had established a firm foothold in the northern part of the peninsula, and the Mikusuki-speaking migrants, who would come to be known as Miccosukee and Seminoles, remained somewhat isolated from colonial control in south Florida.

British, Spanish, French, and finally U.S. interest in Florida was more strategic than economic. Spain failed to maintain control after it regained title to the peninsula in the treaty ending the American War of Independence, and the new United States leaders were determined to secure territory and loyalty. The first so-called Seminole War (1814–1818) was part of Andrew Jackson's continuing attempt to suppress British and other Anglo residents' attempts to create an independent republic.

Spain finally ceded Florida to the United States in 1821. During the early 1830s the United States attempted to exert control over the resistant native population in the Second Seminole War. At the time, the war was the most costly military campaign in the young nation's history. To secure the territory, the United States targeted Indians for removal to western lands. The forced migration (the "Trail of Tears") included slaves who had escaped into Seminole and Miccosukee villages, where they sought and gained protection. This second war inspired some interest by feature filmmakers. The first film to deal with the subject is the unavailable silent film, *Witch of the Everglades* (1911), whose title indicates which side it took in focusing on the war with Chief Osceola. More films followed in the 1950s, the era of popular western films.

As many analysts have pointed out, westerns of the 1950s also contained subtle messages that were framed within the context of the Cold War. They romanticized the triumph of Anglo power over "savage" (non-Christian, traditional, or "backward") people and the process of "taming the wilderness" by replacing native villages with modern structures. Seminoles, including "Black Seminoles," were seen as standing in the way of that process. During the 1950s Florida "westerns" generally mirrored other westerns in their portrayals of white "civilization" versus native "barbarism."

Perhaps the best-known Florida western is the 1951 film *Distant Drums*, starring Gary Cooper as Captain Quincy Wyatt. After leaving the military, Wyatt had married a Creek princess (referred to by using the derogatory term *squaw*) and the couple had a child. When General Zachary Taylor's representatives find Wyatt in order to pull him back into battle, he explains that a group of drunken U.S. soldiers had killed his wife because "the men were young and liquored up and thought all Indians looked alike." Wyatt's bitterness is tinged with understanding and forgiveness toward the soldiers. After all, how could they know that a princess is so much better than the rest of the tribe? (No white man would marry her otherwise, apparently.) Having drifted away from the military to raise his son, Wyatt is called upon by "Old Rough and Ready" to help expel the rest of the Seminoles from a Florida fort where Spaniards and Americans were imprisoned. The Zachary Taylor character explains that the larger military mission is "to bring peace to this territory."

The film begins with a commentary about the "savage and bloodthirsty foe" the U.S. military had to confront, and then proceeds to show the natives as incompetent warriors. Constantly charging into open spaces to be picked off by U.S. soldiers, Seminoles communicate troop movements by drumbeats and fight for reasons that are never addressed in the film. Their attacks on whites are arbitrary and unjustified, while the white soldiers (and the white women they protect) must act defensively to bring order to the chaotic frontier. The movie ends with a U.S. military victory. Larry Cooper plays Chief Oscala, a curious corruption of the name of the actual chief, Osceola. A romantic subplot links Wyatt with a buxom, blond Georgia woman that he frees, along with Spanish captives, from "injuns."

As a Cold War-era western, *Distant Drums* provides predictable interpretations of Indian removal and war in Florida. Seminoles are wild, dirty, brutal scalpers, tied to superstition and "backward" ways of life, including ritual infanticide. In the era of Joseph McCarthy, this triumph over the "enemy within" may have resonated well with audiences. Moreover, unlike many westerns that capture colorless, arid, rocky terrain, *Distant Drums* is in vivid color, showing lush tropical scenery and exotic wildlife still reminiscent of the old Florida.

Over the next four years, three more films focused on this war. In *Seminole* (1953) the story is partly about Chief Osceola's capture and imprisonment, leading to his supposed death in Florida (he actually died in South Carolina). But the film is really about conflicts between soldiers and strict commanders at Fort King, the military garrison near Ocala. In *Seminole Uprising* (1955) the plot also revolves around U.S. soldiers battling the natives and a romance between a kidnapped woman and a "renegade" Seminole. She finally succumbs to love for a soldier she mistakenly assumes is part Indian.

65. A scene from *Seminole* (1953). By permission of Photofest.

A slightly different approach to the Second Seminole War appears in the movie *Naked in the Sun* (1957). Filmed as the civil rights movement was beginning, the plot concerns the alliances between Seminoles and escaped slaves during the 1830s, and it centralizes Chief Osceola as a heroic figure. While the slave trapper in the film is definitely the villain, both for his objectives and his act of kidnapping Osceola's wife, the Seminoles continue to be portrayed as more violent than whites. The Osceola character surrenders to U.S. authorities but escapes from Fort King.

Other films of the same era focus on the danger of encountering Seminoles, but set the stories in different times. In *Shark River* (1953) and *Yellowneck* (1955) Seminoles threaten Civil War deserters trudging through the Everglades on their way to Cuba. Again the Florida natives are portrayed as scalpers, but somewhat more skilled at guerrilla warfare.

Another era in Florida history is dramatized in the film *Wind Across the Everglades* (1958). Set in the early twentieth century, when south Florida was becoming accessible by train, the film depicts a struggle between the proponents of "modernization" and "traditionalists" in the Everglades. Walt Murdoch (Christopher Plummer) has the job of limiting the environmental impact of development and of popular styles he criticizes as primitive. When he arrives in town, a bevy of plume-hatted women also disembark from the train. Murdoch, angrily tearing a feather from one the hats, explains: "Only Indians wear feathers in their hats. We call them savages. But we're civilized!" Sent by the Audubon Society to identify, count, and protect the birds in the area, Murdoch spends the rest of the film confronting Cottonmouth (Burl Ives), the Everglades leader of a scruffy band of ex-criminals and social rejects who are dedicated to killing birds and selling their feathers.

One of Cottonmouth's band, Billy One Arm (Cory Osceola), is a Seminole Indian driven out of the tribe for infractions. Forced by Cottonmouth to lead Murdoch into a trap, Billy develops a bond with the outsider. Murdoch explains that he knows how Indians were forced from their lands to poor land and "finally to this no land at all." Making a comparison between the exploitation of the birds and the loss of Seminole lands, Murdoch wins Billy's admiration for being unlike "other white men." (This is explained, of course, in Billy's stilted English.) Expressing regret he has no "peace pipe" to smoke with Billy, Murdoch offers him the next best thing, one of his Cuban cigars. After learning of Billy's treachery, Cottonmouth kills him with a local poison whose very mention terrifies the Seminole. Aside from the wife who comes to claim his body, this is the only role for Seminoles in the film. The movie does avoid portraying the indigenous people of Florida as "bloodthirsty savages"; instead, it presents them as defeated subjects.

Seminoles also have roles in films set in more contemporary Florida. The earliest is probably *Key Largo* (1948). Loosely based on a Maxwell Anderson play, the film changes the plot. In Anderson's play a father and son migrate to Florida after growing up on Oklahoma reservations, and they are arrested as black vagrants and sentenced to road-gang work. In the film the men are the "Osceola brothers" who are arrested in a brawl: "They just went to Palm Grove and got a little snoot full and started to take Florida back for the Indians. Came mighty near succeeding, too." They break out of jail, and their escape is understood as a cultural response: "Thirty days in jail for them is like thirty years." With Charlie Winook and his family—Seminole "royalty" from Crawfish Island—the Osceola brothers decide to give themselves up to the police. When the film's villain (Edward G. Robinson) kills a sheriff's deputy and the two escaped Seminoles, he blames the deaths on other Indians.

Here again the Seminoles are victims—of historical wars that left them destitute, of Anglo justice systems that penalize them for being Indian, and finally of the brutal behavior of an Italian-American mobster. A long-time Key West resident (Lionel Barrymore) and his daughter-in-

66. Humphrey
Bogart greeting
Seminoles in
Key Largo (1948).
By permission
of Photofest.

law Nora (Lauren Bacall) treat the Seminoles with paternalistic patience while crediting them with special skills. "Indians always know when a hurricane is coming," Nora notes. As in other movies of the period, natives themselves are only able to speak choppy English, and they lack the sophistication necessary for survival in the white man's world. Anderson's play, written in the 1930s, better reflects the views of that new era in government-tribal relations, depicting the natives as "noble savages," who well understood their history and their options.[1]

In the interim between the play and the film adaptation, some Seminoles had survived by participating in several tourist attractions. These first re-creations of tribal villages had been established in the 1920s, and by the late 1930s and early 1940s were being criticized by state and federal agencies as exploitative and culturally destructive. They, nevertheless, thrived through the 1940s.[2] (The Seminole Tribe of Florida was officially recognized by the federal government in 1957.) As tourist attractions Seminoles also became identified with alligator wrestling and by their patchwork clothing, adopted in the 1920s and 1930s. Producers of the 1941 movie *Moon Over Miami* were sufficiently familiar with the nearby reservations to include a nightclub dance scene with gold digger Betty Grable leading the "Seminole Dance." Unfortunately, none of the elements—the dance, dress, music, or performers—is Seminole.

Movie images of Florida's Native Americans are mainly confined to Seminole males, and more importantly, to those who either oppose or associate with white businessmen or other "protectors." In fact Florida's Native Americans have been widely admired in other regions of the United States for their long resistance to the removal policy, and Osceola has been revered for his stand against white control and for his martyrdom. No films so far have provided starring roles for Florida's indigenous women, despite their power and roles in decision making among native groups. The female characterizations in films with Native Americans tend to place them in the background. Occasionally, as in *Key Largo* or *Joe Panther* (1976), elderly Seminole women are portrayed as venerated members of the community, but their speaking roles are limited, and their actions are confined to family tasks. They are never portrayed as conflicted over identity and assimilation or as participants in decisions made by indigenous or white men. In *Naked in the Sun*, Osceola's wife is portrayed as a victim, whose abduction is the central cause of the Seminole leader's fight with the U.S. military.

Between the late 1960s and 1980, few Florida films included Seminole themes. The only film in the 1960s to deal with Seminole culture is the bizarre portrayal of a so-called half breed, played by Chad Everett in the title role of *Johnny Tiger* (1966). The main star, however, is Robert Taylor, cast as teacher George Dean. Transferred with his three urban children to a Seminole reservation in south Florida, Dean eventually changes his attitude about the "primitive thinking" he encounters there.

When Dean first sees the Seminole children dressed in traditional clothing, he asks them to recite their ABCs. When they can't he muses, "they're raw, totally raw, with untouched minds. But at least they haven't been taught the wrong things." Dean's goal is to transform the "primitive" into the "civilized," to "lift them out of the dark ages." He zeroes in on Johnny Tiger as an ideal subject through whom he can demonstrate his ability to be the agent of transformation. Johnny lives outside the reservation, working at various jobs, including alligator wrestling. Resentful that his grandfather rejected his father because of his involvement with a white woman and heavy drinking, Johnny is the conventional native character caught between two worlds. In him Dean recognizes a natural intellect, which he no doubt attributes to the fact that Johnny is half-

67. Chad Everett stars as a Seminole who wrestles alligators for tourists in *Johnny Tiger* (1966). By permission of Photofest.

white, and prepares him for college entrance tests so he can pursue an education. Johnny romances Dean's teenage daughter (Brenda Scott) with her father's blessing (he's a "smart" Indian, after all). After initially rejecting him, she finally succumbs to love while reviewing his essay on Darwin's *The Origin of Species*.

No actual Seminoles apparently play any of the main speaking roles in *Johnny Tiger*, but they mill around or lurk in the background. As an effort to critique arrogant white men who think they should transform indigenous people, the film fits with some others in this era of emerging Native American rights and controversy over the Vietnam War. The local doctor, played by Claire Bloom, is more tolerant of indigenous ways and values, and she divides her time between trying to seduce Dean and seeking to alter his cold and critical thinking. When she takes him to talk to the village elders about sending children to school, the pair watches a medicine man concocting something in a huge black cauldron. Dean comments that it is the "accumulated ignorance of the ages." But the doctor tells him that a pharmaceutical company offered Mr. Billy a lot of money for the tranquilizer he makes; he took stock options instead.

Dean never shows any interest in learning about the Seminoles' values or language, but his attitude toward them is finally—and quickly—transformed at the end of the film. This is because Johnny Tiger's father (Ford Rainey) gives his own life to save Dean's son from a raging fire. Dean then encourages Johnny to return to the tribe and accept its leadership. In the final scene Johnny and his wife pack up books and supplies to go deeper into the Everglades, and the white man's goal of bringing his education to the wilderness triumphs.

A later film, *Little Laura and Big John* (1973), has a small but significant reference to Seminoles in south Florida. Here, John Ashley inaugurates his criminal career by killing his Seminole partner in poaching. "Who's going to hang anybody for killing an Indian?" he reasons. In reality Ashley did not know the Seminole he murdered and robbed.

The 1974 film *Ride in a Pink Car* (not available for viewing) stars Glenn Corbett as Seminole Gid Barker, who returns from the Vietnam War to find his wife remarried and the town suffering from crime and corruption. As he takes it upon himself to set things right, he has to deal with men who despise his indigenous roots. Here the setting of rural Florida and the characterization of a Seminole veteran allowed the filmmaker to criticize both the Asian war and persistent bigotry at home.

68. The last scene of *Johnny Tiger* (1966) shows Robert Taylor watching Johnny Tiger (Chad Everett) leave the Seminole reservation. By permission of Photofest.

69. Ray Tracey in a
publicity shot for his starring role in *Joe Panther*
(1976). By permission of
Photofest.

During the 1980s media focus on indigenous rights and knowledge of
the consequences of U.S. expansion for native populations changed some
portrayals of Native Americans in popular culture. More sympathetic Native American figures were created that challenged long-held views of indigenous people as inherently violent and consistently defeated. *Band of
the Hand* (1986) tells the story of teen criminals confined to an Everglades
rehabilitation program run by a Miccosukee who teaches jungle and urban survival skills that combine his "native" abilities with his Vietnam
War experiences. He fails when he moves out of his "element," and is
killed by young Miami hoodlums.

Joe Panther is the only film thus far to place Seminoles at the center
of the story. As a young man Joe Panther (Ray Tracey) lives in a village
that survives in part by performing alligator wrestling for tourists. (The
tourists don't know that the gator has a broken jaw and is incapable of
inflicting harm.) But Joe wants more from life, and he dreams of working
on a fishing boat and becoming part of "the white man's world." Without shedding his native dress, he goes to a marina to look for work on
a charter boat, and Captain Harper (Brian Keith) promises to hire him
if he captures an eleven-foot alligator. Not interested in witnessing the

contest between Indian and gator, Harper has apparently set an impossible task.

The bargain struck, Joe seems unaware of his own complicity in reinforcing the pattern of accommodation to white demands. He agrees, enlisting the help of his best friend, Billy Tiger (A Martinez). An elder Seminole (Ricardo Montalban) reminds him of the story of the Trail of Tears and the history of perseverance of his people and suggests that he carefully consider his plans. But Joe is determined and fulfills his assignment after a long, harrowing combat. He lands the job, only to become unwittingly involved in the business of smuggling Cubans into the United States. The crew has implemented the scheme without Harper's knowledge, and Joe gets to experience the good and bad of white man's ways. The overall message of the film, however, is that becoming part of a business outside the reservation is liberating. On the reservation camera shots of interiors and exteriors portray a dark and cramped existence. At the docks the open waters and sunshine suggest a sense of infinite space and optimism. Moreover, Harper turns out to be a valuable father figure and guide to the world outside the reservation.

In many westerns from the 1930s to the 1950s, plots include the rescue of white women from violent Indians, and this theme continues in some contemporary films. In *The Substitute* (1996) Tom Berenger works undercover as a substitute teacher in a rough, ethnically diverse Miami high school. When his girlfriend is kneecapped by a six-and-a-half-foot Seminole student, Berenger avenges her. In *Wild Things* (1998) part of the complicated plot refers to the murder of "Seminole Davey," the supposedly violent boyfriend of a rural white girl (Neve Campbell). This provides the motivation for a revenge plot.

The most recent film including Seminoles is the award-winning *Adaptation* (2002). Of course the viewer doesn't know if screenwriter Charles Kaufman is portraying the Seminoles as he expects his audience to envision them or as he thinks the author of *The Orchid Thief*, Susan Orlean, perceived them. Perhaps to heighten the confusion, the film actually uses Navajo men from New Mexico to play the roles of Florida Seminoles, and none of the film was shot in Florida. Orlean's book focuses on south Floridian John Laroche (Chris Cooper), who is in league with Seminoles to steal orchids from a government preserve. For the screen adaptation, in addition to creating a close relationship between Orlean and Laroche, Kaufman makes the Seminoles drug abusers. The Seminoles in this film seldom speak. Instead they glare, stand idly, and isolate themselves. And the blond Orlean character (Meryl Streep) has a discomfiting encounter

70. Jay Tavare, as a Seminole, encounters Meryl Streep in *Adaptation* (2002).

with one of the Seminole characters when she visits their garden shop. As he touches her hair, she freezes in fear, even as he claims to see the depth of her unhappiness and her search for change. In *Adaptation* whites once again enter the dangerous world of the native and the unknown.

Through the 1950s the inclusion of Florida's first residents followed an interesting but consistent path in movies. As villains in plots, they succumbed to brave white male domination over the land. In films dealing with white settlement and control, whites fight Florida Indians in "just" wars that rid frontiers of threats to new settlers. Indians are not only in the way of white advancement, but also incapable of understanding that whites know what is best for them. Indian warriors are seldom portrayed as defenders of land and sovereignty; instead, they appear as primitives who are naturally prone to violence and who refuse to accept their destinies.

In films of the last fifty years, plots about white domination over stubborn native tribes have waned, but the image of natives as defeated people has not. With few exceptions Florida Indians are portrayed on reservations, apart and different from other Floridians. Imagined as universally impoverished and dependent on whites, they appear in films as relics of Florida's precivilization, stubbornly standing in the path to modernization defined by white men. Films also suggest that their continuing refusal to accept white values and systems has limited their success.

In a larger sense the incorporation of Florida Indians into films also presents an image of the state as mysterious and not entirely "civilized." Although they live on reservations elsewhere in the state, as well as outside reservations, in films they are confined to regions of the Everglades. These settings attempt to convey the wilder, darker, untamed environment that coexists with nearby urban complexity. However, in more recent films, especially in the crime genre, the dangers lurking in the swamps seem less threatening and more controllable than the multitude of dangers in the cities. Indian movie characters have, therefore, sometimes moved off the reservation to fight urban crime (*Band of the Hand*), to become involved in crime (*Joe Panther*, *The Substitute*, and *Wild Things*), and to use their sovereign status for their own advantage (*Adaptation*).

Audiences interpreting movie images of Florida's natives will understand nothing about their origins or about the divisions between the Seminole and Miccosukee tribes. Viewers will gain little understanding about their histories of loss, their collective identity as unconquered people, or their contemporary concerns. Their legal challenges to environmental degradation, continuing conflicts with the state about sovereignty, and internal debates about gambling casinos and other businesses are just a few of the modern issues that are missing from film images of Florida's first settlers. Native Americans rarely play starring roles, and their experiences are seldom central to plots. Instead their presence in films serves as a reminder that an element of the state is not completely assimilated or understood.

Chapter 7

Ethnic Identities

African slavery was introduced into Florida during the Spanish colonial period to meet the labor needs first of the military, then of the economy. Ponce de León reportedly brought the first slaves by way of Cuba in 1513. As British settlers moved into the northern part of the continent, and then migrated south, they brought more slaves, some of whom escaped into Spanish-claimed territories, where some lived with the Seminoles. The acquisition of Florida by the United States in 1819 expanded the slave plantation economy in north Florida. By the time Florida achieved statehood in 1845, 52 percent of the African-American population was concentrated in three northern counties, and the slaves constituted 34 percent of the state's population in 1860.

In the first decade of the twentieth century, as filmmaking began in Florida, the state's black and white populations were closely balanced (443,634 whites and 308,669 blacks), but white migration surpassed African-American growth in subsequent decades. In 1920 the white population of Florida was 638,153 and the black population was 329,487, and by 1930, the white population surpassed one million (1,035,390), while the black population grew to only 431,828. Nevertheless, the large number of African-Americans in the state should have provided them with a higher profile in films, but racism limited their presence.

Early Anglo filmmakers like D. W. Griffith and Lubin Studios tended to portray African-Americans as minstrel shows and vaudeville acts had, reflecting racist exaggeration by white actors in blackface. Although few early films are available, they undoubtedly reinforced stereotypical images, as some of the titles suggest: *The Gator and the Pickaninny* (1900), *Rastus in Zululand* (1910), and *Coontown Suffragettes* (1914). While African-American filmmakers, like John Noble and Oscar Micheaux, and a few white filmmakers like Richard Norman, did hire African-American actors and developed plots supporting racial equality, most early films set in Florida either excluded African-Americans or used white actors in blackface in roles as servants. These characters typically were used for "comic" relief.

An early example of African-American portrayals appears in the gender-bender *A Florida Enchantment* (1914). The maid for the female lead is billed as a "mulatto," but is actually a white actress in blackface. She steals one of the pills that is "a secret to happiness for all women" and turns into a man. However, while the mistress who also took a pill develops masculine traits and love for women, the mulatto woman/man displays violent and aggressive behavior, beating up a black man and challenging her new master/mistress. As a servant she has been treated rudely, and her master/mistress tolerates no change in the power relationship after ingestion of the pill encourages the maid to talk back. Her disheveled appearance and her actions are exaggerated to suggest an ignorant child.

After talkies began, white filmmakers slowly added more African-American actors, but kept them in servile roles. Florida films like *Girl Missing* (1933) and *Palm Beach Story* (1942) are good examples of the "mammy" and "yassah" roles played by African-Americans who have minor parts. During President Franklin Roosevelt's administration, fair treatment of African-Americans received more federal government support, and roles for African-American actors very gradually became more serious. In the meantime African-Americans had produced their own so-called race films that dealt with human conflicts exacerbated by segregation and prejudice. As World War II drew to a close, most African-American film studios had been taken over by large white studios, and roles and plots previously common in race films found their way into Hollywood films.

Chloe, Love Is Calling You (1934) is a Florida film that represents the sensibilities (or lack thereof) about race and racism in the era between the world wars. Chloe (Olive Borden) is supposedly the mixed-race daughter of a black nursemaid, Mandy, who is played by African-American actress Georgette Harvey. Mandy, her friend Jim (Philip Ober), and Chloe go to the Everglades so Mandy can avenge her husband's lynching fifteen years earlier. The target is Colonel Gordon, who runs a turpentine camp and lost his daughter in the swamp, also fifteen years before. While Mandy carries out voodoo rituals, Chloe is wooed by white and African-American men. When it is discovered she is really the Colonel's lost daughter and not mulatta, she is free to marry the white suitor. Although shocking to many viewers at the time for its depiction of interracial romance, the movie actually reinforces the taboo, as well as a number of racial stereotypes.

Few Florida-set films by white filmmakers critiqued racism or placed African-Americans in leading roles until after World War II, when some directors became committed to addressing prejudice in the United States. Awarded a Golden Globe for best screenplay, *Bright Victory* (1951) offers a moral lesson on racism with a plot about a returning soldier blinded by a sniper in the war. As Larry Nevins (Arthur Kennedy) struggles to deal with his blindness, he gains vision about the racial bigotry he learned growing up in the small town of Semolina, Florida. Without being able to see, he befriends an African-American man while recuperating in the hospital. When he returns home and hears his mother (Nana Bryant) utter racial slurs, his father (Will Geer) explains that she and her son learned racism growing up in that community. In the end Larry deals successfully with both his physical and mental disabilities.

The history of African-American workers in the state has been of little interest to filmmakers. An exception is *Charcoal Black/Black Rage* (1972), a rarely seen film that focuses on black turpentine camp workers and their brutal exploitation. More often, African-Americans play minor and subservient characters in movies. A 1974 film dealing with racism in prison is *The Longest Yard* (1974), starring Florida resident Burt Reynolds as a prisoner in the fictitious, racially segregated Citrus State Prison. But here Reynolds is the star, not the African-American actors.

The Disney film *Treasure of Matecumbe* (1976), an adaptation of the 1961 adventure book *Journey to Matecumbe*, is actually more focused on Florida racism. In this story a white boy (Johnny Doran) living in post–Civil War Kentucky finds a treasure map in his attic. His African-American friend Thad (Billy Atmore) joins him on the quest to find his family riches in the Florida Keys. As Thad's uncle (Robert DoQui) pursues them through the mosquito-ridden swamps, he is captured by the KKK and

71. Burt Reynolds (*holding the football*) and other prison inmates in *The Longest Yard* (1974). By permission of Photofest.

nearly lynched. The friendship between the boys helps them overcome several near-catastrophes.

Significant roles for adult African-American actors in Florida-set films have taken longer to achieve, despite the increased focus on racism as a theme in movies. As recently as 1980, for example, the popular film *Caddyshack* included only one role for an African-American—the shoeshine "boy" at the country club. Films made during the early 1980s reflect a transition point in the treatment of racial issues in Florida. The popular teen film *Porky's* (1981) lampoons 1950s Florida racism in a small Everglades town, as high-school teenagers challenge local bigotry against Jews, Cubans, and blacks while also spewing every imaginable racial slur. Another film from the same year, *Honky Tonk Freeway*, includes a scene with Ticlaw's citizens (including Asians and blacks) banding together to lure in tourists. Their parade features not only an Indian in Western Plains garb, but also a black woman in Aunt Jemima dress, flipping pancakes.

In contrast, 1981 also marked the release of *Body Heat*, which features African-American actor J. A. Preston as the detective who unravels William Hurt's complicity in crime. This casting was part of a national movie trend of the 1980s, giving more prominent and positive roles to African-Americans. Occasionally films also portray African-Americans as wealthy or middle-class Floridians. For example, in *Summer Rental* (1985) John Candy's family is disappointed to learn that the plush beachfront condo they think they've rented is actually owned by a wealthy black family. African-American college students finally appear in one of the Spring-Break movies in 1983 and in *Revenge of the Nerds II* (1987).

Integrated casts and starring roles for African-Americans in Florida films followed with significant speed during the late 1980s and 1990s. Film veteran Ossie Davis plays Paul Newman's best friend in *Harry and Son* (1984). Black and white cops team up in *Running Scared* (1986); black, white, and Latino survivors of nuclear war compete in George Romero's *Day of the Dead* (1983); black and white playmates unite to capture and then befriend Russians cast adrift in *Russkies* (1987); black and white buddies visit Florida for a fishing tournament in *Gone Fishin'* (1997); and black and white ex-cons team up in *Out of Sight* (1998). Gradually films also stop focusing on race as an issue for the characters.

But these friendships all involve men. With the exception of *Ruby in Paradise* (1993), friendships between black and white women are rare in Florida films. In addition, romantic relationships between whites and African-Americans appear only occasionally in films. One of the exceptions is *Things Behind the Sun* (2001), in which the white female lead continues a close friendship with her former lover, played by Don Cheadle. In *The Break* (1995) a white tennis pro (Vincent Van Patten) reunites with his lost love, an African-American woman. *The Sleepytime Gal* (2001), an independent film, contains scenes suggesting that Rebecca (Martha Plimpton), a white corporate attorney from New York, has a brief fling with Frankie (Jimmy Dupree), the African-American radio station owner. Her assignment in Daytona Beach is to get papers signed transferring station ownership, but she is also searching for her birth mother. Frankie tells her about the good old days, when the "race station" played music that African-Americans couldn't hear at local clubs or on white stations. He also reminisces about a woman who used to work at the station, and it is clear from flashbacks that they had an affair. The woman, unbeknownst to Rebecca, is her birth mother.

Since the 1980s the popularity of black comedians, actors, and musicians has provided opportunities for starring roles in Florida films. Eddie Murphy stars in two Florida-based films, *The Distinguished Gentleman* (1992) and *Holy Man* (1998). In the first the outrageously implausible plot suggests there are flaws in the Florida voting system (!?), permitting

Murphy to get elected to Congress because he has the same name as a dead white Congressman. In *Holy Man* the setting is a Florida television-shopping network. Losing money and ratings, the network is revitalized by the addition of Murphy, an itinerant spiritualist who blends consciousness-raising insights with his sales pitches and becomes a national celebrity. Although Murphy's race is otherwise never referenced, a competing station boss bribes a black welfare mother to claim that Eddie fathered her children and abandoned his family.

Film roles for African-Americans who are stars in music or comedy have continued through the last two decades. In 1987 the rap group Fat Boys released the comedy *The Disorderlies*, an obvious effort to "knock off" the Jerry Lewis film, *The Disorderly Orderly* (1964). In the Fat Boys' version, the rappers are hired by the son of a wealthy, ailing white man to care for his father in south Florida. The son hopes they will soon kill his father because he assumes they are incompetent, but their bumbling accidentally saves the day.

By the 1990s African-Americans appear more frequently in Florida films, playing roles associated with power and success, such as judges, doctors, attorneys, cops, and small businessmen. *Bad Boys* (1995) and *Bad Boys II* (2003) pair Will Smith and Martin Lawrence as cop partners in Miami. The first *Bad Boys* includes little in the plot or dialogue about ethnicity, but the sequel carries the issue to an extreme. Latino villains and local black racism dominate the story line and banter. Similarly *All About the Benjamins* (2002), starring rapper Ice Cube, uses a Florida setting for another crime story, with a black bounty hunter and his petty criminal sidekick solving jewel heists and murders committed by whites. The film's camera angles and scenery evoke the hit television series *Miami Vice*, but like the *Bad Boys* films, *All About the Benjamins* forgoes the obvious racial compromise of including a white and black cop team.

Stereotypical portrayals of black criminals have by no means ended, but the story lines became more complicated in the 1990s. Florida's contribution is *Just Cause* (1995), starring Sean Connery as Paul Armstrong, a law professor who suspects a miscarriage of justice due to racial bias in the murder and rape case against Bobby Earl (Blair Underwood), the African-American defendant. The plot succeeds in keeping the audience sympathetic toward the accused until the ending. Along the way certain members of the NAACP are treated as opportunists who seem to care less about the crime than the history of racial bias in the justice system. Attempting to portray rural justice as an oxymoron, the story is in a time and place that would lead to the assumption that the black defendant is being railroaded, but it concludes by demonstrating that he was just successful at duping white folks. With this turn of events, the film provokes more than one interpretation. On the one hand white liberals (like the law professor-turned-adjudicator) and the NAACP types are fools for jumping to the conclusion that the accused black man is innocent. They are too willing to assume justice could never overcome racism. On the other hand the film's message could be that local police, no matter what race, are better than "outsiders" at identifying violent criminals.

Another "outsider" confronts rural Florida racism in *Rosewood*, the 1997 film by John Singleton. This movie is based on real events involving the 1923 massacre of African-Americans in the town of Rosewood. The small black community was one site of many acts of violence against Florida's black population in the 1920s, a decade plagued by lynchings across the state. A state investigation of the Rosewood events seventy years later ultimately led to greater awareness of racial oppression in this era of Florida history, while also raising further questions about the tragedy. Debates continue about the motives for the crimes, the number of

72. Blair Underwood (*left*) and Ruby Dee, who plays his mother, confronted by the local sheriff (Laurence Fishburne) in *Just Cause* (1995). By permission of Photofest.

73. The lynch mob that terrorizes African-Americans in *Rosewood* (1997). By permission of Photofest.

deaths, and the role of survivors, including law enforcement officials and other whites.

In interviews about his dramatization of events, Singleton explained that his film was not meant to be a documentary. His primary goal was to be "truthful to the essence of what happened."[1] According to the film that essence included economic exploitation, racist law enforcement, ignorance, suspicion, and jealousy, all resulting in mob violence, death, and destruction. The entirely fictitious character inserted into the events by Singleton is Mr. Mann, a World War I veteran played by Ving Rhames. Mann drifts into Rosewood, looking for a place to settle at the same time that rumors spread about a black escaped convict. Mann's arrival also coincides with the claim of a young white woman that she has been assaulted by a black man, an allegation that is eventually expanded to include rape. Singleton said he added Mr. Mann to this true story because of all the African-Americans who fought overseas during the war and then returned to the south with "a whole new mind set."[2] However, the introduction of this character minimizes the role of local African-American men and women in organizing their own escapes.

Another important character in *Rosewood* is Mr. Wright (Jon Voight). As the white owner of the general store and a lecher who turns humanitarian, Wright exhibits a more subtle, and perhaps more modern, form of racism. In his interactions and conversations with Mr. Mann, Wright represents the opportunistic businessman who has exploited blacks in the community and willingly accepted racial segregation in public. In private, however, Wright has sex with his black assistant in the back of the store, emulating the plantation owners of the antebellum South. Only when the town's events spin out of control does Wright feel compelled to take sides, and he wrestles with the decision until nearly the end of the film.

Although *Rosewood* alters details of the events, it still provides a dramatic history lesson for audiences unfamiliar with this era of racist repression. The portrayal of white ignorance and violence is explicit and shocking. Although film receipts during its theater run failed to meet expectations, *Rosewood* has enjoyed more success as a video release.

A less well known film dealing with small-town racism in the 1960s was also released in 1997. *Night Orchid* is an independent film that deserves credit (and viewing) for tackling a subject that still needs more exposure.

Another aspect of African-American history is explored in *Sunshine State* (2002). The location and plot are based on historic changes in the area around American Beach, located on Amelia Island along northeast coastal Florida. Originally established in 1933 as a vacation spot for employees of a major African-American insurance company, American Beach ultimately faced decline as the result of a devastating hurricane, the desegregation of Florida beaches, and increased development of beachfront properties.

In this film, director John Sayles cast former Florida resident Angela Bassett in a starring roles as Desiree. Her generational conflicts with her mother and her parents' entire generation are similar to conflicts motel operator Marly Temple (Edie Falco) has with her own parents in trying to live up to their expectations. Desiree left the fictional Lincoln Beach as a teen, impregnated by a star football player (Tom Wright). As she returns for a visit, he also returns, allying himself with white developers while pretending to help out the local black folk by buying up their property. Older black residents try unsuccessfully to halt white expansion while white small business owners try unsuccessfully to halt corporate chains. Sayles shows that while the struggles faced by both blacks and whites coincide, the families maintain their segregation, never uniting to form a common front against forces directed at their communities.

Although Spanish-speaking people live in every county of Florida, *Sunshine State* includes no Latinos. The major characters are middle-class

African-Americans and whites, but Sayles doesn't portray this small-town environment as an area simmering with racial conflict. Instead he uses the spoken reminiscences of Ralph Waite, as Marly's father, and Bill Cobb, as Desiree's old family friend, to suggest that their generation saw the civil rights movement as disruptive, but in different ways. Cobb laments the loss of good "race men," who catered to black consumers and contributed to black identity, while Waite complains about the domination of blacks in sports. With its casting and plot, the film is more than a story about current controversies over Florida's environmental changes; it is also a story about points of view that are generational rather than racial.

Sunshine State stands out as a Florida film that highlights African-American women. As Desiree reluctantly establishes a new bond with her mother and her mother's delinquent teenage ward, the audience comes to learn about the roles and expectations of African-American women across generations. Viewers also gain some knowledge of how financially successful African-Americans invested in their own communities during the era of segregation.

In addition, Sayles's film touches on Native American issues. An American Indian construction worker is far removed from any tribal identity, despite what others expect. However, he drives the tractor breaking ground on a new development site, only to unearth bones from an ancient Indian burial ground, halting the project.

Since the 1960s filmmakers have continued to make biographic dramas of famous African-Americans to capture audiences and, in some cases, to demystify the heroes, but major studios have been reluctant to finance these films. *Ray* (2004), the biopic about singer Ray Charles, initially had difficulties finding a studio to produce it, so director Taylor Hackford and his cowriter James White carried out the project independently. Later Universal Pictures finally agreed to distribution. Starring Jamie Foxx in an Academy Award-winning performance, the film opens with the singer as a teenager waiting at a Florida country store for a bus to Seattle. Tracing his rise to stardom, the film uses flashbacks to show his impoverished rural life before his brother's drowning death and his blindness, and one scene has him playing with a white Florida country band. His strong-willed mother's determination to make him self-reliant included sending him to St. Augustine's School for the Deaf and Blind (as it was known then). Throughout the film Charles is portrayed not only as a brilliant performer but also as a man who would not allow himself to be limited by circumstances. His drug abuse is explained as an effort to repress bad

74. C. J. Sanders as the young Ray Charles and Sharon Warren as his mother in front of their north Florida home in *Ray* (2004).

memories, but the film offers no explanation for his philandering. In any case Florida seems to have had little effect on Ray's path to stardom; he becomes successful only by leaving the state.

Ali (2003), another biopic that (like *Ray*) received mixed reviews, includes a segment showing Cassius Clay/Muhammad Ali (Will Smith) training at Miami's 5th Street gym for his first championship bout in 1964. Part of that training involved jogging at night, and director Michael Mann has Ali stopped by white cops who yell an all-too-common question, "What are you running from?" There is little else in the film that connects the famous boxer to Florida.

In contrast, the fictional crime drama *Out of Time* (2003), starring Denzel Washington, exemplifies another trend that will hopefully continue, with African-Americans in leading roles, creating interesting and powerful characters in complex plots. Washington plays small-town police chief Matt Whitlock, caught up in a complicated sexual and criminal relationship as his Latina wife and fellow cop (Eva Mendes) sues for divorce. Matt sweats through love scenes and tense chases that use Miami and its suburbs for sets. Chae (pronounced "Che" and played by John Billingsley) is the (white) medical examiner and Matt's best friend who consistently helps him out of difficulties and provides some comic relief. The only explicit references to race, however, are in scenes involving a white woman who comes to the police station during an arson investigation. She is incapable of differentiating between any of the black men she sees at the station and the man she saw wandering in her neighborhood at night; they all look alike to her. *Out of Time* is very much a movie of its time and place, with African-American and Latina leads, and villains who can be of any race. Another groundbreaking aspect of the film is the portrayal of an African-American femme fatale.

Even though Florida is a very ethnically diverse state, home to migrants from all over the Caribbean and Latin America, filmmakers who set their movies in Florida typically include only migrants from Cuba in their story lines. Cubans have moved to Florida for economic and political reasons for well over one hundred years, but they appear infrequently in films until the 1980s. In films from the 1950s, there are references to ties between organized crime and Cubans in Havana (*Miami Exposé* [1956], *Miami Story* [1954], and *The Brothers Rico* [1957]) and to Cuban revolutions (*Santiago* [1957] and *The Gun Runners* [1958]). But focus on Cubans or Cuban-Americans did not increase in films even after large numbers of migrants arrived in Florida during and after the 1959 Cuban revolution. Nor did their visibility rise significantly in the 1970s, when more than one half million had already taken residence in the state.

The earliest film to refer to the large influx of Cubans to Florida was actually about New York Puerto Ricans. *Popi* (1969) stars Alan Arkin as a struggling Puerto Rican in New York City. After busing tables for a banquet of Cuban exiles and getting accidentally caught up in the festivities, Popi learns about the many benefits then offered to Cubans who migrated to Florida illegally. To improve opportunities for his sons, he hatches a scheme to go to Miami and have the boys "rescued" as exiled Cubans from a boat just offshore, their parents supposedly drowned at sea. The boys, speaking through Popi as an interpreter, describe having witnessed their father drown en route. But the scheme initially comes apart over language. The boys don't speak Spanish well, and their first words are vulgarities, which Popi and Anglo state social workers translate to the media as, "We are men of courage." The boys become local celebrities and are invited to the White House. But Popi's efforts to secure better lives for them conflict with his desire to stay with them, and the boys are caught speaking English with their father. The Florida Welfare Department, fearing embarrassment after a huge media blitz, secretly and quietly returns the family to New York. Thirty years later the Elian Gonzalez case contained some striking parallels to this story.

The fault line in portrayals of Cubans and Cuban-Americans is clearly *Scarface* (1983), a story that opens with film footage of Cubans coming to Florida during the 1980 Mariel boatlift. This was another time of con-

75. Two brothers pretending to be Cuban refugees in *Popi* (1969). By permission of Photofest.

flict between the United States and Cuba over immigration policy. Even though the proportion of violent criminals in the boatlift of one hundred twenty-five thousand people was actually small, reports by the media and government claimed that Cuba was "emptying its jails and mental institutions," in a plot to disrupt the United States. Perceptions of a criminal invasion affected Miami-area politics, and some leaders of Miami's Cuban-Americans found themselves on the defensive as a result of negative reactions to the presence of Cubans in the area.

Tony Montana, Al Pacino's character in the film, is an ambitious, violent, volatile figure, whose main objective is making his own opportunities to live the American dream. Montana's criminal career path contrasts with the job choices made by his mother and sister, who pursue factory work and beautician training. He sees himself as the protector of his mother and sister, even though they neither want nor need his protection.

Scarface has achieved a cult status with some audiences, particularly admirers of "gangsta" rappers. The popularity of Tony Montana as a heroic figure, the ultimate "macho man," who lived and died hard, is evident in the sales of T-shirt images, posters, and other promotional products, and the rerelease of the film on DVD in the 1990s. Despite the film's con-cluding disclaimer that its ruthless criminals do not represent the larger Cuban-American community, the fictitious story did contribute to nega-tive images of Miami and Cuban-Americans. Moreover, it set the tone for subsequent films and television shows that depict Cuban-Americans more often as criminals than as contributing members of civil society.

After *Scarface*, Cuban-Americans as drug traffickers and kingpins be-came stock characterizations in Florida crime films. From *Blue City* (1986) to *Bad Boys II*, Cuban-Americans, sometimes in bizarre associations with the Cuban government, are portrayed as primarily responsible for the drug traffic that apparently thrives only in south Florida. Occasionally a Russian immigrant, a Colombian, an Argentine, or a Latino with ambigu-ous national origins gets added to the mix, but the overall emphasis has been on Cuban-American men. Even when portraying cops or politicians fighting illegal drugs, Cuban-Americans are typically cast as corrupt.

Cuban-American women fare only slightly better. They play charac-ters in service to white families (*Blood and Wine* [1996] and *Big Trouble* [2002]), cops (*Out of Sight*, *Wild Things* [1998], and *Out of Time*), and the stereotypical fiery/sexy girlfriends who manipulate men. Cast in differ-ent roles, Jennifer Lopez has become a leading Latina character who plays a U.S. marshal in *Out of Sight* and a nanny in *Blood and Wine*. In the latter she has affairs with both her boss and his son. When she finally extricates herself, she seems to have "gone straight," returning a stolen necklace, but it turns out that she is a thief who has removed one of the diamonds.

76. Jennifer Lopez as a U.S. marshal in *Out of Sight* (1998).

The Cuban refugee experience in Florida has interested filmmakers only as a source of comedy. *The Perez Family* (1995) attempts to examine with humor the difficulties that Cuban exiles experience assimilating in Florida. The funniest thing about the film, however, might be that it continues the practice of casting non-Cuban actors in the leading roles. In another comedy, *Miami Rhapsody* (1995), Spaniard Antonio Banderas plays a Cuban nurse who comes to Florida during the Mariel boatlift and falls in love with the daughter (Sarah Jessica Parker) of a wealthy Jewish family. Colombian-born John Leguizamo plays a Miami Latino, Pestario ("Pest") Vargas, in *The Pest* (1997). Pest is a con artist who owes money to Scottish gangsters and tries to earn fifty thousand dollars by serving as a human target for a visiting sportsman from Germany. Leguizamo dons many ethnic disguises while twisting around some ethnic clichés.

A recent comedy includes roles for Latinas from all over the country, and the Florida Latina hails from South Beach. *Chasing Papi* (2003) pits three women from different towns in the United States against each other as they vie for the attention of a Don Juan-type who is romancing them all. The Miami woman (Sofia Vergara) is a cocktail waitress who dresses more seductively and is brasher than her Latina competitors—a Chicago attorney and a wealthy unemployed New Yorker. The film doesn't attempt to identify the women by any country of origin, however.

The most famous Cuban-American performer for audiences of older generations is, of course, Desi Arnaz. Although he starred in no films set in Florida, some films that associate Miami with Cubans find it necessary to invoke Desi's name. *The Birdcage* (1996), the American remake of *La Cage aux Folles* (1978), uses South Beach for the setting of the drag club. Agador (Hank Azaria), the houseboy working for Robin Williams and Nathan Lane, is from Guatemala. When Williams enters the kitchen one day to find Agador listening to Cuban music and dressed in short shorts, a halter top, and red wig, Agador explains that he is "both Lucy and Desi." Reference to Desi Arnaz is also made in *Revenge of the Nerds II* when the boys rent the "Ricky Ricardo suite," and in *Bad Boys*, when two Latino detectives discuss Lucy and Desi. One observes that "Lucy was the queen, baby. Think about it," but the other responds, "She was a bimbo. What are you talking about? Desi was the whole brains behind the whole thing."

More often filmmakers emphasize the Cuban brains behind south Florida crime. Just as *Scarface* and *Revenge of the Nerds* suggest that the south Florida area has been negatively affected by the presence of low-class Cubans, other Florida films suggest that Cuban immigrants can achieve upward mobility, but only through criminal behavior. These portrayals of Cuban-Americans reinforce stereotypes found in other films about Latinos. Images abound of Latino men who are violent, duplicitous, and money-hungry, yet curiously nice to their mothers and sisters. Occasionally films refer to exile terrorist groups engaging in vendettas. These images are similar to historic film depictions of Italian-American men, who are generally outsiders from Chicago, New York, or Detroit, and have no other business in Florida but crime.

Film portrayals of south Florida as an overwhelmingly Cuban enclave do not quite match statistical realities. While the non-Latino white population in Dade County has been declining in the last fifteen years, so has the percentage of Cubans in the county. The second largest Latino group is Nicaraguan, including those who migrated in large numbers in the 1980s, along with other Central Americans escaping civil wars. To be sure, there are plenty of divisions, but also many alliances within and between immigrant groups. In addition, most significant issues do not involve crime or violence. And in films the simplistic pitting of groups against each other on the basis of ethnicity obscures the more complex interplay of other forces confronting individuals and groups.

In the first half of the twentieth century, a few filmmakers noted another ethnic group that had migrated to the west coast of Florida and developed Tarpon Springs. The interest in Greek-Americans extended only to their roles as sponge divers, however. Perhaps that was because the profession provided the opportunity to develop story lines about a dangerous occupation that offered attractive settings of boat marinas, the open Gulf, and underwater scenes. All the films also include a requisite scene of the yearly Epiphany dive for the cross by young Greek Orthodox men hoping to secure a year of prosperity.

The first of these movies, *Down Under the Sea* (1938), focuses on the conflicts between deep-sea divers and "hookers," men who scooped sponges in shallow waters off Tarpon Springs. The plot's conflict between men who follow the law and those who violate it also involves a conflict over a woman. Along the way the film depicts the lives of Greeks in the Tarpon community and the efforts of one man, a graduate of the University of Florida, to leave the sponging life and enter Columbia Law School.

Appearing a decade later, *Sixteen Fathoms Deep* (1948) stars Lloyd Bridges as a Navy veteran of World War II looking for work at the sponge docks of Tarpon Springs. Here the plot revolves around the efforts of sponge boat operators to secure independence from unscrupulous boat owners, led by an exploitative businessman (Lon Chaney Jr.) who con-

77. Robert Wagner (*left*) and Gilbert Roland on a Tarpon Springs boat in *Beneath the 12-Mile Reef* (1953). By permission of Photofest.

trols the sponge sales. As in *Down Under the Sea*, there are evil Greeks and good Greeks, but their religion and dedication to hard work are treated with respect by the filmmakers.

The better-known *Beneath the 12-Mile Reef* (1953), starring Robert Wagner and Gilbert Roland, approaches Tarpon sponging from yet another angle. The issue is the conflict between Greeks and "Conchs," the Anglo businessmen competing for access to the best sponging sites along the west coast. In all the films Greek men appear to spend every hour of free time in bars, dancing and eating, and the older generation is always much wiser and more honest than the younger. The Greek women are only there to serve and act as love interests.

In film characterizations of ethnic groups identified with Florida, some negative stereotyping has decreased over time. Plots that include Seminoles and Miccosukees tend to be set in modern times, so Florida's first residents are no longer portrayed as savage warriors. Nevertheless they continue to be used in movies to represent wild, unknown, or incongruous aspects of the state's culture. Depictions of African-Americans by white filmmakers have changed more significantly during the past century, thanks to both industry and audience sensibilities. Although there are white and black film producers who still create movies with racially stereotyped characters and situations, the trend is clearly toward plots that are racially neutral. Changes are more apparent in portrayals of African-American males than females, however, as male starring roles and diverse class representations surpass those of women.

Despite over more than forty years of popular identification of Florida with Cuban immigrants, this group has seen the least progress in overcoming negative film stereotyping. On the contrary, Cuban-American Floridians are more likely than any other group to be depicted in the movies as criminal and corrupt. Negative cinematic images of Cubans and Cuban-Americans can be traced to early film stereotypes of other Latinos. Because of geography and immigration, Mexicans were the first Latinos portrayed in Hollywood films. During the 1920s U.S. movies consistently characterized Mexican men as untrustworthy and villainous and Mexican women as lusty and seductive. In response to these derogatory images, Mexico censored Hollywood movies and even boycotted film production companies. Ultimately Mexican resistance to negative stereotypes in U.S. films helped stimulate the rise of a vibrant Mexican industry. Hollywood responded to Mexican pressure by creating more movie plots that used generic Latin American settings and Latino characters with unspecified nationalities.[3] This did not, however, eliminate derogatory images of Latinos in films or other areas of popular culture.

To deflect similar accusations of bias in Florida films, some filmmakers have also created fictional countries or developed plots with Latinos of vague nationalities. However, the growing identification of Florida with Cubans has prompted others to continue the tradition of characterizing Latinos—particularly Cubans and Cuban-Americans—as villains. At times, as in *Scarface*, Cuban-Americans in south Florida have successfully brought attention to film biases, but the overall images have become too pervasive to deal with on a case-by-case basis. Moreover, some films also characterize Cubans still on the island as villains—especially government officials—a depiction that most of the Cuban-American community no doubt applauds.[4] The continuation of the economic and political embargo by the United States against Cuba officially designates that country as an enemy of the United States, further legitimizing negative characterizations. It also ensures limited availability of more positive images of Latinos produced by Cuba's thriving film industry.

Although a variety of characters of different ethnic backgrounds are featured in Florida films, opportunities exist for filmmakers to expand the roles to include people from more ethnic groups that now reside in the state. Among the Floridians missing from films are the ninety-six thousand Asians, two hundred ten thousand French and Creole speakers, one hundred twenty-nine thousand Germans, twenty-five thousand Polish speakers, thirty-two thousand speakers of Arabic, and more than thirty-eight thousand Filipinos.[5] The state's 3.1 million Hispanics (with fifty-five thousand Portuguese speakers) include people from the Iberian peninsula as well as all of Latin America, but filmmakers have historically ignored non-Cubans. And the percentage of Cubans among the Latino population has been declining in recent years, as migration from other regions of Latin America and the Caribbean has increased. Moreover black migration to the state has steadily risen, especially in Broward County. With nearly 2.8 million residents of African heritage, Florida trails only New York. These numbers include both African-American migrants from other states and immigrants from the Caribbean.

If audiences develop their impressions about Floridians based on what they see in films, they will be surprised if they travel around the state. Each of the immigrants has a story of migration to tell; many have experienced dramas that few fictional plots have yet matched. The extraordinary mix of different ethnic groups scattered all over the state has in the past provided the chance for migrants interested in establishing residence and accessing opportunities to assimilate more easily than in many other states. Florida's array of international residents has also apparently made it possible for migrants with more antagonistic goals, like some of the 9/11 hijackers, to blend without being detected. As in other parts of the country, Florida has a history of attributing "good" and "bad" acts of individuals to entire ethnic groups. The state's history is the product of continental and international migration, of racial and ethnic conflict, and of racial and ethnic harmony. Perhaps when the contributions of its many ethnic groups, as well as individual struggles and successes, are better recognized by filmmakers, Floridians and non-Floridians will better understand how much the state is tied to the rest of the world by its people.

Chapter 8

"This stinkpot town. Do you know that women outnumber men ten to one? It's a man's town."

Tony Rome (1967)

Gender-Defined Roles

The earliest Florida feature film to portray switched gender roles was probably *A Florida Enchantment* (1914). The movie also reveals something about the expected social roles and behavior of males and females at the time. When women are transformed into men and adopt male dress, they are accepted as men, engaging in overt flirtation and acts of violence that seem like appropriate masculine behavior. In contrast, when a male takes the magic pills, he becomes childlike, prancing through the streets and daintily lifting his skirt. Despite his effort to feminize himself with lipstick and clothing, he fails to convince the men in the street that he is female, and he/she is chased through St. Augustine by a mob of citizens and police. Such a public display of transgendered behavior is not tolerated.

Later films use the portrayal of men dressed as women for high comedy. This scenario is especially effective in *Some Like It Hot* (1959) because the men in drag are cast with that era's most notorious ideal of female sexuality, Marilyn Monroe. From vaudeville to early television, male co-

medians tried provoking laughs by dressing as females, and the characterizations have become standard in television and films.

In *Girl Happy* (1965) Elvis dons women's clothes to sneak past jail
guards after rescuing his charge (Shelley Fabares) and other jailed women.
Dolled up as a surprisingly attractive female, Presley uses his sensuous
lips and bedroom eyes to carry off the disguise, and he probably delighted
in the scene for two reasons. In 1956, during one of his early concert tours
through three Florida cities, a Jacksonville judge issued an injunction
against Elvis's signature stage contortions for being too prurient. Films
released the singer from such local censorship. By 1965 his displays of
sensuality were so well accepted and identified with virility that he could
dress in drag without audiences questioning his sexual preference. Moreover Elvis so admired Tony Curtis (of *Some Like It Hot*) that he reportedly
dyed his hair black to try to look more like him.

Gays and transgendered characters appear in few Florida films in subsequent decades. In *Midnight Cowboy* (1969) the homosexual acts by Joe
Buck (Jon Voight) may be interpreted as situational. Joe is incensed, after all, when Ratso tells him his cowboy clothes make him "look like a
faggot." "You think John Wayne is a faggot?!" Joe fires back. Once they
arrive in Florida they shed their "New York" and "Texas" clothes, clad-

78. Elvis Presley in a publicity shot for *Girl Happy* (1965). By permission of Photofest.

ding themselves in print shirts that symbolize their new identity with Florida. Joe is also shedding the clothes associated with homosexuality. An alternative interpretation suggests that the audience might accept the character of Joe Buck as a repressed homosexual trying too hard to go straight. In either case Joe displays none of the stereotypically effeminate mannerisms that many filmmakers associate with gays (as in *The Birdcage* [1996]). While making the film, director John Schlesinger was himself struggling with fears that his own homosexuality might be exposed, and this no doubt contributed to the ambiguity of the Joe Buck character.

The few gay or transgender characterizations that followed this movie are limited to the genres of crime and comedies. Moreover, to the extent filmmakers acknowledge the existence of anyone gay or transgendered in Florida, they seem to have decided that all converge in the areas of Miami-Ft. Lauderdale and Key West. *Lady in Cement* (1968) makes this connection by showing a Miami "go-go club" run by a gay man and his partner, a former professional football player. In *Revenge of the Nerds II* (1987), the only significant role for an African-American is as an effeminate male whose behavior presumably forced him into the company of other nerdy "outsider" males. *The Birdcage* is set in a South Beach nightclub and stars Nathan Lane and Robin Williams as lovers with traditional male and female family roles. Unable to "masculinize" himself sufficiently for a visit with prospective in-laws of Williams's son, drag-queen performer Lane dons a more conservative woman's dress and wig to play his lover's wife. When the ruse is revealed, the response of uptight, but not upstanding, Senator Kevin Keeley (Gene Hackman) is disgust, while his wife is more accepting. Male reporters following the Senator delight in the extraordinary news value of the scandal as they watch it unfold.

This rejection of transsexuals by "real men" attempts to be played for even higher comedic effect in *Ace Ventura: Pet Detective* (1994). Here it turns out that a Miami police detective, played by actress Sean Young, is really a man with "issues." His obsession with his missed kick in the Super Bowl pushes him over the edge, leading him to disguise himself as a woman to carry out a revenge scheme. In a final scene, as s/he is forced to undress in front of a crowd of men, someone notices the backside tape job used to suppress his male genitalia. The response of the men gathered is to gag and retch in unison at the sight (and perhaps in painful sympathy). Since Ventura (Jim Carrey) has previously kissed him/her, his response is even more horrified, as he exaggerates (in true Carrey fashion) the need to somehow remove any trace of those male lips from his mouth.

An occasional gay or transgender character appears in crime films. In

79. Nathan Lane in *The Bird-cage* (1996). By permission of Photofest.

Traces of Red (1992) Jim Belushi plays a Palm Beach cop who goes to Key West to find a witness. Among the people he interviews, two are gay. In *Illtown* (1996) the drug kingpin is portrayed as gay. And drag queens, either as performers or undercover cops, are peripheral characters in other crime films. An example is *Big City Blues* (1999) with Giancarlo Esposito as a drag queen trying to decide whether to go through with a sex-change operation. And a maid service in *Smokin' Stogies* (2001) is named the "Cleaning Queens" because the workers are men in drag.

In another film, the sexual preference of one of the male leads is left open to question, but the real story also contains ambiguities. *Bully* (2001), based on an actual murder conspiracy in the Hollywood-Ft. Lauderdale area, does a credible job of telling this bizarre story. The victim is Bobby (Nick Stahl), a late-teenage bully who has brutalized and humiliated his friend Marty (Brad Renfro) over the years. We don't know if there was a real or latent homosexual relationship between the two older teens, but Bobby reportedly includes his friend in making videos of nude men to sell at porno shops, and he engages in other homoerotic behavior. Urged on by his girlfriend and with the assistance of other friends, Marty

80. The out-of-control teenagers in *Bully* (2001). By permission of Photofest.

kills Bobby on the beach. Here, in reality as in the film, is a horrific case of murder and mayhem by a group of seriously maladjusted kids, with hints of young men fascinated by homosexuality.

Given the commonly negative images of gays in Florida films, even small signs of improvement in tolerance are worth noting. *A Murder of Crows* (2001) is set largely in New Orleans, but its story line takes attorney Lawson Russell (Cuba Gooding Jr.) to Key West, where he goes to a Bell South office to get phone records. Russell finds the supervisor, an obviously gay man, very cooperative. As Russell turns to leave the telephone office, the gay supervisor and a woman receptionist both clearly check out his butt, and he looks back and flashes them both a wink.

In contrast, Florida films that portray lesbian characters or females who dress as men are less common. In *The Barefoot Mailman* (1951), twenty-one-year-old Adie Titus (Terry Moore) dons a young boy's attire to try a safer way to get home along the south Florida coast in the early twentieth century. The method works against the local predatory males ("beachcombers") who attack the hiking mailman and other travelers. Once she reveals herself as a female, she becomes a victim, as well as a prize fought over by the mailman (Jerome Courtland) and the film's villain (Robert Cummings).

Film audiences might have assumed there were no lesbians in Florida, at least until *Monster* was released in 2003. Based on the story of Aileen Wuornos, who was executed for killing six men in Florida, the film seems to have misrepresented the real-life relationship between Wuornos and her female companion, Tyria Moore. Some observers have suggested that the filmmakers were hampered because Moore refused to let them portray her, but the film depicts a number of documented events based on Moore's experiences, including a wiretapped phone call between the two after Wuornos was jailed. Many articles, books, and film documentaries about Wuornos are available for anyone interested in checking the accuracy of this independent and award-winning film. Whatever its factual errors, *Monster* is important in part because it dramatizes the story of a rare type of criminal, the female multiple killer. However, in the absence of other feature films that portray lesbian lives in Florida, the film can leave audiences with an image of small-town northern Florida as a place where disturbed women can be driven to lives of crime *and* homosexuality. Criticized by some for portraying Wuornos too sympathetically, the film also includes scenes and references to rape that are rare in Florida films.

Despite the overwhelming popularity of crime films with Florida settings, few of the victims are women, and even fewer of the crimes portrayed are rape. In fact the first female rape victim in a Florida film is a vacationing college student in *Where the Boys Are* (1960). Later the horror/slasher film *Eyes of a Stranger* (1981) uses rape sequences as another element of horror. Produced much later, the film *Just Cause* (1995) examines

81. Charlize Theron (*right*) as Aileen Wuornos and Christina Ricci as Selby in *Monster* (2003). By permission of Photofest.

the case of an African-American accused of rape. Finally a film about a
Florida rape inspired this book. Allison Anders's *Things Behind the Sun*
(2001) incorporates elements of her own personal experience as a child
victim of rape.

The dearth of crimes about rape in Florida films does not mean that
women are not portrayed as victims. They are murdered, conned, turned
out as prostitutes, used as bait to catch criminals, and verbally and physi-
cally abused by husbands, pimps, and boyfriends. In fact the beautiful,
bikini-clad, sun-tanned female victim framed against an idyllic Florida
setting provides exactly the contradictory image that jolts the audience.

From early films through the 1960s, women's roles in Florida films
tended to follow the standard wife/victim/whore characterizations. In
addition to the female tourists who traveled to the state in search of
wealthy husbands, female residents also set their sights on rich spouses.
To find a rich husband, Jewel Courage (Olive Borden) is caught up in
a ruse concocted between a chauffeur and a millionaire in *The Joy Girl*
(1927). Predictably she finds true love and marries the suitor with money.

Since the 1960s women have become increasingly popularized in films
as criminals. Especially following the box office success of *Bonnie and Clyde*
(1967), filmmakers and studios looked for similar themes of women who
worked with men as "gun molls." *Ma Barker's Killer Brood* (1960) actually
inaugurated this trend, but the film was not a critical or box office success. The real-life "Ma" Barker died with her son Freddie in Florida during a shootout with federal agents in Oklawaha, near Lake Wier. *Bloody
Mama* (1970) and *Public Enemy #1* (1991) attempted to capitalize on audience interest in female criminals by offering two more versions of "Ma's"
role in the Barker gang. All of the films inaccurately portray Ma Barker
as the brains behind the crimes committed by her sons and Alvin Karpis.
Public Enemy digresses the most from reality, casting the attractive star
Theresa Russell as a sexy but hardened leader, and suggesting an incestuous relationship with one of her boys. The final shoot-out in Florida is
dramatically "enhanced" in all of the films, but at least *Public Enemy* ends
with a disclaimer about the fictitious nature of the events and persons
depicted.

Little Laura and Big John (1973) makes an attempt to portray the 1920s'
crime spree of Laura Upthegrove (Karen Black), the girlfriend of the real-
life robber/rumrunner/murderer John Ashley. In the film she is not only
a partner, but also at times an instigator. In reality her role was less clear.
For example, one version of history suggests that John, his nephew, and

82. Lurene Tuttle as Katherine Clark Barker holed up in a Florida cabin with one of her sons in a final scene in *Ma Barker's Killer Brood* (1960). By permission of Photofest.

other young men who formed the Ashley Gang robbed a bank in south Florida with one of the men dressed as a woman.

Fictional women murderers have appeared in Florida movies in the last few decades. In *Black Sunday* (1977) the coconspirator of the Super Bowl plot is a Palestinian woman (Marthe Keller) who determines to see the plot through despite the mental illness of her ally, a Vietnam vet (Bruce Dern). She wields a machine gun with ease and is responsible for most of the deaths in the film.

Predictably, films set in Florida have maintained many of the conventions about gender roles that have pervaded movies since the beginning of the industry. For the first half of the twentieth century, films invariably characterized male dominance and female submission and set the conflicts between men and women at the level of sexual tension. Male roles centered on action and work, and plots revolved around struggles for power and control, with action primarily taking place in exteriors and workplaces. Occasionally, men who made wrong decisions in romance or marriage needed to be set straight. D. W. Griffith's *The White Rose* (1923), filmed in New Iberia and Hialeah, Florida, as well as in Louisiana, tells the story of Bessie (Mae Marsh), a young cigar-stand girl who falls in love with her seducer, Joseph Beaugarde (Ivor Novello), a wealthy young man studying for the ministry. After he returns to his plantation to marry someone else, Bessie gives birth to his child, loses her job, and ends up wandering near his estate. She is sheltered by black servants (white actors in blackface) who believe she is near death and summon Beaugarde. Finally convinced that he has made a terrible mistake, he sets things right by marrying Bessie. With women confined to roles that required them to pursue marriage, plots demanded that men do the honorable thing by saving women and/or marrying them.

In Florida films, notions about manliness assume forms that follow national patterns. In Florida westerns, men fight wars against male Seminoles in the Everglades and other rural areas. In pirate films, European men battle each other on the high seas. In films that dramatize the Florida land boom, men buy and sell land and cheat each other. In crime films, leading men murder, fight, scheme, and enforce the law.

The women in early films, however, were mainly confined to interior spaces of the home. As love interests or wives or maids, white female characters either engaged in domestic work or searched for men who would ensure them homes. As wives, their focus was making their husbands happy. An early example of the self-sacrificing woman rescued by an honorable man appears in John Noble's *The Song of the Soul* (1920), which tells the story of a man horribly disfigured after rescuing a blind girl lost in the swamp. He later marries her, and they have a child. After finding a surgeon who can help her regain her sight, her husband displays great anxiety about his wife's reaction if she sees him. So she makes the ultimate sacrifice. When she regains her sight, she looks only at her child, then into a blinding light that sends her back into darkness.

In Florida westerns, when Anglo or Seminole women are placed in exterior settings, they are portrayed as victims, needing male protection. This convention continued in many other movies during the second half of the century. The women in films that highlight the Greek community in Tarpon Springs play similar roles. While men run the businesses, go out on boats, gather sponges, and buy and sell them, women either stay home waiting for them or work in restaurants where they enjoy watching men fight over them.

For decades in crime films, the women characters are either victims or arm candy, unless they play a femme fatale. The femme fatale character is typically a manipulative, untrustworthy opportunist who uses her sexual attraction to lure men into doing some kind of dirty work, usually murder. Through the narrative of the story, the female character is often

83. Michèle Morgan as the femme fatale in *The Chase* (1946).

understood as someone whose behavior is the result of having been victimized somewhere along the way by a vicious or scheming man. If she finally meets the right man—typically the male lead, she is so softened and "domesticated" by his desire that she loses her rough edges and opts for love instead of money or revenge. The central character in film noir, however, is always the male lead, a man desperately torn between moral choices. The earliest Florida film noir is probably *The Chase* (1946), starring Robert Cummings as a down-and-out ex-serviceman pulled into a criminal environment by good deeds, first for a mobster and then for a woman. The femme fatale, played by Michèle Morgan, uses her loneliness and beauty to entice chauffeur Cummings into taking her to Havana. The inability of the antihero to understand the motives and duplicity of the femme fatale is part of what defines this character type.

While most filmmakers chose other settings for classic films noirs in the 1940s and 1950s, *Body Heat* (1981) marked a revival of the style, focusing on Florida. Kathleen Turner's femme fatale character in the film was followed by others, including Madeline Stowe in *China Moon* (1991) and Gina Gershon in *Palmetto* (1998).

The female lead in *Hard Choices* (1984), an independent film, exemplifies a character seen in other recent films—the surprise villain. In this scenario nothing in the early development of the character would lead the audience to expect that the woman could be a criminal. The plot of *Hard Choices* focuses on a social worker (Margaret Klench) who helps a young man drawn into crime by his brother in Tennessee. The audience tends to trust this female character because of her job and behavior. But using a gun, she helps her client escape from jail, and she brings him to Florida, where she continues a past pattern of drug abuse and plans a future of drug running. More recently, unexpected female perpetrators have been featured in films like *Wild Things* (1998), *Wild Things 2* (2004), and *Out of Time* (2003).

Over the past twenty years women's movie roles have included both conventional roles as saviors and more innovative parts as working-class women or professionals. John Sayles's *Baby It's You* (1983) is set in the 1960s and dramatizes the changing expectations of women during that decade. Jill (Roseanna Arquette) is a Jewish girl attending high school in New Jersey and looking forward to college. When she becomes involved with a dapper Italian-American (Vincent Spano) who is a petty criminal and calls himself "The Sheik," he warns her that his goal is to reach Miami, "because that's where Frank Sinatra stays these days." He can't answer her question, "They got any good schools in Florida?" because all he cares about is singing at the Fontainebleau Hotel. After he's forced into a hasty departure, she visits him in Miami Beach, but finds him lip-synching at a club, when he's not working in the kitchen. Jill has not just outgrown him; she finally sees him as deluded. As she continues her education in the north, he becomes a memory of her naive youth.

Diane Keaton in *Marvin's Room* (1996), Claudia Schiffer in *The Blackout* (1997), and several women in *Sunshine State* (2002) play their parts as caregivers. In other films, the traditional role of motherhood is complicated by economic desperation. The leading women in *CrissCross* (1992) and *Striptease* (1996) try to improve their financial situations and take care of their children by working as nightclub strippers.

Female roles as police officers, judges, federal agents, politicians, editors, attorneys, and reporters include both minor and major characters. Both *Up Close and Personal* (1996) and *To Die For* (1995) draw on elements of television anchor Jessica Savitch's life to create quite different narratives about Florida experiences. In the former Tally Atwater (Michelle Pfeiffer) gets her career and romance on track at a Miami television station. In the latter Suzanne Maretto (Nicole Kidman) is an ambitious sociopath who honeymoons in Miami after marrying Larry (Matt Dillon). Spying a famous news anchor at a hotel conference, she gets invited to his table to drink with him and his friends. He recounts a story about

84. Diane Keaton plays the caregiver for her father (Hume Cronyn) in *Marvin's Room* (1996). By permission of Photofest.

a famous newscaster who "earned" her first big break through oral sex, and Maretto plans to try that tactic in her search for a job back home. There she hounds the boss of a small public access cable station for a job, but finds him (Wayne Knight) too unappealing to try out the strategy. Instead she seeks fame by luring a teenage boy into killing her husband.

Another media personality is the subject of *The Sleepytime Gal* (2001). In a series of flashbacks Frances Lake (Jacqueline Bissett) recalls her career as a young disc jockey for night owls at a Daytona Beach radio station. As she dies of cancer, she searches for the daughter (Martha Plimpton) she gave up for adoption. At the same time, her daughter searches for her birth parents in Daytona Beach. But they never connect in this story of remorse and lost chances. And while Frances dwells on the past, she is critical of her son (Nick Stahl), unable to notice that he is either gay or bisexual.

In terms of gender-defined roles, Florida movies fit with national film trends during the twentieth century. Through the 1960s, westerns, crime films, and other dramas generally cast popular male actors in leading roles as heroic, honest, strong, and successful. In films noirs, they tend to be flawed, yet sympathetic, characters who are understandably drawn or forced into criminal acts by beautiful and manipulative women.

The ideal man in movies is expected to protect women and find a wife that he will "settle down" with and support as the family breadwinner.

Only in comedies do male leads fail to demonstrate expected behavior and abilities. Secondary male characters in dramas and adventures may be violent, dishonest, weak, or cowardly, especially in comparison to the film hero. However, as part of the conventional film narrative, these men are destined to come to a bad end.

While many of these images of male traits persist in movies, the development of independent films led to parts for men as characters that increasingly reject traditional gender roles. Leading male characters can suffer from addictions, self-doubts, and cowardice, and they can fail at marriage and in business. In short, heroes and villains can now share common traits.

Traditionally film roles often depicted women as prioritizing marriage and the comfort of their male partners, as well as emphasizing dependence on men for financial support and guidance. Movie women were virginal until marriage—the ultimate goal—and seldom displayed sensuality or sexuality after marriage. In films through the 1950s neither gold diggers nor femmes fatales capture their men by having sex with them. Instead they use flirtation and scheming.

Again, the independent film industry stretched the gender-defined roles for women. Leading roles expanded to include female characters who are single, ambitious, and independent, and who are not necessarily interested in marriage or motherhood as a priority. While plots previously reinforced images of the ideal female as subservient to men and willing to work only until she landed a husband, these views have become less common.

Nevertheless traditional gender-defined roles have certainly not disappeared from movies. The parts available for leading male actors still far surpass those for women. Moreover, since the most common film genre set in Florida remains the action-driven crime film, male characters continue to display strength, fearlessness, and many other supposedly masculine traits. Movies with principal or secondary roles for female characters often emphasize romance or problems faced by unmarried women in nontraditional careers. Finally, while gay and transgendered characterizations have increased in films during the last thirty years, leading roles have been confined to either comedies or dramas that focus on their problems. Although society might debate gender stereotypes, they continue to shape film roles.

Chapter 9

*"[It's] wall-to-wall old people here. . . .
They're never going to die. . . .
Air conditioning keeps them in
cold storage."*

Folks! (1992)

Workers and Retirees

Working people play roles in most films, but the nature of their jobs obviously varies widely. As in society generally, people are defined in part by the work they do, and occupational choices can be shaped by race, ethnicity, gender, and even region. Florida, for example, undoubtedly has more charter boat captains than North Dakota. Many occupations, as well as the retirement that follows, are identified with Florida and figure in films. To some extent movies also reflect dominant economic activities of the eras in which they are set. In the early twentieth century turpentine camps dotted the woods of north Florida, and they appear in several films set in that period. As the tourist industry expanded after World War II, so too did the number of films with characters working in that sector.

The first movies set in Florida generally depicted wealthy residents rather than working-class people. Early silent films like *A Celebrated Case* (1914), *My Lady Incognito* (1916), and *The Confidence Man* (1924) made use of the state's urban setting to tell crime stories and provide moral critiques of the upper class. Well into the 1940s, films portrayed Florida as an important destination, where people from other states connected with rich residents. This theme has not entirely disappeared from movies, but Floridians from other classes have increasingly found their way into the mix of film characters.

Since the 1920s one of the most common occupations in Florida films is the real estate agent. Silent films highlighted Florida's real estate boom in the 1920s, and "talkies" continued to feature often unscrupulous characters manipulating buyers into land deals. As railroads and paved roads brought more upper-class visitors to the state, filmmakers zeroed in on land boom areas along the eastern coast of Florida as settings for several adventures. W. C. Fields's silent movie *It's the Old Army Game* (1926) about Florida and New York real estate deals is set in St. Augustine, and both *The New Klondike* (1926) and *The Cocoanuts* (1929) feature stories about the land boom in south Florida. In most films, male agents lure potential buyers, but in *The New Klondike* a woman (Brenda Lane) plays an important role as the "bird dog" whose job is to "point out human birds for the real estate sharpshooters." The "bird dog" also helps close a deal by disguising herself as a destitute widow eager to sell her land.

Movies generally portray real estate agents and developers negatively. In *The Cocoanuts*, Groucho Marx plays a hotelier-turned-realtor whose shenanigans trying to sell worthless land provide some choice throwaway lines. Real estate agents and developers fare no better in subsequent movies. In *The Barefoot Mailman* (1951), Robert Cummings plays a man who seems well-to-do and honest, but his efforts at trying to con locals into buying worthless land are finally revealed and avenged. As characters, men associated with shady land deals have been lampooned and vilified in more films as the state has become more populated. Contemporary debates about the loss of access to beaches and urban sprawl have ensured that developers continue to be targeted as bad guys in films. There are no portrayals of female developers in films, but Joan Collins appears as a realtor in *The Empire of the Ants* (1977), trying to sell remote island property to gullible buyers.

In the past thirty years some filmmakers have begun to understand the necessary association between developers and government officials, some of whom are dishonest. Politicians on the take have prominent roles in *Honky Tonk Freeway* (1981), *A Flash of Green* (1984), *Coastlines* (2002), and *Sunshine State* (2002). Decision making about Florida land policies actually involves government officials at all levels and various interest groups, as well as businessmen, but the complexity of these interactions is apparently too difficult to portray in movies that conventionally focus on individuals rather than processes. As a result, what emerges from

Florida films dealing with relationships among developers, real estate agents, and politicians are images of these Florida characters as greedy and dishonest.

In the early twentieth century the Sunshine State also increasingly became a destination for tourists, and early movies occasionally depict Floridians who interact with vacationers. Initially they are black and white servants working in hotels or police trying to handle the crimes that tourists commit. White Floridians are otherwise present only as members of the upper-class society who mingle with wealthy tourists. In most cases the rich appear frivolous, status-conscious, and idle. Directed at lower- and middle-class audiences, these films express messages that dominate many films of the era. Wealthy people act as though they deserve better treatment, but they demonstrate no particular attributes that make them merit it. Many plots suggest that rich people deserve to be exploited or lampooned. W. C. Fields made use of these perceptions in *It's the Old Army Game*. Finally forced to spend time with his family, he drives them onto the well-manicured lawn of an estate, where they set up a very messy picnic. "Imagine," Fields muses, "a man built a house in the middle of a beautiful lawn." Fields then proceeds to raid the house, whose owners are obviously away for the season, and he tosses valuable objects on the lawn, leaving the area in shambles.

Although Hollywood had displaced Florida as a film production center by the 1940s, filmmakers continued to focus on wealthy south Florida men as potential victims of gold-digging women. While film codes encouraged filmmakers to make sure that the plots ultimately prioritized love over money, the view of south Florida as awash in unsuspecting millionaire men waiting to be parted from their money remained a constant theme.

In contrast, few Florida films deal with males attempting to hustle wealthy women. One exception is *The Happening* (1967), a crime drama featuring four Miami Beach bums, one of whom survives by romancing wealthy older women. A more recent exception is the film *Wild Things* (1998), in which a male Lothario (Matt Dillon) tries to con a wealthy widow (Theresa Russell) out of an estate she inherited from her developer husband. In both cases these con men end up getting what they deserve, and the films reject the happy ending of love and sacrifice.

Movies seldom explain how the wealthy "marks" made their money. Was it on Wall Street, through organized crime, or in Florida real estate? And are they really Floridians or are they seasonal visitors? Since box office stars usually portray central characters in the films, neither the

85. Ronald Reagan playing a farm worker in *Juke Girl* (1942). By permission of Photofest.

millionaire patsies nor the working-class gold diggers from other states are characterized entirely negatively. These portrayals, however, started to change after the 1940s, as nearly all wealthy men and women living in Florida increasingly become stylized as either corrupt or criminal and, as a result, decidedly unsympathetic figures.

Florida has long attracted farmworkers among its many migrants, but they are rarely portrayed in films. *Juke Girl* (1942) may be the only one to organize its plot around migrant workers. Although it was filmed in California (the mountain ranges in the background are a dead giveaway), the Florida setting was probably chosen in order to exclude images of Latino farm laborers who dominated work in the California fields. It seems clear, however, that the filmmakers did not visit Florida fields in the 1930s or early 1940s, a time when mostly African-Americans labored there for low wages. The only African-American in *Juke Girl* is Jo-Mo (Willie Best), a buffoonish character who sells small packets of "good luck jo-mo" [sic] on street corners. Nevertheless the movie presents a clear critique of the exploitation of farm labor, as well as the living conditions at the tent-city camp.

The film opens with Steve (Ronald Reagan) and Danny (Richard Whorf) walking down a railroad track and heading for Cat Tail, Florida, the "Salad Bowl of America." After getting work on a farm, they face the loss of their jobs when the tomato packager threatens to reduce the price he'll pay the grower. Steve and Danny go to the grower's aid and hijack a truck to cart the tomatoes to Atlanta, paying Jo-Mo fifty cents to kick up dust on a field to aid their escape. Steve and Danny eventually split up over strategies and priorities and then reconnect, but when Steve urges Danny to stay and continue working on the farm, he declines, saying, "I'd go crazy in the swamp." The plot suggests that the world of migrant labor is violent and dangerous, with fistfights, murder, and even an attempted lynching. It also suggests that the produce growers are natural friends of the migrant workers and that both groups are equally exploited by packagers and processors.

Ann Sheridan plays the sarcastic juke girl in the familiar role of a hardened, unhappy woman who survives by singing at juke joints. As she becomes entangled in Steve's conflict, she emerges as a more dependent, docile woman, eager to please him and make him a home. Although no match for the film adaptation of John Steinbeck's *Grapes of Wrath*, *Juke Girl* is still worth seeing for a rare focus on a central issue in Florida.

The Yearling (1946) was the first significant film to portray rural Floridians as hardworking, respectable citizens. Adapted from Marjorie Kinnan Rawlings's Pulitzer Prize-winning book, the film initially began production in the Ocala forest in 1941, but faltered due to problems with the environment, actors, and directors. With a new cast and a new director, production finally renewed in 1945. This time the studio hired a number of locals as consultants, including Troy Hudnell, who were supposed to teach rural dialect and mannerisms to Gregory Peck, the new Pa Baxter.[1]

"Southern" drawls, twisted vocabulary, and ungrammatical constructions are presumably immediate clues that identify film characters as rural—and usually, also uneducated. Rural southerners became negatively stereotyped in much more significant ways as city dwellers increasingly defined urbanization and technology as measurements of progress or "civilization." These stereotypes identified so-called hillbillies and other rural people as more violent, lazy, gullible, dirty, hard-drinking, and prone to incest and shotgun weddings.[2]

Throughout the nineteenth century, rural white Floridians were portrayed in similar ways as southern hillbillies, even though they did not live in "hills" (those isolated regions lacking modern amenities). In Florida rural folk were long referred to as *crackers*. The origin of this term is uncertain, but it was used by white observers to identify rural white

86. Jane Wyman, Claude Jarman Jr., and Gregory Peck in *The Yearling* (1946). By permission of Wisconsin Center for Film and Theater Research.

Floridians in the nineteenth century and much of the twentieth century. One Civil War-era writer described crackers as "much less human than the Negroes, more ignorant, dirty, and lifeless; many of them look as if they had already been buried for months."[3] In 1880 a travel writer wrote about the "hybrid bipeds . . . called crackers," who "spend a portion of the [summer] season in raising a little corn and potatoes . . . which [are] consumed by their numerous families." Moreover, "Many of them never 'hire out,' but subsist entirely by hunting, fishing, or gathering berries, for which pursuits their wild natures and unsettled habits well adapt them." According to this author, crackers were ignorant, illiterate, dishonest, and stingy. Chewing tobacco or dipping snuff, male crackers kept dogs as constant companions and hogs as their main livestock. In addition to broad-brimmed hats braided from palmetto leaves, they wore deerskin vests and brown jean coats and breeches, and their mustaches and whiskers were always unkempt.[4]

Early twentieth-century films typically portray hillbillies as moonshiners who engage in irrational feuds (usually involving a hog) and as people who reject city ways out of ignorance and superstition. Men and women always have their trusty rifles handy and are quick to use them against outsiders. When Marjorie Kinnan Rawlings lived among Florida crackers, she did see guns, moonshine, and lives untouched by much of modern technology. But she also came to know rural Floridians as honest, hardworking, and considerate. Moreover, her interest in the struggles and strengths of rural Florida women meant that she made them central characters in several of her Florida stories.

Despite the differences between the Rawlings book and the film adaptation in character development (and in the simplification of the story), the movie version of *The Yearling* has become a classic for its realistic portrayal of the rural Florida environment and its people. Ma and Pa Baxter and their neighbors are challenged by the elements—heat, heavy rain, disease, and accidents—and work hard to sustain themselves and rear productive and independent children. Most are honest and kind, but also pragmatic and stoic.

In contrast the south Florida crackers in *Wind Across the Everglades* (1958) include men who survive by killing wild pigs and other animals and women who stop by occasionally on large boats loaded with produce, selling scarce goods and their bodies. Most of the swamp people are violent, filthy, and ignorant rejects from various other jobs. Villainous leader Cottonmouth, giving orders from his big rattan chair covered with a bear

87. A group of Florida crackers, led by Chuck Mitchell (*second from right*), in *Porky's* (1981). By permission of Photofest.

pelt, seems completely lacking in sentimentality and has no qualms about using his many weapons.

A more sympathetic cracker from the early twentieth century appears in *Gal Young "Un* (1979), the second Rawlings story made into a film by Victor Nuñez. The central character is Mattie Siles (Dana Preu), a pipe-smoking, middle-aged rural woman who has inherited a working farm, a modern house, and income from her father's turpentine camps. The story centers on Mattie's loneliness and gullibility, as she is duped into marriage by a manipulative young moonshiner with his eye on her financial assets. The film follows Mattie's increasing exploitation by the no-good Trax (David Peck) and her foolish willingness to endure his absence and cruelty. When he brings another female, called Gal (J. Smith-Cameron), to live with them and then abandons the two women for another moonshining trip, we anxiously await the point at which Mattie will finally say "enough." She is either unbelievably naive or desperately stoic. The ending finally relieves the viewers' frustrations about Mattie's behavior, but she takes too long to react. Moreover the film's ending also fits stereotypes about rural women. Like a Mammy Yokum-style hillbilly, Mattie dons her floppy felt hat and grabs her shotgun. In seeking revenge against a shiftless, no-good, moonshining man, she follows the conventional behavior of rural southern women as portrayed in early silent films, such as *The Moonshiner* (1904) and *A Mountain Wife* (1910). After destroying the still, Mattie sets fire to Trax's modern car and aims her rifle at him as he approaches. Refusing to believe she would shoot, he comes closer, and she blows off his toe. Trax makes tracks, as well as he can, and Mattie and Gal form a loose bond based on their common experience.

Written in 1938, and filmed much later as the women's rights movement progressed, Rawlings's story digressed from early plots that had women challenging, then acquiescing to patriarchal control. In hillbilly-gal silent films, as one analyst noted, the vast majority of the stories "ended in traditional matrimony, with the former gals becoming 'ladies' because they accepted the weaker role and financial dependency."[5] Mattie's story rejects that outcome, leaving the impression that Mattie finally realized she did not need a man in her life.

In most films from the 1980s and 1990s, Florida crackers tend to be portrayed as violent, racist, and lazy, and they speak with deep southern drawls. Another Rawlings film, very loosely based on the story of her life in rural northern Florida, was released in 1983. *Cross Creek*, starring Mary Steenburgen as Marjorie Rawlings, reinforces some traditional views of rural Florida men and women, but also portrays them sympathetically.

88. Mary Steenburgen as Marjorie Kinnan Rawlings and Rip Torn as Marsh Turner in *Cross Creek* (1983). By permission of Photofest.

Rip Torn, as Rawlings's neighbor, supplies her with moonshine and infuriates her when his hog roots in her garden. But he also tries to take care of his poor family and treats Rawlings with respect. His wife is depicted as someone more refined than he, but slowly losing her mind. The audience is led to believe that this is a result of the boredom and sense of isolation created in the backwoods. Rawlings's associations with rural Floridians provided her with rich sources for characters, but this particular film fails to portray either the author or her subjects with the depth that her writing and her biographers have revealed.

Contemporary films present rural Florida women as repressed by dominant men or as hardworking, devious, and ambitious, like the Suzis in *Wild Things* and *Miami Blues* (1990). Cracker men include the bib-overall, hick stereotypes who still haunt bars, shoot pool, and threaten crimes, as in the films *The New Kids* (1985) and *Trash* (1999). In comedies cracker men are objects for audience derision; in dramas they are agents of danger.

Some directors have recognized these stereotypes and challenged then. When Joe (Joe Pesci) and Gus (Danny Glover) finally arrive at their rundown fishing camp in *Gone Fishin'* (1997), Joe observes, "It sure doesn't look like paradise, Gus." The two soon meet the owner, a skinny man in baggy clothes, who spits tobacco juice from his front porch and directs them to their rental—a dilapidated trailer. The next morning as Joe and Gus leave, the owner's appearance is the same, but his disheveled wife joins him on the porch rocking chairs. She has almost completed a crossword puzzle and asks him for help: "What's blank 'Shrugged,' five letters?" Her husband responds, "*Atlas Shrugged*, by Ayn Rand." Clearly the message here is that not all crackers are ignorant. Country singer Willie Nelson also has a role in the film, playing a fishing expert Joe and Gus admire on television. When the men are kidnapped and tied up in a swamp cabin by a thief and murderer, Nelson suddenly appears out of nowhere to save them, carrying them to safety in an airboat. Like a misty apparition Nelson acts as savior and adviser, leading the men to freedom and notoriety for catching a thief. Similarly, the rural community depicted in *Dunsmore* (2003) is described by an outsider as looking like "Mayberry RFD," but its sheriff reads Aristotle.

For many decades African-Americans have used the term *cracker* to describe any southern white racist. But for most Floridians cracker has generally lost its pejorative and rural meanings, to become part of a modern self-identity. The reasons for this are twofold. First, as migrants to the state increasingly included people from other countries, more Floridians have used the term to differentiate themselves from all "outsiders." Second, the proportion of Floridians born in the state has just about kept pace with the number of migrants over the last thirty years. Being a Florida cracker now usually means someone who was born in the state, regardless of the kind of job the person has or where s/he lives. Some might debate whether one becomes a cracker by virtue of living in the state for most of her/his life, but that debate raises the much larger question of what particular attributes it takes to be a Floridian.

Aside from workers in the tourist industry, few other lead characters come from the working class, but the circus provides an exception. *The Greatest Show on Earth* (1952) is a popular, award-winning film about circus people who winter on the west coast of Florida. Although the characters in the film are not residents of the state, the film no doubt reinforced the association of Florida with circus people. Jerry Lewis stars in and directed *Hardly Working* (1980), a film about a down-and-out Florida clown. After failing in other jobs (all of which are taken from his past films), he gradually learns a skill as a postal worker. It's the perfect opportunity, he is told by his brother-in-law, because "no one loses a civil service job unless he wants to." Lewis fails to find fulfillment delivering mail, however, and decides in the end that it is better to be a clown than a mail carrier. The bizarre film *Wilder Napalm* (1993) casts Dennis Quaid as the circus-

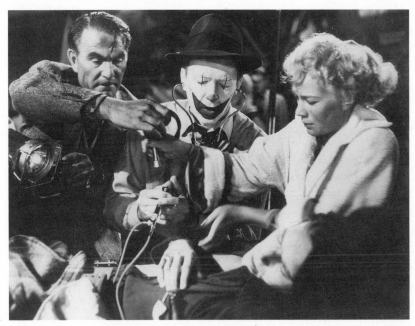

89. James Stewart (*center*) and Betty Hutton as circus performers in *The Greatest Show on Earth* (1952). By permission of Photofest.

clown brother of Arliss Howard, stopping to exchange pyromaniac skills on his way to Frostproof, Florida. And in *The First of May* (2000) Julie Harris plays a former circus performer who escapes her nursing home to find a lost love at the circus.

Service workers like Jennifer Jason Leigh in *Miami Blues* and Goldie Hawn in *CrissCross* (1992) are seldom the main characters in films. Leigh's character once worked at Burger World and has delusions of better things while she survives as a hooker. *CrissCross* dramatizes an adolescent boy's discoveries about himself and his surroundings during one hot summer in Key West. As the boy's mother Hawn struggles to survive on low wages as a waitress and as an unsuccessful stripper. When the boy gets caught up in drug deals run by local fishermen, and his mother becomes romantically entangled with an undercover agent, the helplessness and hopelessness faced by working-class people in Florida are starkly portrayed. All of these characters—the men working the fishing boats, the men running the restaurant and dealing drugs, the boy, his fleeing alcoholic father, and his mother—try to escape their current conditions. Their efforts invariably fail.

Ruby in Paradise (1993) also highlights service workers. Ruby (Ashley Judd) gets a job in a tourist shop, but she also briefly works in a laundry and considers working as a stripper. Victor Nuñez, the film's writer/director and a Florida native, pointed out in an interview that his inspiration for story lines comes from his characters, not the location: "You can show people that something they thought was their private, personal pain is also universal. One of the things I have always admired about growing up in north Florida is the ways normal people have in connecting to their deeper selves."[6]

Dramas about the struggles of working-class Florida men have become more common in the past twenty years. *Harry and Son* (1984) stars Paul Newman and Robby Benson. Newman plays an aging demolition worker who considers his life a failure. Emotionally distant from his children, Harry suffers continuous mental and physical decline, while his son works to establish a bond that never materializes. A similar characterization of the remote father casts Peter Fonda as a beekeeper trying to run a honey-canning business in north Florida in Victor Nuñez's 1997 film *Ulee's Gold*. Like other recent films that focus on working-class characters in Florida, the movie tends to contrast the expectations of peaceful, idyllic environments with the harsh realities of making ends meet.

Florida dramas and comedies usually portray politicians and bureaucrats as corrupt, hypocritical, or inept. The social worker assigned to help

90. Ashley Judd (*right*) and Allison Dean play clerks in a tourist shop in *Ruby in Paradise* (1993). By permission of Photofest.

91. Eddie Murphy in *The Distinguished Gentleman* (1992). By permission of Photofest.

the Kwimper family in *Follow That Dream* (1962) immediately tries to seduce Elvis instead of assisting the family, and then conspires to get even when he rejects her. The corrupt (and lusty) U.S. Senator played by James Garner in the comedy *The Distinguished Gentleman* (1992) is replaced by a petty criminal (Eddie Murphy), who gets elected because he has the same name. Corrupt Department of Transportation officials and a corrupt governor deal with a corrupt mayor in *Honky Tonk Freeway*. A city councilman (Gordon Clapp) in *Sunshine State* takes kickbacks from developers and fails at every attempt to commit suicide. Immigration officials take bribes to release detainees in *Scarface* (1983). County Commissioner Elmo Bliss (Richard Jordan) schemes for a development project in *A Flash of Green*. Congressman David Dillbeck (Burt Reynolds) is in league with sugar interests in *Striptease* (1996). Florida films seldom portray politicians and bureaucrats, but as this list demonstrates, they most commonly appear in comedies or in contemporary films about land projects. Whether audiences would prefer to see more of these characters or not, filmmakers seem uninterested in characterizing them in any positive way.

Most workers eventually retire, and given the popular and valid image of the Sunshine State as a retirement center, we should anticipate that films would reinforce that perception. However, films have few starring roles for older people, and when they do get such parts, they are typically in the sci-fi and comedy genres rather than in dramas. For the most part retirees and older people are simply part of movie backgrounds, where they reflect the image of Florida as home to an aging population.

The *Cocoon* films (1985, 1988), *Folks!*, and *The Crew* (2000) cast older white stars and character actors in the roles of retirees with various types of mental and physical problems. In *Cocoon* and its sequel, characterizations predictably include an aging Lothario, a bitter widower, and two couples (one with a debilitating disease). Moreover, male characters lead the way to rejuvenation by breaking into the closed pool area and bathing with the pods. The women are later converts, following their husbands' leads. And with their new youthfulness, the men focus on sex and sports, while the women enjoy family and makeovers. The aliens in the pods appear with no genitalia, but are always referred to as "he"—masculine life-givers of energy and health. Although statistics show that women have longer life spans, the women die before their husbands in both *Cocoon* films.

Cocoon initially depicts the retirees as suffering from disease, mental decline, boredom, and neglect—common images of retiree life. To extend their lives and health, some leave Florida—which is not a paradise for the elderly, after all—to find a more promising utopia on a distant planet. But the debate about staying or leaving always centers on the question of whether or not they should go through a "natural" aging process and die "normally." Given the increase in surgical procedures and life-extending drugs in recent years, this debate now seems vaguely quaint. As in other retiree films, none of the characters here is a Florida native.

In the movies Florida retirees all come from somewhere else, and few live in their own homes. Instead they reside in trailer parks, nursing homes, and boarding houses. In *Folks!*, when Tom Selleck tries to rescue his Alzheimer-stricken father (Don Ameche) from various disasters in his south Florida trailer park, the story is an attempt at humor. It is difficult, however, to find humor in children's efforts to care for parents with Alzheimer's.

Apparently one means of rejuvenation for elderly women is to team up with troubled young boys. In *The First of May*, when retiree Julie Harris runs away to the circus, she joins up with a young boy running away from a foster home. Together they reconnect with Julie's old circus folk, meeting with the gruff and greedy manager, played by Mickey Rooney. Joe Di Maggio, in his last film appearance, gives the boy tips on playing baseball. Once the foster parents find their son and also take in Harris, a "normal" three-generation family is formed. In *Marvin's Room* (1996) the

92. Diane Keaton and her nephew (Leonardo DiCaprio) driving on the beach in *Marvin's Room* (1996). By permission of Photofest.

character played by Diane Keaton is temporarily rejuvenated by a bond she establishes with her nephew (Leonardo DiCaprio), enjoying a rare moment of excitement as he careens her car along the beach and into the surf. Finally, in *Great Expectations* (1998) the "grande dame" character (Anne Bancroft) has mental problems that keep her from seeing the reality of her environment, her condition, or the people around her. But she finds some comfort and companionship in frequent visits over the years by Finnegan Bell (played by Jeremy Kissner and Ethan Hawke).

The Crew may be the best film featuring Florida retirees. Burt Reynolds, Richard Dreyfuss, and Seymour Cassel play former northern wise guys who are living out the remainder of their lives in a South Beach rooming house. To avoid expulsion as their neighborhood is gentrified, the men revert to their old mobster tactics. But nothing works exactly as it did in their youth, including their bodies, so mistakes get them into deeper trouble. Joey "Bats" Pistella (Reynolds) is a curmudgeon who wants to die. He occasionally becomes catatonic, but always revives with a brilliant new insight. Losing another job at Burger King doesn't help his mood, but as Bobby (Dreyfuss) argues in a voice-over, "Once you're over sixty you shouldn't have to answer to a young punk named Skippy." Bobby is depressed and lonely, searching for a lost daughter he ultimately finds in Miami, while Tony "The Mouth" Donato (Cassel) only speaks after sex with hooker Ferris Lowenstein (Jennifer Tilly). The film offers lots of gags and jokes about aging men and also causes us to wonder just how many retired criminals live in Florida.

If Santa Claus decided to retire, where would he go? *Ernest Saves Christmas* (1988) assumes the answer is Florida. When Santa arrives by plane in Orlando, Ernest P. Worrel (Jim Varner) helps Santa find a successor to fly the sleigh. After many difficulties, the deliveries finally get arranged, and a northern transplant gets one of his holiday wishes—it snows in Florida on Christmas.

One sizable population of Florida retirees is quite underrepresented in movies. Jewish retirees from the north started to make Miami Beach a popular destination in the 1940s, and the Jewish population of all ages has expanded throughout the state. Despite this there are very few depictions of Jewish retirees or workers in Florida films. Walt's love interest in *Wind Across the Everglades* is a Jewish girl, Naomi, the daughter of the general store owner. In *The Godfather: Part II* (1974), one of the aging Miami mobsters, loosely modeled after Meyer Lansky, is Jewish. In *The Crew,* Ferris Lowenstein blackmails the retired mobsters so they will kill her Jewish stepmother. Occasionally in films groups of aging Jewish women appear as targets of politicians seeking votes in community centers or as part of the background, sitting on the porches of rooming houses. A rare case of a film with Jews in central roles is *Miami Rhapsody*

93. Richard Dreyfuss, Seymour Cassel, Dan Hedaya, and Burt Reynolds play retired mobsters in *The Crew* (2000). By permission of Photofest.

(1995), which features Sarah Jessica Parker as the middle child of afflu-
ent Miami Jews. She visits her grandmother's nursing home, where her
mother's lover (Antonio Banderas) energizes the aging Jewish residents.
Like *The Pest* (1997) the film takes great liberties with stereotypes in its
attempt at comedy. In a more recent comedy, *Meet the Fockers* (2004),
Dustin Hoffman and Barbara Streisand play Ben Stiller's Jewish parents
living in Cocoanut Grove. As a couple of free spirits, Roz Focker teaches
sexual techniques to senior citizens in her home, and her retired husband
Bernie practices *capoeira* and takes care of household tasks.

Non-Floridians might associate certain kinds of jobs and professions
with the state either because they have been to the state or because they
develop opinions from other sources. If they have been tourists, the
chances are good that the only people they have met are associated somehow with the tourist industry. Non-Floridians visiting friends or family
members in Florida get to know the state in a slightly different context,
understanding that jobs in the state resemble those found elsewhere. But
movies set in Florida also play to audiences whose only knowledge of the
state is likely to depend on what is portrayed by the mainstream media
in news stories, in state tourist promotions, and in novels and films.

In Florida movies many workers and retirees struggle with financial
and personal problems, giving them little time to enjoy the pleasures offered by living in the Sunshine State. The contrast between work and leisure is particularly evident in Miami crime films, as men and women in
law enforcement fight crime amidst tourists relaxing by pools, dancing,
fishing, gambling, and playing golf.

Over the course of the twentieth century, films set in Florida gradually expanded the range of occupations pursued by leading characters. In
the early decades of the twentieth century, few movie plots centered on
Floridians, and these typically portrayed nineteenth-century plantation
owners or professionals of the era. As the state land boom captured the
attention of filmmakers, dishonest low-to-middle-class real estate agents
were added to the cast of characters and have remained in main and secondary roles ever since. Similarly, as the state has become more identified with tourism over the past seventy years, the number of principal
or secondary movie characters who serve tourists has increased. These
roles are more likely to include bellhops, wait staff, small motel and hotel
owners, and charter boat captains, than wealthy owners of big tourist
businesses.

Even before the Great Depression, filmmakers had tired of plots that
focused only on the rich, and after World War II, films told more sto-

ries about members of the working class—circus workers, sponge divers, amateur athletes, and farmers. At the same time, the popularity of crime movies ensured that the most common characters in Florida films are associated with law enforcement, and the main characters are likely to be cops involved in action-packed adventures, not judges or attorneys busy with paperwork. The wealthy have traditionally been depicted negatively in films and that perspective has not changed much, especially if their riches have been acquired illegitimately. However, movies rarely portray the bulk of the state's middle-class workers—in education, government, health care, communication, manufacturing, travel, and other professions. And working-class Floridians—in mining, ranching, farm labor, and construction, to name a few—seldom fit into the crime stories that dominate the big screen.

Although Florida has also been associated with retirement for many decades, filmmakers have shown little interest in telling stories about retirees. Retirement-age Floridians have appeared with greater frequency in the last thirty years as part of the background of movie scenes, often in contrast to the more active lives of the main characters. In addition, stereotypes abound in films about gray-haired, bald, quirky, poorly dressed, confused, and inactive retirees.

Once again we must credit independent filmmakers with successfully depicting some of the state's more interesting, if less well known characters. In both major and minor roles, some of these characters are memorable, including the beekeeper in *Ulee's Gold*, souvenir shop workers in *Ruby in Paradise*, and the military reenactor and the traveling alligator handler in *Sunshine State*. As these films demonstrate, opportunities clearly exist for future filmmakers to expand the list of jobs held by Florida characters. However, financial considerations tend to encourage studio executives to follow successful movie formulas, as measured by box office receipts. Thus the mix of jobs and professions portrayed in films has been somewhat repetitive, undoubtedly reinforcing the viewers' perception of the state as mainly populated by criminals, cops, tourists, real estate developers, and old folks.

Chapter 10

Warriors and Heroes

From the wars against the Native Americans to the Civil War, Florida has experienced military action, and the state is also home to many veterans of foreign wars. Florida's connections to piracy, war, and warriors captured the attention of filmmakers throughout the twentieth century.

U.S. wars against the Seminoles in Florida are the subject of several 1950s' films, including *Distant Drums* (1951), *Seminole* (1953), *Seminole Uprising* (1955), and *Naked in the Sun* (1959). Most members of the U.S. military are portrayed favorably in these films, as justifiably dedicated to the task of subduing resistant enemies. Two films also deal with Civil War soldiers, but much less favorably. Both *Shark River* (1953) and *Yellowneck* (1955) portray Civil War deserters as unsavory cowards who ultimately get what they deserve at the hands of the indigenous people whose territories they traverse.

During the Spanish-Cuban-American War (1895–1898), Florida was an embarkation point for Cuban exiles returning home to fight and for U.S. troops sent to support the independence war. A rare film dealing with the era is *Santiago* (1956), starring Alan Ladd as gunrunner Caleb "Cash"

Adams. Court-martialed and discharged from the Army after an incident during one of the Indian wars, Adams becomes a mercenary, and in 1898 he is selling guns to Tampa Cubans for the independence war against Spain. When forced to take supplies directly to Cuba, he meets José Martí (who actually died in 1895), falls in love with a Cuban woman, and becomes dedicated to the cause. Since Florida played a central role as a site for political organizing and fund-raising by Cuban exiles and as a staging area for Rough Riders and other fighters, it is surprising that filmmakers have shown so little interest in developing plots that deal with the era.

In comparison, the two world wars sparked more interest by filmmakers. Although fewer films deal with U.S. soldiers from the Great War, an early example is *The Flying Ace* (1926). The hero is Billy Stokes (J. Lawrence Crimer), who earned his reputation as a pilot in Germany and as a crime-solver in Mayport, Florida. Two years later *The Mating Call* was released, starring Thomas Meighan as returning war veteran Leslie Hatton. During his absence his wife has annulled the marriage and remarried, but she still loves him. The new husband, Lon Henderson (Alan Roscoe), heads the local Ku Klux Klan, and when one of his despondent lovers drowns herself on Hatton's farm, Henderson decides to get even. He brings Hatton before a KKK tribunal, which exonerates him. Hatton moves on with his life and his new bride, a Russian aristocrat he met at Ellis Island.

The fictional character Mr. Mann (Ving Rhames) in *Rosewood* (1997) also served in the Great War. The film provides no understanding of what he has been doing since his separation from the service, but it sheds light on how the war affected many African-American troops. Mann is bitter about the assignments African-Americans received in the segregated service. The white owner (Jon Voight) of Rosewood's general store fought in the Philippines during the Spanish-Cuban-American War, and he tries in one conversation with Mann to establish a loose bond, based on their common experiences. But Mann makes it clear their war experiences were incomparable.

U.S. veterans of the Spanish Civil War (1936–1939) have seldom interested filmmakers in the United States. A Florida exception is a minor role in the comedy *Two Much* (1995), which has Sherman Dodge (Eli Wallach) sharing problems that his son (Antonio Banderas) has created for himself in Miami. Sherman and his fellow vets continue in their old age to write letters protesting government policies.

By World War II Florida contained a number of military bases and training schools that drew thousands of men and women. One of the

94. Ving Rhames as Mr. Mann, a veteran of World War I, in *Rosewood* (1997). By permission of Photofest.

early dramas to highlight this military role for Florida is *Over 21* (1945). The film features Polly Wharton (Irene Dunne) as a novelist and screenwriter who joins her husband Max (Alexander Knox) in Florida. He has resigned as editor of a northern newspaper to do his part for the war, and he is struggling through Army Officers Candidate School at Tetley Field. To save the newspaper and to offer her spouse the chance to graduate and go off to war, Polly writes his editorials. The moral here is that every family member needed to play a part in the war effort.

The positive experiences of soldiers who passed through the state during World War II drew many of them back after the war. These migrants included men like Chuck Scott (Robert Cummings) in *The Chase* (1946). An honest man now without work and suffering from post-traumatic stress disorder, he performs a good deed and is pulled into a deadly affair. Frank McCloud (Humphrey Bogart) in *Key Largo* (1948) is also a vet, carrying a message to his friend's wife (Lauren Bacall), who migrated to the Keys during the war. In *Slattery's Hurricane* (1949), Will Slattery (Richard Wid-

95. A publicity photograph for *Slattery's Hurricane* (1949), starring Richard Widmark (*far left*). By permission of Photofest.

mark) has ended up in Miami after his dismissal from the Navy. He had been charged with violating orders as a pilot, but while he's in Florida, the Navy reverses itself and awards him the Navy Cross. Now a civilian pilot, he recklessly flies into an approaching hurricane to provide weather information, and his success encourages him to reenter the service.

Ray Douglas (Lloyd Bridges) is another Navy vet, a diver looking for work in the waters of Tarpon Springs in *Sixteen Fathoms Deep* (1948). Florida is his destination because he wants to be where there is "blue sky and blue water," not smokestacks obscuring the air. Hired as a sponge diver, he becomes entangled in the conflicts between boat owners and sponge dealers. In all these postwar films the veterans continue to display heroism in civilian life. They are honest and willing to work hard if someone gives them a chance. Audiences probably appreciated, and even identified with, their difficulties in making the transition from military to civilian life. Viewers no doubt also expected that the popular leading men would ultimately succeed, and they do.

Ronald Reagan displays a different kind of heroism in postwar Florida in *Night Unto Night* (1949). Cast as John Gaylord, he worked on penicillin research during the war, but for what agency is unclear (he often wears military-style khaki shirts). Now John has developed "low-grade" epilepsy, and he sets up a research laboratory at a house near the Everglades. His landlady is Ann (Vivica Lindfors), whose Navy husband died in a torpedo attack just off the Florida coast. John helps her overcome hallucinations that her husband is haunting the mansion, and they fall in love. But John's epilepsy is getting worse, and his visiting psychiatrist sees the only cure as faith and love. Reluctant to tell Ann about his disease, John sinks into depression and decides to commit suicide during a raging hurricane. Ann talks him out of it, and the audience is left with the impression that his battle will continue, but perhaps be won.

In the postwar period the number of films critiquing bigotry exceeded any previous era. As American audiences became more knowledgeable about Nazi ethnic cleansing and as the U.S. military desegregated, some filmmakers focused on prejudice in American society. One of Florida's contributions uses the experiences of a war veteran to make a point about racism. *Bright Victory* (1951) stars Arthur Kennedy as a hero of the North Africa campaign who has been blinded in battle. His civilian struggle combines coping with blindness, planning a future, and learning about his own racism. In this case blindness enables him to judge people and form friendships without "seeing" race.

Films highlighting heroism during World War II continued to be produced through the 1950s, and two are set primarily in Florida. *Wings of Eagles* (1957) stars John Wayne as a Navy pilot whose career in Pensacola spans both world wars. In *Underwater Warrior* (1958), Commander Forest (Dan Dailey) reminisces about his 1942 experiences training at the Underwater Demolition School at Fort Pierce. The film provided an opportunity to inform audiences about an aspect of military training that is otherwise seldom mentioned in films. Jimmy Stewart plays a veteran of World War II who steps up to meet Cold War demands in *Strategic Air Command*, abandoning his professional baseball career and rejoining the military to defend the United States against the new Soviet enemy. Although he sees no significant action, his test flights are dangerous, and his sacrifice is portrayed as heroic. In fact the many discussions about aircraft capabilities and in-flight scenes make the film seem like a recruiting effort.

In contrast to previous conflicts, the Korean War (1950–1954) has inspired few filmmakers to focus on Florida heroes of that bloody war. Indeed, since the 1960s, Florida veterans are more likely to be portrayed as troubled, at the very least. An example is the film *Chattahoochee* (1989), loosely based on the actual experiences of Korean War veteran Chris Calhoun. After the war Calhoun suffered from post-traumatic stress disorder that led to a suicide attempt and commitment to the state mental facility, Chattahoochee, in 1956. During his stay there (to 1962), he and other "patients" suffered through rapes and other violence at the hands of the staff. Calhoun wrote reports that were smuggled out of the institution by some honest staffers and by visitors, who finally got the attention of reporters at the *Tampa Tribune* and of Governor Farris Bryant. An investigation led to a number of significant reforms, and the facility later closed.

Calhoun's story is played out in the film by the character Everett Foley (Gary Oldham), who is arrested after terrorizing his neighborhood and trying to commit suicide. His real motivation, however, is having the police kill him so his wife can collect the death benefits. His wife, played by Frances McDormand, visits him at the hospital and chastises him for leaving her to fend for herself and their daughter: "If you'd been a better shot, we wouldn't have to go through all of this." The horrific scenes at Chattahoochee reveal just a portion of a dark era in Florida's treatment of the mentally ill, but the film vividly shows the determination of one man to start a program of reform.

The Cuban revolution in the latter part of the 1950s inspired a film starring World War II hero-turned-actor Audie Murphy. *The Gun Runners* (1958) also features Eddie Albert as profiteer "Papa" Hanagan, who tries to coerce Sam Martin (Murphy), an unsuccessful charter boat captain and former navy officer, into smuggling guns to Cuba for the revolutionary forces.

After the revolutionaries succeeded in overthrowing the dictatorship backed by the United States, relations with Cuba deteriorated. The use of surrogate forces during the Bay of Pigs fiasco in 1961 prompted the production of *We Shall Return* (1963), starring Cesar Romero as Carlos Rodriguez. Romero (believed to be a descendant of Cuban Independence War hero José Martí) plays a wealthy Cuban planter who goes to Miami with his son and his future daughter-in-law before the Bay of Pigs invasion. In Miami they meet up with another son, a member of a Free-Cuba group that is part of the operation. One reason for the failure of the invasion is the betrayal by his son, whom Romero feels justified in killing.

The 1962 Cuban Missile Crisis is the setting of the comedy *Matinee* (1993). The central character is B-movie filmmaker Lawrence Woolsey (John Goodman), who is always trying new techniques to lure people to the movies by making the experience more titillating. In October 1962 he travels to Key West to open his new "Atomovision" horror film, entitled "Mant," which tells the story of a man transformed into a giant ant.

96. John Goodman
as a shock filmmaker
in *Matinee* (1993).

Ever the showman, Woolsey hires two men from a fake "Citizens
Against Decent Entertainment" (one of whom is actually director John
Sayles) to "protest" outside the theater. Woolsey dresses his trashy blond
companion as a nurse and places her in the lobby to gather release signa-
tures from viewers, in case they have a heart attack from the horror they
are about to see. Woolsey has attached electric shocks to the seats, recorded loud vibrating thunder ("rumblerama"), and installed vapor-pro-
ducing machines. He also hires a local kid to dress as the Mant and terror-
ize the audience. As he explains to the theater manager (Jesse White), the
"yokels" are bound to come to the movie since everyone in Key West is
on pins and needles because of the missile crisis. Huge convoys of trucks,
machine-gun batteries, and missiles appear in the area, and the base is
on alert. And people do come to see the movie. At the critical moment

an atomic explosion appears on the screen, synchronized with the special effects. The audience panics, destroying the theater. But the theater manager pronounces the event a success and wants Woolsey to bring in more films, "with two separate screens—that's the wave of the future."

The main Key West character is teenager Gene (Simon Fenton), who has trouble fitting in at the high school because locals disdain the "base kids." Gene falls for another "outsider," a Florida native named Sandra (Lisa Jakob), who refuses to participate in the duck-and-cover drills at school "because it's insane." Gene asks himself, "What is she, a Communist?" But outsider Gene suddenly becomes more interesting to his classmates after his father is deployed during the crisis and considered a hero. A new friend explains to Gene that they should take girls to the film so they can comfort them when they're scared. After all, he says, "everyone knows that Key West is the make-out capital of the world." As the rumblerama begins, Gene and Sandra run into the theater's fallout shelter, where they are locked down temporarily and discuss whether they will be forced to procreate and carry on humanity.

Matinee is one of the few films to deal with the missile-crisis era, despite the potential for some entertaining plots. In Florida, fallout shelters were built at a frantic pace, and there were panicky raids on grocery stores, and extraordinary discussions by the media, government, and families about imminent doom.

The Vietnam War still has its detractors and supporters, and filmmakers reflect this ambiguity in stories about the effects of the war on veterans. The frightening plot to target spectators at the Super Bowl in *Black Sunday* (1977) is orchestrated by a former Vietnam POW (Bruce Dern) in league with the Black September Movement. As the Goodyear blimp pilot the vet seems coherent to his coworkers, but he appears wacky during conversations with his coconspirator, a Palestinian woman. A more positive view of a vet is presented in *Ride in a Pink Car* (1974), whose hero is a Seminole and Vietnam vet who turns his town back into a safe place to live.

In *Band of the Hand* (1986), a Miccosukee who is also a Vietnam vet runs an Everglades "rehabilitation" program for urban juvenile delinquents. After surviving the war, Joe (Stephen Lang) dies at the hands of urban pimps and pushers. When he moves from the jungle to Miami, he remarks, "This is where the war is." Joe is committed to using a combination of paramilitary training and community service to reform young criminals, but his "hearts and minds" plan has limited success.

Vietnam experiences continue to haunt film characters. In *CrissCross*

97. Peter Fonda in *Ulee's Gold* (1997). By permission of Photofest.

(1992), the father of twelve-year-old Criss (David Arnott) is a Vietnam veteran who became an alcoholic after the war and abandoned his family. His son finds his father working at a monastery but fails to convince him to reestablish a bond. In *Ulee's Gold* (1997), the title character (Peter Fonda) feels remorse at the deaths of the rest of his squad in a Vietnam battle, as well as the death of his wife, but his real problem is survivor's guilt. While Ulee is committed to providing for his family, his choice of a honey-canning business in rural Florida seems to indicate a greater interest in isolation than in wealth. His relationship with his children and granddaughters is cold and aloof. Despite his desire to focus on caring for honeybees, he is drawn into heroic action once again by solving his son's criminal problems and his daughter-in-law's drug addiction. A less heroic Vietnam vet is portrayed by Bruce Dern in *Monster* (2003), as the alcoholic friend of Aileen Wuornos.

Soldiers affiliated with various covert activities or overseas assignments also appear as heroes in Florida films. Matt Hunter (Chuck Norris) comes out of CIA retirement in the Everglades to almost single-handedly defeat an attempted takeover by Russian mercenaries in the Cold War film *Invasion U.S.A.* (1985). In *Only the Strong* (1993) former Green Beret Louis Stevens (Mark Dacascos) uses his military discipline and the *capoeira* skills he learned while stationed in Brazil to train high school kids and clean up drugs and gang violence in his Miami neighborhood. In *The Substitute* (1996) a CIA contract agent (Tom Berenger) turns to teaching after his operation against a Cuban drug processing plant fails. As a substitute teacher in Miami, he rids a high school of drug pushers and gangs.

Heroes saving us from potential wars and scary creatures are commonly the stars of films that fall into the category of science fiction or horror movies. Perhaps the most famous Florida film in the sci-fi genre is *Revenge of the Creature* (1955). Gill Man has been brought from the Amazon to the Jacksonville Ocean Harbor research center for study and tourist gaping. One of his visitors is a student, Helen Dobson (Lori Nelson), working on a master's degree in ichthyology. Unfortunately it seems that Gill Man has some interest in crossing over to another species and becomes enamored of Helen. His pursuit results in efforts to track him down and destroy him. Not only the scientists, but also members of the local community join in the effort, and Gill Man is pushed back into the waters—to rise again in a sequel.

A less well known film, *Night of the Blood Beast* (1958) pits scientists against forces from outer space. An astronaut launched into space from Cape Canaveral has somehow picked up aliens who have impregnated him and are reproducing at a rapid rate. The heroes in this story save the human race.

Cape Canaveral/Kennedy becomes the center of disaster in *Lightning Bolt* (1967). Moon rockets are mysteriously exploding in midair minutes after launch, and a well-known nuclear scientist has disappeared. Secret agent Harry Sennet (Anthony Eisley) goes to Miami to investigate and finds that beer trucks near the cape actually contain powerful laser guns that have been destroying the rockets. Sennet locates the submarine base of the mad scientist who is building a giant laser cannon and saves the world.

George Romero's *Day of the Dead* (1983) is based on the premise of nuclear war destroying humanity and creating zombies. This companion to his other *Dead* films dramatizes the lives of the state's only nuclear holocaust survivors, living in a fourteen-mile underground bunker in south

Florida. The survivors include Anglo males, a Latino who is losing his mind, a Jamaican who manages to stay stoned, and a white woman who tries to exert authority and use reason. The men, who hurl racial epithets at each other, constantly criticize her. The dilemma, of course, is figuring out how to survive on the surface among the mutant zombies feeding on human flesh. Some zombies are brought down into the bunker in an attempt to "civilize" them, but a few escape and go on a bloody rampage. The woman, the Jamaican, and a white man are the only survivors, and they escape to an unpopulated island where, we presume, they will do their patriotic duty to carry on the species.

Florida's east coast has been the focus of manned and unmanned space flights since the 1950s, but in films about space travel, references to the state are usually peripheral. An early film highlighting the Kennedy Space Center was the drama *Countdown* (1968), directed by Robert Altman and starring James Caan. The movie was released just before the classic film *2001: A Space Odyssey* (1968) set a new standard for space films. *Countdown* suggests that a faster way to the moon is to launch a moon shelter and the manned craft separately. The only trick is for the astronaut to find the shelter on the moon and try to survive until the next spaceship gets there. This turns out to be more difficult than anticipated.

Four months after the real first moon landing, *Marooned* (1969) was released. In this plot, used in many previous science fiction movies, the astronauts are stranded in space. Technical difficulties keep three Apollo astronauts (Gene Hackman, James Franciosa, and Richard Crenna) from returning to earth after a five-month stay at a space lab. Oxygen depletion leaves two survivors, and the president orders the NASA project supervisor (Gregory Peck) to send an experimental rescue craft to bring them back to earth in the midst of a Florida hurricane. In a rare friendly depiction of Russians during the Cold War, they are assisted by a roving Russian cosmonaut. The three astronauts are depicted as heroes, as are the Russian cosmonaut and the rescue craft's pilot (David Jansen).

A favorite among space exploration conspiracy theorists, *Capricorn One* (1978) is about a space launch that never took place. All of the astronauts are pulled out of the rocket just as it is ready to shoot for Mars. While they are sequestered in a western desert, simulated accounts on stage and screen portray to world audiences their supposed voyage to and exploration of Mars. The real heroism here is the determination of one survivor (James Brolin) to make it back to civilization and tell the truth.

The Right Stuff (1983) is a critically acclaimed account of the Mercury 7 astronauts. When the movie was released, it helped reinforce the im-

98. Astronaut Gus Grissom (Fred Ward) and his wife (Veronica Cartwright) in a Cocoa Beach motel in *The Right Stuff* (1983).

age of American frontier heroes at a time when debates raged about government commitment to military ventures in the Caribbean and Central America. The interest of the media in these pilots who had migrated to Florida to train as the first astronauts is accurately captured in the film, which portrays the men as dedicated and heroic. *Apollo 13* (1995) creates a tension-filled dramatization of the near disaster in the "Houston, we have a problem" mission, when Jim Lovell, Fred Haise, and Jack Swigert lived through an explosion during a planned moon landing.

Race to Space (2001) is a family film about conflicts between a son (Alex Linz) and his immigrant German space scientist father, Dr. Wilhelm Von Huber (James Woods), during the era of animal test flights. The boy, Billy, befriends one of the experimental chimpanzee astronauts thus interfering with his father's scientific efforts. Von Huber disciplines his son, but his heavy-handed approach is softened by his American coworkers. Mostly filmed on site, the movie also uses California sets, which accounts for a goof that shows Alan Shepard's jet taking off from Florida with a background of mountain ranges.

Servicemen (and women), veterans, and astronauts comprise categories of heroes that should provide a rich source of plots and character studies for films set in Florida. But while hundreds of movies have been made about war veterans, few of these are about Floridians. In films World War II vets are hardworking and courageous migrants to the state. Later films about Vietnam vets dramatize their lives as negatively affected, a theme common in many films about this group of vets. Instead, Florida's more recent film heroes are generally federal agents, cops, and other crime fighters whose strategies and tactics "save" the people of the state from drug dealers, murderers, and monsters. In this sense films not only reflect new sensibilities about the heroes in historical eras, but also avoid messy ambiguities about the goals and results of foreign conflicts. Today a filmmaker considering making a film about the Seminole Wars would be less likely to frame it in the simple terms of "savagery" versus "civilized" slaughter that Cold War audiences accepted in the 1950s. During World War II filmmakers dramatized both the battlefield and the home front, thereby connecting with audiences that felt intimately involved with war efforts. But contemporary films set during the two World Wars typically focus on the battlefield rather than the home front, reinterpreting the actions of heroes, but not questioning the virtue of the wars. The Korean War and its vets have generated less interest among moviemakers using Florida characters. And although the question of heroism in the Vietnam War continues to provoke controversy in political discussions, the battlefield and its heroes seem to have faded from films.

Whether the heroes and veterans of more contemporary wars will inspire filmmakers remains to be seen. For now, what is left in portraying Florida heroism is the heroic crime fighter. Often the enemies are still foreigners—Latino drug traffickers and pushers—who are conquered by dedicated U.S. citizens. With a variety of scenarios to develop and indecisive victories in the continuing battle, this war has long-term cinematic advantages.

Chapter 11

"This isn't just a football game to the warden. . . . It's a fear and violence philosophy."

The Longest Yard (1974)

Athletes

With its consistently balmy climate, Florida provides an ideal location for any sport that doesn't require snow or hills. The film genres that center on sports in Florida cover musicals, comedies, and dramas, and the athletes and sportsmen characterized include (in order of the number of films) baseball and football players, fishermen, golfers, boxers, tennis pros, sailors, and race car drivers. Without exception, these characterizations focus on men in various sports, but their activities result in widely varying levels of success and failure.

The first baseball team to establish spring training in Florida was the Philadelphia Athletics, which went to Jacksonville in 1901. *The New Klondike* (1926), the silent film about baseball players becoming real estate moguls, is set in south Florida, where other teams migrated for spring training in the Teens and Twenties. The players in the film are characterized as naive, but eager and honest. In contrast the owners and managers are duplicitous and villainous.

The audience understands the players' growing interest in real estate during this boom period; buyers and sellers are everywhere. Baseball lots and housing lots become interrelated. Wherever spring training camps went up, adjacent land was cleared and made available for speculation. As the film card reads: "Buy a lot, Sell a lot, Have a lot; Lots—plots—payments—home runs—home sites—first base—first mortgage—options—umpires—bungalows—money—real estate, real estate, real estate." Baseball was a perfect metaphor for the real estate boom.

Frank Sinatra and Gene Kelly star as baseball players who moonlight in vaudeville in the 1949 musical comedy *Take Me Out to the Ball Game.* Set in Jacksonville during the early years of spring training, the movie casts popular film stars of the period in the leading roles. The baseball players want to break their strict training regimen, so they decide to romance the new female owner (Esther Williams). Kelly urges Sinatra on: "After all, if she's a dame, she wants romance; either that or the caveman approach." Williams gets to show off her swimming ballet skills, and Sinatra and Kelly do song and dance routines that their fans will undoubtedly enjoy.

In 1953 another spring training film, *Big Leaguer,* provided an unusual role for film star Edward G. Robinson. Cast effectively in gangster roles during the 1930s and 1940s, here Robinson plays John Lobert, manager of the New York Giants. In selecting the best of the young minor league players to move up, he is subtly pressured by a visiting niece (Vera Ellen), who is attracted to one of the players. The competition is a bit ugly for a prized contract in the majors, but why not? At this time major league players could earn as much as $150 a month! Baseball was arguably the most popular sport in 1953, and this film includes cameo appearances by several well-known ballplayers. Although the Giants were among the first teams to integrate, the cast of *Big Leaguer* is all white.

Fear Strikes Out (1957) includes brief scenes of Jimmy Piersall (Anthony Perkins) at the Red Sox spring training camp in Sarasota. The film attempts to portray sympathetically this young athlete's struggle with mental illness, but Piersall disliked its misrepresentations. Two popular baseball heroes of the time, Mickey Mantle and Roger Maris, play themselves in *Safe at Home!* (1962). In this plot Hutch Lawton (Bryan Russell) moves in with his widowed father, Ken Lawton (Don Collier), the operator of a charter fishing boat in Florida. Ken claims to be a friend of the famous players and promises to deliver them for a Little League banquet. Hutch can't convince the players to lie and cover his father's mistake. Instead Mantle and Maris invite the Little Leaguers to their spring training camp.

As baseball lost ground to football in popularity, fewer films featured the national pastime. Not until *Field of Dreams* (1989) attracted large au-

99. Jim Morris (Dennis Quaid) pitching in Orlando in *The Rookie* (2002).

diences did a filmmaker produce another baseball story set in Florida. Pete Rose's banishment from baseball in 1989, combined with subsequent scandals related to the sport, might have contributed to the decision of filmmakers to replace baseball dramas with comedies. Florida's only recent contributions to baseball movies have been family films. The first was the fantasy/drama *The Last Home Run* (1996), in which Seymour Cassel plays Jonathan Lyle, a Florida physician dying from an incurable disease. While watching a group of young kids play a baseball game, he is miraculously transformed into one of them. Allowed to be young and play baseball again—but for only five days—Dr. Lyle brings to his new-found youth the wisdom of his real years. Fulfilling a lifelong fantasy to play good ball, he and the others learn that winning is not the most important thing in life.

Finally, the recent film *The Rookie* (2002) tells the real-life story of Jimmy Morris (Dennis Quaid), the oldest rookie pitcher in the major leagues in many decades. Morris was signed by the Tampa Bay Devil Rays, but this Disney film includes only a few scenes in Florida. It's hard to say whether this movie helped or hurt perceptions of the Tampa Bay team.

While professional football was played throughout the twentieth century, the popularity of the sport in film tended to center on college teams until the 1960s expansions. The Miami Dolphins played their first game in 1966, and six years later they won the Super Bowl. Until that championship in 1972, no films appeared about football in Florida. Even then, the initial films that followed were not really about pro football. The first, the comedy *The Longest Yard*, focuses on some bigger issues than football and portrays the sport and players as agents of change. By uniting against the common enemy, the prison team of white and black inmates develops a winning strategy.

The second film about football in Florida is often cited during Super Bowl season, especially since the attacks of September 11, 2001. In *Black Sunday* (1977) an Israeli intelligence officer (Robert Shaw) unravels the terrorist plot but is hopelessly clueless about the importance of the Super Bowl. He suggests that the best way to deal with the threat is to cancel the game. Dolphins owner Joe Robbie (playing himself) responds: "Cancel the Super Bowl?! It's the most ridiculous suggestion I've ever heard! That's like canceling Christmas!" More than any other film, *Black Sunday* heightened sensitivities to the potential target created by a well-attended sporting event.

The Miami Dolphins figure in the plot of *Ace Ventura: Pet Detective* (1994). Some of the players (including Dan Marino) appear as themselves, but the plot unravels the past of a fictional ex-player, Ray Finkle, who became obsessed with revenge after he was held responsible for missing a kick that would have won a Super Bowl for the Dolphins. However, Finkle blames Marino for causing the loss because of a bad hold ("laces out!"). His obsession put him in the Shady Acres Mental Hospital in Tampa.

100. Dan Marino (*center*) with his kidnapper (Sean Young) and Ace Ventura (Jim Carrey) in *Ace Ventura: Pet Detective* (1994).

After escaping and killing a female hiker, he took not only her name, but also her female identity. He is now Lieutenant Lois Einhorn (Sean Young), and s/he kidnaps Dan Marino and the team's dolphin mascot.

Fictional football players are major characters in several other films set in Florida. An African-American college player being courted by pro teams provides part of the story line for *Black Spring Break* (1998), and a former college-star-turned-developer is one of the characters in *Sunshine State* (2002). Finally the most recent movie focusing entirely on football in the state is the drama *Any Given Sunday* (1999). Rather than compromise the real Miami team, this film creates a pro team called the Miami Sharks. The players and the coach indulge in wild parties with drugs and hookers, while failing on the gridiron and at the gate. The head coach (Al Pacino) and the owner (Cameron Diaz) try to shake up the team, but in the process, issues of racism and politics are revealed.

Unlike the spectator sports of baseball and football, golf directly engages Floridians in numerous ways. A recent study concluded that Florida devotes some 205 thousand acres of land to over twelve hundred golf courses, more than any other state. The business accounted for $4.4 billion in Florida's economy during 2000. Golf courses also use at least 173 billion gallons of fresh and recycled water every year.[1] Moreover, the popularity of golf has increased in recent years and attracts even younger enthusiasts.

A sport usually identified in films with the wealthy, golf has long been synonymous with Florida leisure. In *Doorway to Hell* (1930) a Chicago gangster (Lew Ayres) briefly retires in Florida to live in a mansion and play golf at a private club. The best-known recent films about Florida golfers are *Caddyshack* (1980) and *Caddyshack II* (1988), set at the fictional Bushwood Country Club. In the first the focus is on an uncouth developer, a country club bigot, an anal-retentive judge, and club employees—a groundskeeper and a caddy. In the second Jackie Mason plays a nouveau-riche millionaire who is denied club membership and takes revenge by buying the club and turning it into a general admission theme park. Both films include some outrageous stereotypes, but the first makes it clear that the club is anti-Semitic, antiblack, and anti-Catholic. In the second, by casting Jewish comedian Jackie Mason in the role of an Armenian from New Jersey who encounters discrimination, the film attempts to make a point about what used to be referred to as "restricted" clubs. In both, golf and country clubs are status symbols for old and new money.

The pleasure of golf is emphasized in *Illtown* (1996), a crime drama directed and cowritten by Nick Gomez, who clearly appreciates the sport.

101. Chevy Chase, Bill Murray, Rodney Dangerfield, and Ted Knight in a composite publicity photograph for *Caddyshack* (1980). By permission of Photofest.

The film tells the story of Dante (Michael Rapaport), a drug-addicted dealer in south Florida, whose idea of heaven is a golf course. As the bodies of victims pile up in a drug war, Dante regularly plays golf, and the last scene shows him riding off into the sunset in a golf cart.

A Gentleman's Game (2001) is not set in Florida, but it dramatically portrays an ex-pro golfer who needs to get to Florida to redeem his self-image. In a decisive Florida match years before, Foster Pearse (Gary Sinise) cheated, winning the cup and starting a lifetime of guilt and self-loathing that made him quit the game. Only through association with a young boy interested in becoming a pro does he decide to redeem himself, return to Florida, and deliver the trophy to its rightful owner.

Perhaps the cleverest cinematic use of golf and golfers is by John Sayles in *Sunshine State*. His film resonates with Florida viewers in part because of the pontificating remarks about the virtues of land transformation made by golfer Murray Silver (Alan King) to fellow golfers. Rhapsodizing on the chutzpah of the Spanish conquistadors and other Europeans in transforming nature while exploiting labor, Silver has no doubts about the meaning of "progress." As he emphasizes the inevitability of improving upon nature, the golfers themselves find that their course has shrunk to the small grassy median of a highway.

Another golfer in the film is the sexual partner of Marly (Edie Falco), and he is more focused on becoming a pro than on his relationship with her. He represents another generation of players who will ensure that even more land will be razed, irrigated, and fertilized for golf courses. Indeed, sprawling courses are everywhere in this movie. One infringes upon a historic African-American cemetery, and another is where Marly and past loves once met at night, where she breaks up with her current lover, and where she gives her first kiss to a potential new lover. In the ambivalent view of this film, golf courses can represent the manicured, orderly, expansive use of land for leisure and work, as well as an unwelcome intrusion.

Florida's waterways make boating a popular pastime for residents and visitors alike. Early filmmakers who wanted to include boating scenes reproduced stories about Florida coastal piracy or used a passenger ship or yacht as a setting for throwing characters together in a drama. An example is *Always in Trouble* (1938), starring Jane Withers as Ann Darlington, a child scheming to re-create her family's lost closeness. Her father has become a wealthy oil tycoon and the family is living in splendor in Miami, but the simple things that they once shared have been lost. Ann orchestrates a trip on the family yacht that results in a disaster, stranding her mother, sister, uncle, and an employee on an island off Biscayne. In *Mercy Island* (1941) vacationers go to Florida for deep-sea fishing and get marooned on an offshore island, a plot that reappears in several other films.

After World War II recreational motorboats became more affordable, and sport fishing gained in popularity. When Elvis Presley's family decides to homestead on state property in *Follow That Dream* (1962), they choose a fishing spot near a newly opened bridge so that they can feed themselves. Elvis and his family quickly turn their modest ability to catch fish into a thriving fish camp that provides bait, boats, and other supplies to eager fishermen. In *Gone Fishin'* (1997), when Gus (Danny Glover) and Joe (Joe Pesci) go to Florida to fish in a tournament, their encounters with people who serve the sport are much less friendly. A sleazy salesman cons them into buying an expensive boat, and the snobbish staff at the Rod and Reel Club treats them as inferiors. Lots of people show up at Elvis's fish camp in the 1960s, but it's orderly and manageable. The south Florida fishing tournament of the 1990s is portrayed as wall-to-wall people and boat traffic. Some fishermen are friendly, but many are boorish. Fishermen Gus and Joe are simply incompetent—well-meaning and enthusiastic, but incompetent.

Fishermen and charter boat operators around Key West are the centerpiece of the screen version of the book *92 in the Shade* (1975). The small

102. Danny Glover (*top*) and Joe Pesci in *Gone Fishin'* (1997). By permission of Photofest.

rundown community is filled with lots of weird characters, including the baton-twirling wife of the dock owner. Trying to make a living from the tourist trade is portrayed as a tough business, not only because few tourists show up, but also because many have no idea what they're supposed to do on a boat. Still Tom Skelton (Peter Fonda) dedicates himself to his job as a fishing guide, despite the inexplicable and sociopathic opposition of Nichol Dance (Warren Oates), who wants to kill him. The film suggests that the people involved in this business are an unpredictable lot.

The hero of *Joe Panther* (1976) is not interested in signing on with boats that travel so close to shore. His objective is finding a job with fishing boats that go miles out in the ocean, far from his Seminole village. The work also represents less of a transition for Joe, the audience understands, because it simply replaces his work with nature in the Everglades with work with nature on the high seas.

The charter boat business figures in both *Cocoon* films (1985, 1988), and in the second the business is clearly a failure. Apparently tourists catch on too easily if you "bury" fake treasure chests and conveniently float over them in glass-bottomed boats.

Florida regattas in *Clambake* (1967) and *Summer Rental* (1985) make heroes of Elvis Presley and John Candy. *Racing Fever* (1964) stars Connie Stevens in a story about her romance with a millionaire playboy who races his hydroplane at the Miami International Grand Prix.

Sailing and speedboats appear in many other Florida films, including *Moonraker* (1979). Florida's waters have become overrun with boats of all kinds, making them something of a convention for Florida settings in recent years. Clearly, high-speed boat chases with cops pursuing criminals appear more frequently than sailing scenes. Still, sailors at marinas and sailboats in the sunset, as well as the occasional cruise ship, add a sense of leisure and timelessness to many films. Moreover, the choice of boats tends to serve as a marker of class.

Another sport associated with Florida draws many fans and participants from across the nation, but rarely appears in movies. Daytona Beach is home to one of the most famous racetracks in the United States, but only a few films feature drivers competing at the Daytona International Speedway. Two feature California men as entrants. In *Fireball 500* (1966), most of the action takes place in California, where Frankie Avalon, Annette Funicello, and Fabian have fervent fights. Once they get to Daytona and race in the Firecracker 400, one of them has to end up in a near-death crash and burn, of course. In this case it's Leander (Fabian) who is practically burned alive. He and his girl Jane (Annette) seal their love, and Dave (Frankie) and his girl decide to settle down. This attempt at a serious film about moonshiners and stock car racing did not match the popularity of the Frankie and Annette beach movies (they don't even sing together!).

In *Days of Thunder* (1990), Daytona's Firecracker 400 is hotly contested by Californian Cole Trickle (Tom Cruise) and his archrival, North Carolinian Rowdy Burns (Michael Rooker). This time the inevitable crash and burn involves both drivers, and Cole is treated by a neurologist (Nicole Kidman) who also works on the love center in his brain. Apparently assuming that viewers might expect racing teams and enthusiasts to be southern (overlooking Indianapolis and other northern tracks), director Tony Scott added some dialogue between Harry Hogge (Robert Duvall) and Tim Daland (Dennis Quaid), who discuss Cole's identity. Asking about Cole, Hogge says "You mean he's a Yankee?" Daland explains, "If you're from California, you're not a Yankee. You're really not anything." Sorry, Frankie and Annette.

Only one film focuses on a fictional Florida boxer. A remake of the 1931 film starring Wallace Beery and Jackie Cooper, *The Champ* (1979) moves the setting from California to Florida. A former boxer and now a horse trainer, Billy Flynn (Jon Voight) tries to raise his son T. J. (Ricky Schroder) without the involvement of his ex-wife Annie (Faye Dunaway). His penchant for drinking and gambling coincides with her return in an attempt to reclaim her son. The audience is never quite sure what went wrong between Billy and Annie, but there are hints that Billy is fond of hitting in and out of the ring. He pushes Annie around the first time they reunite, gets in a fight over gambling debts, and slaps his son during a jail visit.

Finally out of ideas, Billy decides to become a prizefighter again, despite the long years out of training. The boxing match between Billy and a fighter who is much more buff lasts more than ten minutes of the film. And it's not just long; it's bloody. Billy dies in the locker room, in front of the son who so admires him. It seems likely the kid will follow the same aimless path as his father, given his experiences, but we're relieved to see that his mother shows up and takes him off to what we hope is a better life. In the most recent boxing movie with a Florida component, Muhammad Ali's Miami fight with Joe Frazier for the heavyweight boxing championship is re-created in *Ali* (2001), with scenes in the same Miami gym where Ali trained.

One of the few Florida films with a tennis theme is *The Break* (1995). Nick Irons (Vincent Van Patten) is a drunk, carousing gambler and ex-tennis pro who is forced into drying out. To cancel a debt owed to Gil Robbins (Martin Sheen), Nick must coach his teenage son—not to win, but to lose. Gil thinks his son's interest in tennis is "not manly enough," so he wants Nick to prove that it is boring and a waste of time. As Nick realizes the kid's talent, he devotes himself more to coaching and wins back the affection of a former girlfriend (Rae Dawn Chong).

Whether locals, tourists, or migrants, sportsmen generally seem to succeed in their favorite Florida sports. Often the sport itself becomes a metaphor for coping strategies that the leading men develop. Plots that use the sports theme can take advantage of outdoor settings that are typically much more controlled and controllable than urban settings. While casting leading men as athletes and creating plots around sports is not as common as we might expect, amateur athletes and recreational sports are part of the background in numerous Florida films. If a movie is set in Florida and includes any outdoor scenes, the chances are good that boating, swimming, golfing, tennis, or some other sport will appear somewhere in the film.

Characters engaged in outdoor sports reflect the settings and plots that appear in many Florida films. While the state's natural environment provides the often dreamlike setting for swimmers and boaters, the manufactured landscape of golf courses serves as a physical reminder of the unrelenting, and apparently unstoppable, effort to create paradise in Florida. In these settings film plots commonly portray sportsmen either as amateur tourists seeking year-round recreation or as professional athletes in search of re-creation. Even criminals find time to go boating or play golf in movies set in Florida. As a result, all film genres frequently use sports to say something either positive or negative about the nature of Florida's environment and the joys or problems of living in the Sunshine State.

Epilogue

As Florida changed dramatically over the course of the twentieth century, so too did portrayals of the state in films. Nevertheless, cinematic change occurs slowly, especially in Hollywood movies. The particular settings, plots, and characters selected by filmmakers reflect not only their own perceptions, but also what they think will attract the largest possible audiences. Given the production and marketing costs of movies, the people behind them understandably tend to follow formulas that have proven successful in the past. This means that a kind of herd mentality prevails in the industry, resulting in familiar sets and story lines that resonate with viewers.

Certain aspects of the Florida environment have remained fixed in the lenses of filmmakers. Whether depicted as a dreamland or nightmare, the Sunshine State is consistently associated with sun and water, which figure prominently in films since the silent era. A common establishing shot for Florida is an aerial view of the coastline bathed in sunlight. Florida's climate can, of course, turn ugly and even dangerous, creating conditions that get title billing in *Slattery's Hurricane* (1949), *Hurricane Island* (1951), *92 in the Shade* (1975), and *Body Heat* (1981). In addition the state's best known living creatures occasionally play leading—though nonspeaking—roles in movies, including *The Yearling* (1946), *Flipper* (1963), *Alligator* (1980), and *Jaws 3-D* (1983).

Water provides a perfect setting for filmmakers to depict every imaginable human emotion, from joy and lust to anxiety and fear. Films portray Florida's waters as places for recreation, rejuvenation, romance, horror, and death. Once again, as with other elements of Florida's landscape, water has become increasingly perceived as a source of danger rather than pleasure. This is clear in the contrasts between both the titles and content of *Where the Boys Are* (1960) and *Nightmare Beach* (1988). Even so, the state's beaches and rivers still offer a potential for escape and romance in films.

Similar changes have occurred in cinematic depictions of the state's manufactured environment. Films produced prior to the 1960s commonly portray Florida hotels and mansions as elegant fixtures in a rich man's paradise. *The Big Street* (1942), *Palm Beach Story* (1942), and *Some Like It Hot* (1959) all feature people who are down-on-their-luck heading for the fancy surroundings of south Florida. The area's spectacular natural environment appears as an ideal setting for the trappings of wealth, including luxurious mansions like those shown in *It's the Old Army Game* (1926) and *Tony Rome* (1967). The influx of middle-class tourists and retirees after World War II eventually turned this upper-class enclave into sprawling stretches of highways, motels, and trailer parks that deteriorate over time in movies. Beginning with *Honky Tonk Freeway* (1981) and *A Flash of Green* (1984), some films even suggest that attempts to manufacture paradise have turned Florida into an environmental nightmare.

After the demise of the state's early film industry that used outdoor settings in north Florida, Hollywood movies typically equate the Sunshine State with south Florida, which usually means Miami and its environs. Even films made elsewhere but set in Florida—like *The Cocoanuts* (1929) and *Clambake* (1967)—frequently locate the action in south Florida. As Miami grew, so too did its prominence in films. Nine movies made between 1924 and 2003 use the city in their titles. These and dozens of other films set in Miami clearly show the city's evolution from upper-class playground during the first half of the twentieth century to a center for crime and retirement in the 1960s and 1970s and, finally, to its resurrection in the 1980s as a vibrant and complex center of shimmering skyscrapers. Even the sordid behavior that occurs at ground level in movies does little to detract from the visual coolness of Miami and Miami Beach as portrayed by recent filmmakers, who commonly expand upon the imagery first popularized on television by *Miami Vice* in the 1980s.

Aside from *Cross Creek* (1983), *Rosewood* (1997), and *Palmetto* (1998), the only Florida locations to get title billing in films are all in south Florida—Palm Beach, Key Largo, and the Everglades. The latter is the principal natural landscape that filmmakers have highlighted in addition to coastal waters. As dominant images of the state shifted from paradise to paradise lost, the Everglades have become more prominent as a movie setting. Viewed either as a mysterious river of grass or as a dense jungle-like swamp filled with deadly alligators and snakes, the Everglades are home to wildlife and people that frequently cause death and destruction in films. From nineteenth-century Seminole Indians in Florida westerns to beastly predators in *Just Cause* (1995), the swampland remains associated with danger.

Whatever the particular location, the physical settings and plots of movies clearly go hand-in-hand to create moods and deliver messages. Films about Spring Break inevitably take place at the beach, as do most movies about tourism. The biggest changes in stories about vacationing in Florida reflect dramatic shifts in both the social class and experiences of visitors. Films made prior to the 1960s portray the Sunshine State as a playground for the wealthy, who are often decked out in evening gowns and tuxedos when not on yachts or at the beach. Following the invasion of middle-class vacationers, the tourist theme gradually lost its cachet in films. Stories set in Florida now often show overcrowded beaches, poor accommodations, and other disappointments.

Despite changes in portrayals of Florida recreation, the state has maintained its image as a place for re-creation. By its very nature, the hope of rebirth is built on a dream. Whether it is a search for the Fountain of Youth, some kind of psychic renewal, material wealth, or romantic love, the desire to migrate and start over serves as a frequent plot device in films set in Florida, from *A Florida Enchantment* (1914) through *Midnight Cowboy* (1969) and *Adaptation* (2002). Significantly the search ends in failure in each of these films, but that does not prevent characters in other films from continuing to dream of rebirth in the Sunshine State.

While recreation and re-creation are common story lines, these plots are overshadowed by the prominence of crime stories. Beginning with the earliest silent movies, all film genres feature a variety of illegal activities that are associated with Florida, from real estate schemes to rum-running. More generic crimes like murder and robbery consistently plague the state in films, but drug trafficking has emerged as the most common crime in dramas and comedies about contemporary Florida.

In crime films, as well as other movies, the portrayal of heroes has maintained some consistency. In Florida westerns, military officers triumph over savage natives. Crime films often highlight the success of detectives, cops, and attorneys. However, since the development of the film noir, the antihero has also become a prominent figure. Films like *The Chase* (1946), *Body Heat, China Moon* (1994), and *Out of Time* (2003) pair the honest and trusting male lead with the femme fatale who manipulates him into committing crimes. Despite the continued popularity of noir films about flawed men, heroes still populate Florida movies. While portraying some of the extraordinary qualities of heroes in sports, space exploration, and wars against foreign enemies, recent filmmakers also explore what makes successful athletes and warriors like everyone else. In short, depictions of many characters have become more complex and presumably more realistic.

The villains confronted by the heroes of crime and war stories vary widely—Seminoles, foreigners, thieves, murderers, extortionists, bootleggers, drug dealers, and con artists, to name a few. As this list suggests, some crimes are identified in movies with certain eras and also with particular ethnic groups. Nevertheless, whatever the crime or the background of its perpetrator, some themes remain constant. Villains in early films typically display decidedly negative qualities that justify their demise. More recently, however, the ethical and behavioral line between "good" and "bad" men has become more blurred; some might say, more human.

Story lines about criminals who migrate to Florida frequently combine the themes of both crime and starting over. Like the characters played by Edward G. Robinson in *Key Largo* (1948), Alec Baldwin in *Miami Blues* (1990), and George Clooney in *Out of Sight* (1998), they see the Sunshine State as a place to revitalize their criminal careers. The same impulse propels some Latino villains, beginning with the Cuban immigrant played by Al Pacino in *Scarface* (1983). Since the 1980s Latino criminals have replaced native Floridians and outsiders (often with Italian names) who previously dominated crime films. Comedies and dramas have stereotyped Latinos in general and Cubans in particular as south Florida drug dealers. When not cast as criminals Latinos are often used as a source of humor—or attempted humor—as in *Bad Boys* (1995) and *The Pest* (1997).

In contrast, film roles for African-Americans have improved dramatically over the course of the century. White filmmakers initially limited speaking roles for African-Americans, caricatured their images by using white actors in blackface, and cast them in subservient roles as ignorant and childlike. Early African-American producers and directors who made movies with Florida settings and characters probably portrayed African-Americans with more humanity, but very few of their films have survived. Only with the rising power and influence of African-American civil rights groups after World War II did images begin to change in films developed by major studios. As a result contemporary films are more likely to portray African-Americans from all classes in a variety of professions.

Roles for African-American men still outnumber those for African-American women in Florida films. Moreover, characterizations of African-American women have seen less change. Although some films now portray African-American women as judges, cops, and other professionals, they are much more likely to be cast as wives, "arm candy," hookers, or senior citizens with various problems. Movies that depict African-American women as strong, heroic, and independent are extremely limited.

White women have fared better, having experienced significant changes in their leading and supporting roles over time. Certainly many films follow the convention of placing attractive young women in bathing suits in the background of Florida scenes, where they seem part of the natural environment. However, Florida movies have also expanded the traditional roles of wife/victim/whore and featured the special talents of actors such as Esther Williams, Doris Day, and Kelly Clarkson. At the same time, the dark and manipulative Florida femme fatale fits in with film images of the Sunshine State as a place that harbors evil beneath its bright and happy facade. In the wake of struggles for women's rights and the rise of the independent film industry in the 1960s, leading roles for women have slowly expanded to include nontraditional jobs. White women in recent films pursue a variety of occupations that take them outside the home and mark them as members of different classes. Contemporary films also provide these women with a greater range of issues to deal with than viewers will see in the first sixty years of moviemaking, which kept them focused on love and marriage.

With the exception of *The Birdcage* (1996) and *Monster* (2003), leading roles are rare for gay and transgender characters. Mainly limited to comedies set in south Florida, these characters sometimes appear in other genres but usually as comic relief. In addition, stereotypical behavior is the norm for gays portrayed in both leading and supporting roles.

In analyzing Florida settings, plots, and characters, we found that some films defy easy categorization. However, it does seem that Florida has become increasingly identified with oddball characters. When director Christopher Guest used some of his wacky ensemble cast from *This*

Is Spinal Tap (1984) for other spoof/pseudo documentaries, he created strange Floridians whose stories could have been taken from newspaper articles. In *Waiting for Guffman* (1996), a small-town dentist in Missouri realizes his calling is the stage, and he moves to Miami and performs in nursing homes. In *Best in Show* (2000), the winning owners in a dog show are a Florida couple, Cookie (Catherine O'Hara) and Gerry (Eugene Levy). When they return home to Fern City, they are rewarded with a key to the city and radio and newspaper interviews. Finally, in *A Mighty Wind* (2003), a group of musicians reuniting their old folk-band find a former singer teaching school in Orlando, and she is only too eager to leave and re-live her glory days.

In several other films that do not fit into obvious categories, the characters are on a quest for Florida. *Coupe de Ville* (1990) is a heartwarming movie about three brothers forced to get along while delivering their father's car to his new home in south Florida. But it isn't the destination; it's the voyage that tells the story. Characters also head for Florida to work or vacation *The Falcon's Adventure* (1946), *Two Thousand Maniacs* (1964), and *Period of Adjustment* (1962), but are diverted by various crises and never reach the Sunshine State.

Some films set in other places use Florida themes to reveal something about characters and add depth to plots. John Sayles sets his film *Lone Star* (1996) in Texas, where he examines issues of racial categorization, immigration, and migration. None of the film's action takes place in Florida, but one of the characters effectively relates the history of Black Seminoles, many of whom were forced from Florida and eventually relocated in Texas during the nineteenth century.

Although scores of films recount stories of migrants moving to Florida, few plots refer to Floridians who leave, or even want to leave, the state. In *The Mean Season* (1985) a Miami reporter (Kurt Russell) is so burned out by covering the local crime scene that he promises his girlfriend he'll move to her hometown in Colorado, but he never gets there. *Get Shorty* (1995) opens with a loan shark, Chili Palmer (John Travolta), leaving Florida to make movies in Hollywood. In *The Devil's Advocate* (1997), it takes Satan (Al Pacino) to lure a small-town lawyer (Keanu Reeves) from Florida to New York City, and the result is a descent into hell.

Some conclusions we reached about movies were entirely anticipated; others were surprising. We expected the narrative structures of films to remain largely constant, and they do. However we did not anticipate how consistently Florida would be identified in movies with the Miami skyline, alligators, and other markers, or how often certain themes would recur in films. Perhaps the biggest surprise was that we discovered many more films than we anticipated, and there are undoubtedly more. Nevertheless we are confident that any missing films will likely reinforce our observations, given the consistency of certain themes.

For those readers inspired to see any of the films discussed in this book, they might consider first reading reviews by professional movie critics who analyze artistic merits, as well as entertainment values. In addition, industry awards often recognized meritorious films. But remember that tastes change over time. *Where the Boys Are* was very popular in the early 1960s, but its prudish plot and banter might seem incomprehensible to audiences today. However, some films now available on video or DVD, especially those made by independent filmmakers, went largely unnoticed when first released, and they are entertaining, even insightful, in their treatment of Florida themes.

For non-Floridians any reference to Florida can stir visions of natural beauty or natural disaster, depending on their particular images of the state. Like other forms of mass media, movies have a powerful ability to both reflect and shape cultural values. But what differentiates them from most other media is that they seek primarily to entertain. Generally avoiding any claims of accuracy, moviemakers only hope to hold viewers' attention for an hour or so. If the story is compelling, the actors strong, and the direction effective, they might achieve that goal. If neither the plot nor the acting is any good, they can still sell theater tickets or home videos, if their publicity hype is sufficiently clever.

We do not presume to rate the films we discuss; we leave that task to critics and audiences. Our goal is to provide a view of the state as seen through the lenses of filmmakers. And some of them might be surprised at the triteness of their plots and the lack of originality in some of their scenes. Audiences appreciate movie characters who are engaging, and Florida certainly has its share of characters. Audiences also enjoy plots with depth, meaning, and complexity, and any newspaper in the state can provide those stories. Many even raise significant issues other than crime. As for settings, Florida is more than the Everglades and Miami. The state contains natural and architectural wonders, as well as unique settings, that most location scouts have overlooked. Future filmmakers might take advantage of all Florida has to offer by considering both what has been done in the past and what remains to be done.

Appendix

List of Films with Florida Scenes

Film	Year	Genre
Absence of Malice	1981	crime
According to the Law	1916	drama
Ace Ventura: Pet Detective	1994	comedy
Adaptation	2002	drama
Ali	2001	drama
All About the Benjamins	2002	crime/comedy
All Fall Down	1962	drama
Alligator	1980	horror
All Shook Up	1999	comedy
Always in Trouble	1938	comedy
Analyze This!	1999	comedy
Any Given Sunday	1999	drama
Apollo 13	1995	drama
Assault on a Queen	1966	crime
Baby, It's You	1983	romance
Bad Boys	1995	crime
Bad Boys II	2003	crime

Band of the Hand	1986	drama
Barefoot Mailman, The	1951	comedy
Because of Winn-Dixie	2005	drama
Bellboy, The	1960	comedy
Beneath the 12-Mile Reef	1953	drama
Beyond Desire	1994	thriller
Big City Blues	1999	crime
Big Daddy	1969	drama
Big Leaguer	1953	drama
Big Street, The	1942	drama
Big Trouble	2002	comedy
Birdcage, The	1996	comedy
Blackout, The	1997	crime
Black Spring Break	1998	comedy
Black Sunday	1977	action
Blood and Wine	1997	crime
Blood Stalkers	1978	horror
Blood, Sweat, and Bullets	1990	crime
Bloody Mama	1970	crime
Blue City	1986	crime
Body Heat	1981	crime
Break, The	1995	drama
Bright Victory	1951	drama
Brothers Rico, The	1957	crime
Bullets for O'Hara	1941	crime
Bully	2001	crime
Cabeza de Vaca	1991	drama
Caddyshack	1980	comedy
Caddyshack II	1988	comedy
Cat Chaser	1989	crime
Caught in the Fog	1928	comedy
Champ, The	1979	drama
Chapter Zero	1999	comedy
Charcoal Black	1972	drama
Chase, The	1946	drama
Chasing Papi	2003	comedy
Chattahoochee	1989	drama
China Moon	1994	crime
Chloe, Love Is Calling You	1934	drama
Citizen Kane	1941	drama
Clambake	1967	musical

Coastlines	2003	drama
Cocoanuts, The	1929	comedy
Cocoon	1985	sci-fi/drama
Cocoon: The Return	1988	sci-fi/drama
Code Conspiracy	2001	action
Confidence Man, The	1924	drama
Cop and a Half	1993	comedy
Countdown	1968	sci-fi
Coupe de Ville	1990	comedy
CREEP	1995	horror
Crew, The	2000	comedy
CrissCross	1992	drama
Cross Creek	1983	drama
Crosswinds	1951	drama
Curdled	1996	crime
Cutaway	2000	crime
Darker Than Amber	1970	crime
Dark Universe	1993	adventure
Daughter of Macgregor, The	1916	drama
Day of the Dead	1985	horror
Days of Thunder	1990	action
Dead Dogs Lie	2001	drama
Deadly Rivals	1992	crime
Dead Reckoning	1947	drama
Death Curse of Tartu	1966	horror
Devil's Advocate, The	1997	drama/fantasy
Disorderlies, The	1987	comedy
Distant Drums	1951	adventure
Distinguished Gentleman, The	1992	comedy
D Minus	1998	crime
Donnie Brasco	1997	crime
Doorway to Hell	1930	crime
Down Under the Sea	1936	adventure
Dunsmore	2003	drama
Dust Be My Destiny	1939	drama
Easy to Love	1953	comedy
8MM	1999	crime
Empire of the Ants	1977	sci-fi/horror
Ernest Saves Christmas	1988	comedy
Eternal Summer	1961	drama
Everything's On Ice	1939	comedy

Eyes of a Stranger	1981	horror
Fabulous Bastard from Chicago	1969	crime
Fair Game	1995	action
Falcon's Adventure, The	1946	crime
Fat Spy, The	1966	comedy
Fear Strikes Out	1957	drama
Felony	1995	crime
Fireball 500	1966	action
First of May, The	2000	drama
Flash of Green, A	1984	crime
Fled	1996	crime
Flipper	1963	adventure
Flipper	1996	adventure
Florida City	2003	drama
Florida Connection, The	1974	crime
Florida Enchantment, A	1914	comedy
Flying Ace, The	1926	drama
Folks!	1992	comedy
Follow That Dream	1962	musical
Footloose Widows	1926	romance
Forever Mine	1999	crime
Frogs	1972	sci-fi/horror
From Justin to Kelly	2003	musical
Funhouse	1981	horror
Fun on a Weekend	1947	comedy
Gal Young "Un	1979	drama
Ghost Story	1981	fantasy
Girl Happy	1965	musical
Girl Missing	1933	crime
Godfather: Part II, The	1974	crime
Golden Arrow, The	1936	drama
Goldfinger	1964	thriller
Gone Fishin'	1997	comedy
Goodfellas	1990	crime
Greatest Show on Earth, The	1952	drama
Great Expectations	1998	drama
Guilty Generation, The	1931	crime
Gun Runners, The	1958	crime
Happening, The	1967	crime
Hard Choices	1985	crime

Hardly Working	1980	comedy
Hard to Handle	1933	comedy
Harry and Son	1984	drama
HEALTH	1979	comedy
Heartbreakers	2001	comedy/crime
Held for Ransom	2000	crime
Her Father's Gold	1916	crime
Hole in the Head, A	1959	musical
Holy Man, The	1998	comedy
Honky Tonk Freeway	1981	comedy
House of the Dead	2003	horror
Hunting for Herschell	2003	crime
Hurricane Island	1951	adventure
Illegally Yours	1988	comedy
Illtown	1996	crime
Image Maker, The	1917	sci-fi/drama
Instinct	1999	drama
In the Shadows	2001	crime
Interrupted Melody	1955	drama
Invasion U.S.A.	1985	crime
It's the Old Army Game	1926	comedy
Jaws 3-D	1983	drama
Joe Panther	1976	drama
Johnny Tiger	1966	drama
Joy Girl, The	1927	drama
Juke Girl	1942	drama
Just Cause	1995	crime
Just for the Hell of It	1968	drama
Key Largo	1948	crime
Lady in Cement	1968	crime
Last Home Run, The	1996	drama
Lauderdale	1989	comedy
Let It Ride	1989	comedy
Licence to Kill	1989	action
Lightning Bolt	1967	sci-fi
Little Laura and Big John	1973	crime
Longest Yard, The	1974	comedy
Lucky Me	1954	musical
Lure of the Swamp, The	1957	drama
Ma Barker's Killer Brood	1960	drama

Mafia Girls, The	1967	crime
Manfast	2001	drama
Marooned	1969	sci-fi
Married to the Mob	1988	comedy
Marvin's Room	1996	drama
Matinee	1993	comedy
Mating Call, The	1928	drama
Mean Season, The	1985	crime
Meet Me After the Show	1951	musical/drama
Meet the Fockers	2004	comedy
Mercy Island	1941	drama
Miami	1924	drama
Miami Blues	1990	crime
Miami Exposé	1956	crime
Miami Rhapsody	1995	drama
Miami Shakedown	1993	crime
Miami Story, The	1954	crime
Miami Supercops	1985	crime
Miami Tail, A	2003	comedy
Midnight Cowboy	1969	drama
Midnight Crossing	1988	crime
Monster	2003	crime
Moon Over Miami	1941	musical/comedy
Moonraker	1979	action
Murder of Crows, A	1999	crime
Murph the Surf	1975	crime
My Girl	1991	comedy
My Life With Caroline	1941	comedy
My World Dies Screaming	1958	horror
Naked in the Sun	1957	drama
New Kids, The	1985	crime
New Klondike, The	1926	comedy
Nightmare Beach	1988	horror
Night Moves	1975	action
Night of the Blood Beast	1958	sci-fi
Night Orchid	1997	crime
Night Unto Night	1949	drama
92 in the Shade	1975	drama
Nothing But the Truth	1941	comedy
Ocean's 11	2002	crime

Off and Running	1991	crime
On an Island with You	1948	comedy
Only the Strong	1993	action
Out of Sight	1998	crime
Out of the Darkness	1915	drama
Out of Time	2003	crime
Over 21	1945	drama
Palm Beach Girl	1926	drama
Palm Beach Story	1942	drama
Palmetto	1998	crime
Perez Family, The	1995	comedy
Pest, The	1997	comedy
Plato's Run	1997	action
Playthings of Desire	1934	drama
Point of Impact	1993	action
Police Academy 5	1988	comedy
Popi	1969	comedy
Porky's	1981	comedy
Porky's Revenge	1985	comedy
Private Resort	1985	comedy
Profit, The	2001	drama (banned)
Public Enemy #1	1991	crime
Punisher, The	2004	action
Race to Space	2001	drama
Racing Fever	1964	drama
Radio Inside	1994	drama
Ramshackle House	1924	drama
Random Hearts	1999	drama
Ray	2004	drama
Reap the Wild Wind	1942	adventure
Revenge of the Creature	1955	sci-fi/horror
Revenge of the Nerds II	1987	comedy
Ride	1998	comedy
Ride in a Pink Car	1974	drama
Right Stuff, The	1983	drama
Rookie, The	2002	drama
Rosewood	1997	drama
Ruby in Paradise	1993	drama
Running Scared	1986	crime
Russkies	1987	drama

Safe at Home!	1962	drama
Santiago	1956	drama
Satan Bug, The	1964	sci-fi
Scarface	1983	crime
Scream, Baby, Scream	1969	horror
Screwball Hotel	1988	comedy
Second Honeymoon	1937	comedy
Seminole	1953	drama
Seminole Uprising	1955	drama
Senior Week	1987	comedy
Sensible Obsession, A	2001	drama
Shackled	1918	drama
Shark River	1953	drama
Sixpack Annie	1975	comedy
Sixteen Fathoms Deep	1948	drama
Slattery's Hurricane	1949	drama
Sleepy Time Gal, The	2001	drama
Smokey and the Bandit II	1980	comedy
Smokin' Stogies	2001	comedy
Some Like It Hot	1959	comedy
Song of the Soul, The	1920	drama
South Beach Academy	1994	comedy
Specialist, The	1994	crime
Spring Break	1983	comedy
Standoff, The	1999	crime
Stick	1985	crime
Sting of Death	1965	horror
Stolen Paradise	1941	drama
Stone Cold	1991	action
Stranger Than Paradise	1984	drama
Strategic Air Command	1955	adventure
Striptease	1996	comedy
Substitute, The	1996	crime
Summer Rental	1985	comedy
Sunday Dinner for a Soldier	1944	drama
Sunshine State	2002	drama
Sweet Daddies	1926	crime
Switch, The	2002	crime
Take Me Out to the Ball Game	1949	musical
Tell It to a Star	1945	crime

There's Something About Mary	1998	comedy
Things Behind the Sun	2001	drama
Thunder and Lightning	1974	crime
Tony Rome	1967	crime
Traces of Red	1992	crime
Trans	1998	crime
Transporter 2	2005	action
Trash	1999	crime
Treasure of the Matecumbe	1976	drama
True Lies	1994	crime
Truth or Dare	1986	horror
2 Fast 2 Furious	2003	crime
Two Much	1995	comedy
Ulee's Gold	1997	drama
Unconquered	1917	drama
Under the Gun	1951	crime
Underwater Warrior	1958	drama
Uninvited	1988	horror
Untamed Fury	1947	drama
Up Close and Personal	1996	drama
Victoria's Shadow	1998	horror
We Shall Return	1963	drama
Where the Boys Are	1960	comedy
Where the Boys Are	1984	comedy
White Rose, The	1923	drama
Whoopee Boys, The	1986	comedy
Why Do Fools Fall in Love	1998	comedy
Wilder Napalm	1993	crime
Wild Things	1998	crime
Wild Things 2	2004	crime
Wind Across the Everglades	1958	drama
Wings of Eagles	1957	drama
Wings of the Navy	1939	drama
Women in His Life, The	1933	drama
Wrestling with Alligators	1998	drama
Yearling, The	1946	drama
Yellowneck	1955	drama
Young Sinners	1931	crime
Yours for the Asking	1936	crime
Zaat	1971	horror

Notes

Introduction

1. For a history of the early film industry in Florida, see Nelson, "Florida and the American Motion Picture Industry."
2. *Tampa Morning Tribune*, July 22, 1913, quoted in ibid., 253.
3. Powers et al., *Hollywood's America*, 28–37.
4. Solomon, "The Way We Live Now."
5. Sherrill, "Dade Ain't Disney."
6. Allison Anders is a cousin of author Susan Fernández, who also migrated with her family from Kentucky to Florida.

Chapter 1

1. King, "The Southern States of North America," 147.
2. Silver and Ward, *Film Noir*, 151.
3. Christopher, *Somewhere in the Night*, 239.
4. Cracknell, "*China Moon*."
5. LaSalle, "*Palmetto*."
6. Handwerk, "Florida Shark Attacks"; Roach, "Key to Lightning Deaths."
7. Douglas, "The Everglades," 225, 226.
8. Rainer, "Talented Cast.'"
9. LaSalle, "*Just Cause*."

10. *St. Petersburg Times*, July 16, 2005.

11. Scheib, *"Frogs."*

Chapter 2

1. Federal Writers' Project, "Florida: A Guide," 214.

2. Ozon, "Interview."

3. Altman, "Miami," 251.

4. Ebert, *"Miami Rhapsody."*

Chapter 3

1. O'Sullivan and Lane, *Florida Reader*, 82.

2. Ibid., 12.

3. Scheib, *"Cocoon."*

4. Jasper, *Restless Nation*, ix.

Chapter 4

1. Bartram, "The Travels of William Bartram," 53.

2. Federal Writers' Project, "Florida," 211.

3. Swarthout, *Where the Boys Are*, 172–73.

4. Our thanks to Gary Mormino for sharing his observations about California's competition with Florida.

Chapter 5

1. Ebert, *"Invasion U.S.A."*

2. Ebert, *"Licence to Kill."*

3. "U.S. DEA History Book"; President's Commission on Organized Crime, "America's Habit."

4. Fumento, "They Shoot Tourists, Don't They?"; "Visitor Crime in Florida."

5. Caramanica, *"Bad Boys II."*

6. Ebert, *"Bad Boys II."*

7. Ibid.

8. Ebert, *"Palmetto."*

9. Mathews, *"Palmetto."*

10. Rainer, "Talented Cast."

Chapter 6

1. Lucy Jones, a graduate student at the University of South Florida, St. Petersburg, provided useful information about *Key Largo*.

2. West, *The Enduring Seminoles*.

Chapter 7

1. Berardinelli, *Rosewood*.

2. Singleton Interview.

3. Delpar, "Goodbye to the 'Greaser.'"

4. Fontova, *Fidel*.

5. For Florida census data, see http://www.census-online.com/links/FL/.

Chapter 9

1. Lucy Jones, a graduate student at the University of South Florida, St. Petersburg, contributed to this analysis.

2. Williamson, *Hillbillyland*, 1–17.

3. Hawks, *A Woman Doctor's Civil War*, 109.

4. Sunshine, "Petals Plucked from a Sunny Clime,"155–58.

5. Williamson, *Hillbillyland*, 234.

6. *St. Petersburg Times*, February 29, 2004.

Chapter 11

1. Haydu and Hodges, "Economic Dimensions of the Florida Golf Course Industry."

Bibliography

Altman, T. D. "Miami: City of the Future." In *The Florida Reader: Visions of Paradise*, edited by Maurice O'Sullivan and Jack C. Lane, 251–58. Sarasota: Pineapple Press, 1991.

American Film Institute. http://www.afi.com.

Anders, Allison. Interview by *Frontline*. Public Broadcasting System, July 2001. http://www.pbs.org/wgbh/pages/frontline/shows/hollywood/interviews/anders.html.

Bartram, William. "The Travels of William Bartram." In *The Florida Reader: Visions of Paradise*, edited by Maurice O'Sullivan and Jack C. Lane, 51–57. Sarasota: Pineapple Press, 1991.

Berardinelli, James. Review of *Rosewood*, February 24, 1997. http://movie-reviews.colossus.net/movies/r/rosewood.html.

Caramanica, Jon. "*Bad Boys II*." http://www.villagevoice.com/issues/0330/tracking.php.

Christopher, Nicholas. *Somewhere in the Night: Film Noir and the American City*. New York: The Free Press, 1997.

Cracknell, Ryan. "*China Moon*." http://apolloguide.com.

Delpar, Helen. "Goodbye to the 'Greaser': Mexico, the MPPDA, and Derogatory Films, 1922–1926." *The Journal of Popular Film and Television* 12 (Spring 1984), 34–40.

Douglas, Marjorie Stoneman. "The Everglades: River of Grass." In *The Florida Reader: Visions of Paradise*, edited by Maurice O'Sullivan and Jack C. Lane, 225–31. Sarasota: Pineapple Press, 1991.

Ebert, Roger. "*Bad Boys II*." http://rogerebert.suntimes.com.

———. "*Invasion U.S.A.*" http://rogerebert.suntimes.com.

———. "*Licence to Kill*." http://rogerebert.suntimes.com.

———. "*Miami Rhapsody*." http://rogerebert.suntimes.com.

———. "*Palmetto*." http://rogerebert.suntimes.com.

Federal Writers' Project. "Florida: A Guide." In *The Florida Reader: Visions of Paradise*, edited by Maurice O'Sullivan and Jack C. Lane, 210–17. Sarasota: Pineapple Press, 1991.

Fontova, Humberto. *Fidel: Hollywood's Favorite Tyrant*. Washington, D.C.: National Book Network, 2005.

Fumento, Michael. "They Shoot Tourists, Don't They?" *Investor's Business Daily*, 1993. http://www.fumento.com/florida.html.

Handwerk, Brian. "Florida Shark Attacks Spotlight Real, But Rare, Danger." *National Geographic News*, June 28, 2005. http://news.nationalgeographic.com/news/2005/06/0628_050628_sharkattack.html.

Hawks, Esther Hill. *A Woman Doctor's Civil War*. Edited by Gerald Schwartz. Columbia: University of South Carolina Press, 1989.

Haydu, John, and Alan Hodges. "Economic Dimensions of the Florida Golf Course Industry." IFAS Extension, University of Florida. http://www.edis.ifas.ufl.edu.

Internet Movie Database. http://www.imdb.com.

Jasper, James M. *Restless Nation: Starting Over in America*. Chicago: University of Chicago Press, 2000.

King, Edward Smith. "The Southern States of North America." In *The Florida Reader: Visions of Paradise*, edited by Maurice O'Sullivan and Jack C. Lane, 144–48. Sarasota: Pineapple Press, 1991.

LaSalle, Mick. "*Just Cause* Wins Case on Connery's Appeal." *San Francisco Chronicle*. http://www.sfgate.com.

———. "*Palmetto* Has Some Bite But Doesn't Fly." *San Francisco Chronicle*. http://www.sfgate.com.

Mathews, Jack. "*Palmetto* Gets Stuck in the Middle of Film Noir." *Los Angeles Times*, February 20, 1998, 8.

Nelson, Richard Alan. "Florida and the American Motion Picture Industry, 1898–1930." Ph.D. diss., Florida State University, 1980.

O'Sullivan, Maurice, Jr., and Jack C. Lane, eds. *The Florida Reader: Visions of Paradise*. Sarasota: Pineapple Press, 1991.

Ozon, Francois. "Interview from Press Kit." http://www.francois-ozon.com.

Powers, Stephen, David J. Rothman, and Stanley Rothman. *Hollywood's America: Social and Political Themes in Motion Pictures*. Boulder, Colo.: Westview Press, 1996.

President's Commission on Organized Crime. "America's Habit: Drug Abuse, Drug Trafficking, and Organized Crime" (1986). http://www.druglibrary.org/schaffer/govpubs/amhab/ahmenu.htm.

Rainer, Peter. "Talented Cast Bogged Down in Mystery Thriller 'Cause,'" *Los Angeles Times*, February 17, 1995.

Roach, John. "Key to Lightning Deaths: Location, Location, Location." *National Geographic News*, June 22, 2004. http://news.nationalgeographic.com/news/2003/05/0522_030522_lightning.html.

Scheib, Richard. "*Cocoon*." http://www.moria.co.nz.

———. "*Frogs*." http://www.moria.co.nz.

Sherrill, Robert. "Dade Ain't Disney." *The Nation*, March 6, 2000. http://www.thenation.com/doc/20000306/sherrrill.

Silver, Alain, and Elizabeth Ward, eds. *Film Noir: An Encyclopedic Reference to the American Style*. Woodstock, N.Y.: Overlook Press, 1992.

Singleton, John. Interview by Film Scouts. http://www.filmscouts.com/scripts/interview.cfm?File=joh-sin

Solomon, Deborah. "The Way We Live Now: Questions for Carl Hiaasen." *New York Times Magazine*, July 25, 2004.

Sunshine, Sylvia. "Petals Plucked from a Sunny Clime." In *The Florida Reader: Visions of Paradise*, edited by Maurice O'Sullivan and Jack C. Lane, 155–61. Sarasota: Pineapple Press, 1991.

Swarthout, Glendon. *Where the Boys Are*. New York: Random House, 1959.

"U.S. DEA History Book, 1975–1980." http://www.usdoj.gov/dea/pubs/history/deahistory_02.htm.

"Visitor Crime in Florida: The Perception vs. the Reality," January 22, 1996. http://www.fdle.state.fl.us/fsac/Archives/visitor_crime.asp.

West, Patsy. *The Enduring Seminoles: From Alligator Wrestling to Ecotourism*. Gainesville: University Press of Florida, 1998.

Williamson, J. W. *Hillbillyland: What the Movies Did to the Mountains and What the Mountains Did to the Movies*. Chapel Hill: University of North Carolina Press, 1995.

Index

Susan J. Fernández is associate professor of history at the University of South Florida, St. Petersburg. She is the author of *Encumbered Cuba: Capital Markets and Revolt, 1878–1895* (UPF, 2002).

Robert P. Ingalls is professor of history at the University of South Florida, Tampa. He is the author of *Urban Vigilantes in the New South: Tampa, 1882–1936* (UPF, 1993) and co-author of *Tampa Cigar Workers: A Pictorial History* (UPF, 2003).